PRAISE FOR *ADVOCATING FOR THE COMMON GOOD: PEOPLE, POLITICS, PROCESS, AND POLICY ON CAPITOL HILL*

"Jane West is a legend. Her advocacy work for persons with disabilities began in Washington, DC, working for disability legislation, including the passage of the Americans with Disabilities Act. In this thorough, practical, and eminently readable book, Jane shares her experiences in advocating for the common good. This is absolutely indispensable reading for anyone seeking to make positive changes in the world of policy. Jane West's book is an instant classic!"
—**Mitchell L. Yell, Fred and Francis Lester Palmetto Chair, Teacher Education and professor, special education, University of South Carolina**

"Jane West has written an extraordinarily comprehensive treatise on the legislative process in the US Congress and how advocacy can be translated into effective policy that can influence the creation and enactment of legislation. Through a combination of insights gained from experience as a highly regarded Hill staffer and significant roles representing major educational and policy organizations, she has created a comprehensive primer on the formal process of how legislation is created, providing insights into how to be a most resourceful and effective advocate."
—**Philip J. Burke, University of Maryland**

"Jane West's *Advocating for the Common Good* is at once theoretical and practical. Based on her four decades of experience across the various levers of power in Washington, West provides valuable insights into how our federal government works in comprehensible terms for a wide audience at a critical time in our nation's history."
—**Maryam Ahranjani, School of Law, University of New Mexico**

"An engaging and inspiring read. Dr. West presents a complicated and layered process through a clear and digestible framework, extending readers' appreciation of the complex relationships among people, policies, process, and politics. I believe that this book will be read, appreciated, and applied by multiple audiences, including those who approach policy making from an academic or research background, those who are advocates 'in the making,' and those who simply want to learn more about the process. There are many of us who think we understand what's going on in our nation's capital, but few of us possess the depth of understanding and experience that Dr. West has acquired and conveys so clearly through this book."
—**Katharine Shepherd, dean and Levitt Family Green and Gold Professor, College of Education and Social Services, University of Vermont**

"This text is a call to action for anyone interested in serving the common good through policy work. Dr. West's framework, the four Ps—the people, the politics, the processes, and the policy—provides a structure to understand what is seen, heard, and learned in policy making. *Advocating for the Common Good* lays a foundation for the essential aspects of policy making by integrating theory with practical action steps to begin and sustain advocacy work. The timing of this text feels strikingly pointed."
—**Elizabeth A. Harkins (Monaco), William Paterson University**

"Dr. Jane West has done something remarkable: she has made policy and the political process accessible and relatable. Her expertise, combined with her lived experiences, results in a book that should serve as a primary resource for anyone interested in learning the keys to advocacy, policy, and politics."
—**Corey D. Pierce, College of Education and Behavioral Sciences, University of Northern Colorado**

"West seamlessly translates an examination of the American political institutions, the policy process and the factors at play, and the practical experience of policy experts into an action plan for developing an advocacy campaign to shape public policy. This text serves as a wonderful introduction for students looking to take their theoretical understanding of policy making beyond their classroom learning to real-world, practical use."
—**Benjamin F. Melusky, Old Dominion University**

"How can a regular citizen advocate for the common good? In this hopeful call to action, West walks her readers though the different participants and processes involved in governmental decision making. Blending theory with practice, she then details the historical context and current strategies used in policy creation, approval, implementation, and evaluation. She finishes with suggestions on how to influence policy in your own areas of passion and encourages all of us to engage in the political process."
—**Barbara Jean Hickman, School of Counseling, Leadership, Advocacy and Design, University of Wyoming**

"This book empowers experts with the understanding of the process to impact policy and provides a bridge to collaborative partnerships between experts and policy makers."
— **Gloria Niles, University of Hawai'i**

"The author builds on the extant body of work on this critical topic, while also incorporating their deep experience in practice. This book thus in essence presents a practice-informed theory, which is much needed in the field of education and public policy."
—**Raquel Muñiz, Boston College, Lynch School of Education and Human Development and School of Law**

"I think Jane West is the perfect individual to write this type of book. She directs the reader from the start of a concept through the fruition of the campaign/law. This is a step-by-step approach to how the system works to develop a law and to meet with elected representatives. West takes the mystery out of a process that to many of us is mysterious and untouchable."
—**Deborah E. Griswold, The University of Kansas**

"Jane West's approach is meticulous and rooted in her experience and knowledge, while also leveraging existing work. A very practical book that can be useful to folks who are fresh on the policy scene and also to academics as part of their syllabi."
—**David Morar, George Mason University**

"Jane West uses her extensive experience in the policy realm to provide a text appropriate for anyone interested in public policy. This is a must-read for anyone wanting to know how government works and how public policies are made."
—**Christine Tartaro, Stockton University**

"Advocating for the Common Good moves beyond the standard description of the policy process by providing invaluable advice on the actual interactions with the people developing policy. Jane West includes stories from her experiences and experiences of several US policy insiders in collaboratively building policy for positive change."
—**Catherine Robert, EdD, The University of Texas at Arlington**

"A key component of becoming a special educator and a school administrator is advocacy, and Dr. West makes a valid point that many educators, constituents, and other entities are novices when it comes to visits and discussions with congressional representatives and senators. The process can often be intimating and daunting. This text provides that practical guide and assistance from the experts on not only how to speak to congressional leaders,

but also how to get involved in policy making procedures. Whether you are a beginner or an adroit advocate, Dr. West brings her political wisdom and experience to the forefront of politics and policy so the readers can formulate their own foundation and adequately establish an advocacy plan for their sector. More than just a 'car manual' on policy making, this book encompasses the application of effective advocacy and cohesive problem solving at a national level."
—**Lisa Bisogno, Northeastern State University**

"While most books focus on the policy analysis and evaluation process, I have not come across a good explanation of how to put this into action, which this book presents. The practical knowledge shared in this book is invaluable for those wanting to use their analysis to affect change."
—**Annah Rogers, University of Alabama**

"The world in which we live mandates that educational leaders understand and can function in the world of federal policy making. This book, written by a veteran of federal political processes in Washington, DC, provides a road map to help train aspiring leaders and advocates on how to make their voices heard and allow the policy making process work for them."
—**Elizabeth Timmerman Lugg, JD, PhD, Illinois State University**

"West very clearly explains how various players interact to develop federal policy with timely and pertinent examples. Having been involved in various aspects of the policy development process, West provides insights on being a policy advocate at the national or state levels that will encourage readers to become more engaged and to advocate for policies for the common good."
—**Linda R. Vogel, University of Northern Colorado**

"Advocating for the Common Good is a tangible and pragmatic overview of the public policy process in the United States. In covering the four Ps (people, politics, processes, and policy), Jane West provides the reader with a fundamental democratic lesson. Citizens should expect their elected and unelected government officials, with their input and counsel, to create policies that improve the status quo and help the republic move toward a more perfect union."
—**Brian L. Fife, Lehigh University**

"*Advocating for the Common Good: People, Politics, Process, and Policy on Capitol Hill* offers a cursory glance at the systems and strategies that shape how public policy is made in the United States. As a practical tool, this is a great read for those beginning their journey to understand and engage in effective policy and advocacy work."
—**Patrick Steck, Deans for Impact**

"In *Advocating for the Common Good*, Dr. West draws on her extensive practical experience in federal policy to provide a useful organization of the landscape of policy making. This theoretically grounded practical manual illustrates how to understand and leverage the four Ps—people, politics, process, and policy—to be an effective advocate."
—**Christine Carrino Gorowara, University of Delaware**

SPECIAL EDUCATION LAW, POLICY, AND PRACTICE

Series Editors
Mitchell L. Yell, Ph.D., University of South Carolina
David F. Bateman, Ph.D., Shippensburg University of Pennsylvania

The Special Education Law, Policy, and Practice series highlights current trends, policies, and legal issues in the education of students with disabilities. The books in this series link legal requirements and policies with evidence-based instruction and highlight practical applications for working with students with disabilities. The titles in the Special Education Law, Policy, and Practice series not only are designed to be required textbooks for general education and special education preservice teacher education programs but are also designed for practicing teachers, education administrators, principals, school counselors, school psychologists, parents, and others interested in improving the lives of students with disabilities. The Special Education Law, Policy, and Practice series is committed to research-based practices working to provide appropriate and meaningful educational programming for students with disabilities and their families and policies that support these practices.

Titles in Series:

Advocating for the Common Good

Advocating for
the Common Good

People, Politics, Process,
and Policy on Capitol Hill

JANE E. WEST, PH.D.

ROWMAN & LITTLEFIELD
Lanham • Boulder • New York • London

Associate Acquisitions Editor: Courtney Packard
Assistant Acquisitions Editor: Sarah Rinehart
Sales and Marketing Inquiries: textbooks@rowman.com

Published by Rowman & Littlefield
An imprint of The Rowman & Littlefield Publishing Group, Inc.
4501 Forbes Boulevard, Suite 200, Lanham, Maryland 20706
www.rowman.com

86-90 Paul Street, London EC2A 4NE

British Library Cataloguing in Publication Information Available

Library of Congress Cataloging-in-Publication Data Available

ISBN 978-1-5381-5522-6 (cloth)
ISBN 978-1-5381-5523-3 (paperback)
ISBN 978-1-5381-5524-0 (ebook)

∞™ The paper used in this publication meets the minimum requirements of
American National Standard for Information Sciences—Permanence of Paper for
Printed Library Materials, ANSI/NISO Z39.48-1992.

This book is dedicated to the hardworking people who toil daily in our nation's capital to keep the wheels of policy making moving in service to the common good.

Brief Contents

Contents

Tables, Textboxes, and Figures

....

TABLES

TEXTBOXES

....

FIGURES

Acknowledgments

I would like to acknowledge my doctoral students, whose appetite for understanding policy making led them to Washington to participate in my course over the years. Their enthusiasm, questions, and insights inspired me to develop this book. Several course participants have gone on to become coinstructors of the course, deepening its content and expanding its reach. I am grateful to Sarah Nagro, Kaitlyn Brennan, Ashley White, and John Andresen.

Without the support of the Higher Education Consortium for Special Education (HECSE), the course would not have been possible. I am forever grateful for their support and faith in me, particularly Katie Shepherd, the HECSE president at the inception of the course, who championed its development. HECSE's leadership stands as a lighthouse for advocacy under the years of guidance from its presidents: Corey Pierce, Cindy Vail, Lisa Mondo-Amaya, Jeff Anderson, Cynthia Wilson, Harvey Rude, Ben Lignugaris-Kraft, Chriss Walther-Thomas, Stan Shaw, Herb Reith, Bill Berdine, Chuck Salzberg, Susan Fowler, Mike Rosenberg, Mike Hardman, and Deb Smith.

To the many congressional staff, executive agency staff, interest group experts, colleagues, and advocates, I am most indebted as they shared their expertise and insights with me over the years and generously met with doctoral students as part of the course. Pat Wright, the extraordinary legislative strategist for the Disability Rights Education and Defense Fund, schooled me in political and policy strategy like no one else could. Rebecca Cokley, national disability rights leader, continues to show me what effective advocacy looks like.

To those policy experts who allowed me to interview them for this book—David Cleary, Jon Fansmith, Lindsay Fryer, Kim Knackstedt, Kuna Tavalin, Ashley White, Michael Yudin, and the staffer who shall remain anonymous—I thank you. Your insights and reflections on your decades of experience inside the policy making process in Washington bring the concepts in the book to life.

I am forever grateful for Sen. Lowell P. Weicker (R-CT) and his staff director, John A. Doyle, who took the chance to bring me on board to work in the Senate in 1983 as an eager and terrified doctoral student at the time. I would not have had the rich opportunities I have had without them. My mentor at the University of Maryland for my doctoral program, Phil Burke, led me to pursue the position in the Senate. His guidance and never-ending support have sustained me.

I offer my heartfelt thanks to my colleagues and friends who held my hand and offered sage advice as I trudged through the process of writing a book: Lani Florian, Mo West, Kathleen Pereira, Kaitlyn Brennan, Megan McCoy, Wendy Bedenbaugh, John Berger, Jim Ford, Elsie Ford, Roy Berkowitz, Jan Smoot, M. A. O'Donnell, and Bill Bowser.

My colleagues at the American Association of Colleges for Teacher Education— Lynn Gangone, Leslie Fenwick, and Jaci King—offered invaluable suggestions and support.

For the insightful reviewers of my proposal and my manuscript offering multiple helpful recommendations, I am grateful. These include Lisa Bisogno, Northeastern State University; Dennis Cavitt, Midwestern State University; Susan DeJarnatt, Temple University Beasley School of Law; Lisa Driscoll, University of Tennessee; Brian Fife, Lehigh University; Christine Carrino Gorowara, University of Delaware; Deborah Griswold, University of Kansas; Elizabeth A. Harkins (Monaco), William Paterson University; Barbara Hickman, University of Wyoming; Beth Kania-Gosche, Missouri University of Science and Technology; Ann Knox, University of Redlands; Timothy Letzring, University of Central Florida; Elizabeth Timmerman Lugg, Illinois State University; Vicki Luther, Mercer University; Nita Mathew, Lake Michigan College; Benjamin Melusky, Old Dominion University; David Morar, George Mason University; Raquel Muñiz, Boston College; Gloria Niles, University of Hawaii; Karen Ramlackhan, University of South Florida; Catherine Robert, University of Texas at Arlington; Katharine Shepherd, University of Vermont; and Christine Tartaro, Stockton University.

Mitch Yell reached out to me in 2019 to explore the possibility of this book. Without his encouragement and guidance, it never would have come to pass. The ever-enthusiastic Rowman & Littlefield Executive Editor Mark Kerr and his associate editor, Courtney Packard, guided me expertly through the process of turning ideas into a finished product.

Finally, I am so grateful for my family. My loving cousins—Martha, Rick, Suzie, Emery, and Ross; my remarkable stepchildren and their spouses—Jon and Joan and Emily and Nick; my extraordinary son, Marc, and his wonderful wife, Brittney; my brother Thomas and my sister-in-law Rosa—were all cheerleaders in my corner. In particular I am forever indebted to my very accomplished brother Thomas, who insisted I start a website, edited my newsletter for more years than I can count, loved the idea for my book, made a video of me describing the four Ps (there is a link in the book), and whose consistent wisdom and support I could always count on. Lastly, I know my late husband, Stan Mayer, would be so proud of me were he still with us. He ever delighted in calling himself "Mr. Jane West."

In closing, I thank my late mother, Sarah West, an amazing trailblazer and an eternal advocate for the common good.

Author's Note

....

Advocating for the Common Good

The idea for this book began to percolate in the fall of 2019. We could not foresee a global pandemic and the full effect of the tumultuous four years of the Trump presidency. We did not anticipate the events of January 6, 2021, the ongoing denial of presidential election results, the escalation in violence and threats, and the emergence of culture wars at the heart of our education system—all reflecting what has become all too common extremism and polarization in our society and our politics. There is a sense that our government is not up to the job.

For forty years, I have been a part of the policy making apparatus in Washington—working in the U.S. Senate, for several federal agencies, and for multiple interest groups. I have had the good fortune to contribute to a system that works, that generates results for the common good. I contributed to the development of the Americans with Disabilities Act and multiple education laws—all of them with bipartisan support. The ethic that dominated policy making was compromise and results.

While today our policy making apparatus may appear more often broken than not, there is ample evidence that functionality remains intact. The media's predilection for reporting drama and dysfunction can obscure this reality. Between May and August 2022, in the lead-up to the highly contested midterm elections, in the midst of intense partisan tension over the Supreme Court's controversial decision overturning the landmark abortion ruling in *Roe v. Wade*, and amid the investigation of former president Trump, Congress enacted three meaningful laws (Desjardins, 2022). The PACT Act to extend veterans benefits, the CHIPS Act to invest in science and technology, and the Safer Communities Act addressing gun safety, all passed with bipartisan support. Our policy making institutions may be weakened, but they still work. The threat to them is real; it is also an invitation to us. It is up to us to reinvigorate them and use them to serve the common good.

Introduction

....

BACKGROUND

The framework offered in this book is the result of a course I developed for doctoral students in 2015 (HECSE Short Course, 2023). Created and offered under the auspices of the Higher Education Consortium for Special Education, the course takes place in Washington, DC, with students from all over the country. The course has stood the test of time, as the annual waiting lists attest. What is unique about the course is the opportunity for participants to directly engage with policy makers and their staffs (some of whom are quoted in this book). Meetings with members of Congress, House and Senate congressional staff, staff from the White House, staff from federal agencies, and government relations experts working at national associations offer students direct access for dialogue to understand the roles and the process of policy making in Washington.

While students leave the course excited and empowered, the experience is a bit like drinking from a fire hose. There is so much new information and so many new perspectives—it is hard to digest and make sense of it all. They return to their campuses and their professional roles and are unsure of how to integrate what they learned with their ongoing work. Out of this realization was born the framework presented in this book—the four Ps. By unpacking the essential aspects of policy making—the people, the politics, the processes, and the policy—it is my hope that advocates will have a framework to use in organizing and deploying their advocacy work, as well as analyzing policy *post facto*.

This book provides a foundation from the policy making literature (political science, public policy, law, congressional studies, and education policy), the structure and procedures that embody the machinery of government, the well-established practical protocols for advocacy developed by Washington's many government relations experts, and my personal experiences, as well as those of others who have worked in the policy making world for years. My intention is to integrate the theoretical with the practical and offer action steps to begin and sustain advocacy.

While relying heavily on the policy areas I know best—education and disability—the four-P framework is designed for use in any policy arena, be it energy, health care, banking, agriculture, or any other. The situational particulars of the people, the politics, the processes, and the policy will be distinctive;

....

however, the framework of the four Ps holds steady across policy spheres. Likewise, it is applicable to policy making at the state level.

I chose the title of this book, *Advocating for the Common Good*, as it reflects what is at the heart of public policy and why it matters. The impetus to define and pursue an elusive common good drives our collective participation in our government. Definitions are multiple and contested, but the dialogue is essential to move toward a more perfect union.

OVERVIEW OF THE FOUR Ps: PEOPLE, POLITICS, PROCESSES, POLICY

The framework of the four Ps provides a structure for making sense of what is seen, heard, and learned when venturing into the unfamiliar terrain of policy making. It is a tool to activate policy advocacy and to analyze policy after its creation.

The four Ps are deconstructed categories—not circumscribed silos unto themselves. Each bleeds into the others. People cannot be clearly separated from politics. Process will circumscribe policy options. Policy cannot be divorced from politics. Articulating the four Ps separately enables putting them back together so that the whole becomes larger than the sum of its parts, as depicted in figure I.1.[1]

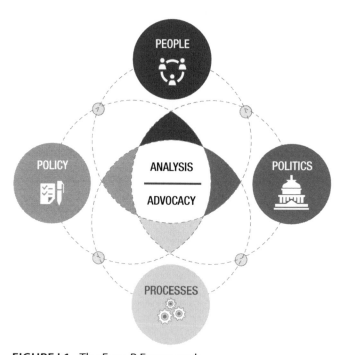

FIGURE I.1. The Four-P Framework
Infographic developed by Vivian Vitullo, Lauren Bruno, Gabrielle Pickover, and Cassandra Willis

---

1. A brief video explanation of the four Ps can be found at https://player.vimeo.com/video/350154153.

Chapter 1: People

At the heart of policy making lies the iron triangle—a well-established configuration for considering the three sectors that routinely interact to move the policy making apparatus—Congress, the executive branch, and interest groups. While the first two sets of actors lie within government, the third set—interest groups—represents organized voices outside of government but always engaged with government. Each government sector includes multiple subunits with distinct and key roles in policy making and implementation. Interest groups run the gamut from professional associations to public interest groups, to business and corporate associations, to think tanks. The relationships developed between those working in the three sectors of the iron triangle are the grease that keeps the wheels of government turning.

Beyond the iron triangle, there are multiple influences on policy making, including social media and the press, public opinion, courts, constituents, grassroots organizations and movements, and experts. Social media is infused throughout the policy making process, alternately magnifying and distorting it.

A lack of diverse peoples in the policy making apparatus is apparent and influences policy outcomes, as policy problems and policy solutions are inextricably linked to the perspectives and experiences of those at the table. Awareness of the voices missing in policy making invites those who have historically been marginalized to claim their seats at the table. As former representative Shirley Chisholm (D-NY) said, "If they don't give you a seat at the table, bring a folding chair."

As advocates approach policy making, inquiry into differences between the culture of their sector and the policy making world invites reflection on differences in variables that create the norms and patterns that shape action. Knowing the differences in dimensions such as communication styles and institutional incentives informs the approach to policy.

Chapter 2: Politics

Politics is an essential ingredient in the policy making process. The implications of which political party controls the House and the Senate, which party controls the White House, how the election cycle impacts members of Congress, and how advocates may participate in elections serve as a backdrop for policy advocacy work. While advocates will want to work with both Republicans and Democrats, knowing how their roles are influenced by the politics of their party and their reelection status facilitates strategic decision making and communication. Though often hard to come by, bipartisanship remains a laudable goal, though it does not ensure policy success.

Chapter 3: Process

Understanding processes of policy making illuminates four aspects of advocacy work: timing; the range of options for progress; the ability to anticipate, plan, and strategize; and opportunities to initiate new proposals. Political science litera-ture offers numerous policy making frameworks, most commonly with six distinct phases: problem definition, agenda setting, policy formulation, policy adoption, policy implementation, and policy evaluation. While this sequential and logical stage model is rarely at play in a straightforward manner, its components can be helpful in analyzing what may appear as a chaotic undertaking. A persuasive and more realistic framework is offered by John Kingdon (2010) in his book *Agendas, Alternatives, and Public Policies*. The intriguing notions of "policy streams" and "policy primeval soup" capture more authentically the roller-coaster ride that pol-icy making can be.

The 1976 version of the legislative process represented in the iconic School-house Rock song "I'm Just a Bill" continues to resonate, providing a comforting, elementary, and unembellished look at what is often complex and bewildering (Jabbow, 2011). Despite the maze of policy making operations, three core processes remain anchors at the heart of legislative action—budget, appropriations, and authorization—with each providing unique opportunities for advocates to work with both the legislative and executive branches.

Swirling around these core legislative processes are the ever-changing maze of congressional procedures and House and Senate rules. In some congressional offices there is a dedicated staff person who is the expert on procedure and rules, advising on matters such as how to fill an amendment tree and whether a recon-ciliation provision might violate the Byrd rule. While this level of knowledge is not necessary to be a good advocate, it is important to know that such rules and protocols exist as they can serve as either barriers or opportunities to an advocacy agenda.

While Congress is charged with writing statutes, the executive branch plays a major role in interpreting and implementing law. In addition, the president holds unique authority granted by the Constitution to issue executive orders that are considered to have the force of law. These may be significant policy determinations and will frequently reverse direction from the previous president if they were from the other political party. Federal agencies write regulations to implement and clar-ify laws, offering the public important opportunities to provide comments, which the agency considers in finalizing the new rule.

Chapter 4: The Policy

The destination of the policy making process is to arrive at policy decisions, decisions that usually represent multiple compromises but also a predominant belief that the policy will be effective. The dance between the policy problem and the policy solution can be revealing. Many astute analysts argue that the solution may precede the problem in that a problem may be conceptualized so that it leads to a predetermined solution.

Multiple policy tools are available to craft a policy solution, including grants, civil rights laws, data collection, research, increases in funding for par-ticular programs, implementation requirements, and accountability requirements.

Choosing the most appropriate policy tools to address the policy problems of concern increases the likelihood of policy success. Whether there is capacity to implement the policy solution, the cost of the policy solution, whether the policy generates conflict with other policies, whether the time line for implementation is reasonable, the reasonableness of accountability requirements, and importantly whose voices were heard and unheard at the policy making table will all inform the likelihood of a policy being successful.

Two case studies offer stark contrasts in terms of policy success. The Americans with Disabilities Act of 1990 and the No Child Left Behind Act of 2001 and its derivatives differ significantly in terms of how the policy problem and the policy solution were defined, whose voices were heard in the policy making process, how best practice and research informed policy, the extent to which the measures built on successful policy that was already in place, the capacity to implement the policy, the anticipation of possible unintended consequences and resistance, the flexibility of the policy to adapt to changing circumstances, and the long-term survival of the policy. Such retrospective analysis can inform advocates as they pursue new policy provisions.

Chapter 5: Advocacy: Putting It All Together

The four Ps promote development of successful advocacy work and the avoidance of critical mistakes, such as urging adoption of a policy for which there is no policy process in play that would move it forward.

Washington is filled with experts in policy advocacy—government relations professionals in every policy arena whose job is to monitor day-to-day policy developments and forecast upcoming opportunities for members of their organization. The very practical aspects of successful advocacy for constituents, experts, and association members are well established. The first step is doing the homework to have an up-to-date understanding of the policy terrain—the people, the politics, the processes, and the policies in play. Setting up meetings with policy makers initiates the development of long-term relationships that serve both the advocate and the policy maker in two-way communication that can strengthen policy outcomes. A coherent message for a policy maker includes a statement of the problem, how it is playing out in the relevant district or state, data about the scope of the problem, suggestions for solutions with evidence that they will be successful, a powerful personal story to exemplify the problem and the solution, and specific "ASKS" or requests of the policy maker. Follow-ups include thank-you notes, requests for updates on action related to the "ASKS," sharing good news from the field and back home, and invitations to further engage, perhaps by visiting a successful program associated with the policy challenge.

Multiple policy artifacts are available for analysis and deeper understanding of the policy matter at hand. For Congress, committee reports, hearing records, the *Congressional Record*, and lists of bills introduced and their status are all available online. Reports from the Congressional Research Service and the Government Accountability Office provide in-depth analysis. The executive branch is replete with policy announcements about new initiatives, executive orders, rule making, guidance, funding competitions, and more—all found in the *Federal Register*. Equipped with such in-depth information, advocates are prepared to participate in town hall meetings and serve as expert resources for policy makers.

While the COVID pandemic and the events of January 6, 2021, at the Capitol have resulted in multiple unfolding new access protocols, robust advocacy continues, with online communication reported to be effective and at times preferable, as it allows frequent communication without requiring travel.

By taking a seat at the policy making table, equipped with an understanding of the four Ps, advocates are ready to make their voices heard. Experience, knowledge, and a view from the ground can inform policy so that the probability of its success grows.

REMEMBER: ELECTIONS CHANGE CONGRESS AND THE EXECUTIVE BRANCH

Every two years when there is an election, things change. If it is a midterm election, a new Congress is seated. If it is a presidential election year, both a new Congress and a new president with all their political appointees take office.

Much of this manuscript was finalized in 2022 when President Biden was in office and during the second and final year of the 117th Congress. In January 2023, after the 2022 midterm elections, a new Congress was seated—the 118th Congress. The majority in the House of Representatives shifted from Democrats to Republicans while the majority in the Senate remained Democrats. In both bodies, new members of Congress were elected. As the makeup of the bodies changed, so did committee chairs and committee members. Rules of the House and Senate changed; names of some committees changed; some new committees were formed; and some old ones were eliminated.

As a result of elections, every two years there are changes in Congress. Every four years, and often more frequently, there are changes in political appointees in an administration, even if the incumbent president wins reelection. As you read, note that there may be differences in real time from what is presented in the book. Your best bet is always to check online, where you will find up-to-date information.[2]

---

2. Websites www.senate.gov and www.house.gov are good resources for current information for Congress as is www.whitehouse.gov for the executive branch.

CHAPTER 1

People

....

Let us never forget that government is ourselves and not an alien power over us. The ultimate rulers of our democracy are not a President and senators and congressmen and government officials, but the voters of this country.

—Franklin D. Roosevelt, Address at Marietta, Ohio, 1938

The machinery of government is complex, arcane, and often out of reach, making it hard to remember that it is people who make the policy making apparatus work—or not work. It is people who create the rules, people who break the rules, and people who change the rules. People are at the heart of each of the other Ps—politics, process, and policy.

When I worked on Capitol Hill, there was a saying: "Members of Congress put their pants on one leg at a time too." In other words, they are just people. When I bring doctoral students to Capitol Hill for the first time, there is always a sense of shock that the congressional staffers they meet with are so accessible, down to earth, interested in what they have to say, and forthcoming. As we leave, I routinely hear comments like "He's so nice," "She's so thoughtful," "She's really smart," and "He's so young."[1]

The people involved in policy making are organized into identifiable entities or sectors—bodies of Congress, executive agencies, organizations outside of government, and more. Each set of people has particular functions and roles in the policy making apparatus, which may include developing policy options, advocating for those options, generating pressure, messaging targeted audiences, developing and managing legislation, implementing legislation through executive orders, rule writing, distributing funds, providing guidance, monitoring policy implementation, and continually engaging in policy dialogue and debate.

---

1. Many staff begin their service on Capitol Hill in their twenties, coming from election campaigns or as constituents of the elected member. Work hours are notoriously long, and the job can be grueling, often outpacing the compensation. The experience of working on Capitol Hill is a significant résumé builder for other policy jobs in Washington, which provide greater compensation and more reasonable work hours. In conjunction with the turnover caused by election cycles, a regular coming and going of young staffers in congressional offices is common.

....

THE IRON TRIANGLE

The iron triangle is a well-established configuration deeply embedded in political science and public policy literature (Birkland, 2016; Kingdon, 2010; Kraft & Furlong, 2021). Each point on the triangle represents one of three key sectors that form the core of policy making interaction. Congress, with the essential function of writing laws, sits at the pinnacle of the triangle. The executive branch of government, including its multiple bureaucracies, marks a second point of the triangle. Interest groups and their various iterations are at the third point of the triangle, representing organizations outside of government that seek to influence and shape policy making.

People who work in a particular policy area in each of the sectors represented by the iron triangle form networks of ongoing interaction. Congressional committee staff, representatives of relevant interest groups, and civil servants and political appointees in the executive branch (including federal agencies and the White House) may work together for years on a number of issues in a policy arena. It is not uncommon for individuals in a policy area—for example, higher education—to move from congressional staff to executive agency staff to interest group staff, thus establishing long-standing relationships. Each sector is examined below.

> "The concept of the iron triangle reflects my experience. This is a small world. People move from different points on the triangle in different portions of their careers. You are often working with the same people though their roles will shift. Preexisting relationships and an understanding of where people stand make a big difference. It is this informal interaction that is how policy really gets made, particularly when it comes to the details." (Jonathan Fansmith, author interview, August 16, 2022)

Congress

Comprising two legislative bodies, Congress is a bicameral entity. Though made up of two bodies, it is one of the three branches of government, and theoretically the most powerful in the policy making process, given its authority to make laws and appropriate federal funds. The United States House of Representatives—generally referred to as "the people's house"—is composed of 435 members, each representing a district of approximately 700,000 constituents. Because the number of representatives is based on population, some states have large delegations (such as California, which as of 2022 had fifty-three) and some have small delegations. The least populated states have only one representative; as of 2022, these were Alaska, Delaware, Montana, North Dakota, South Dakota, Vermont, and Wyoming. The Constitution requires that every state receive at least one House seat. Elections occur for all House seats every two years.

Every decade, the results of the Census are used to determine congressional districts. States may gain or lose seats, or districts within states may be redrawn, depending on Census results (Eckman, 2021). In a process called apportionment, or reapportionment, states use the results of the Census to distribute seats in the House of Representatives based on population. Finally, the state may redistrict, or redraw the lines of a district, related to ensuring an equal population for each district within the state. Thus, every decade states stand to win or lose seats in the House of Representatives. As a result of the 2020 Census, seven states will lose a seat in the House, five states will gain a seat, and the state of Texas will gain two seats (Council of State Governments, 2021). The process of redistricting has become increasingly contested and driven by partisan politics as the country's polarization has grown. In *Laboratories of Autocracy*, David Pepper argues that gerrymandering (setting boundaries in electoral districts that favor one party over another) has become so intense in states that it threatens the core of democracy, as it enables the minority to govern the majority (Washington Journal, 2022).

The United States Senate is composed of one hundred members—two from each state—each serving a six-year term. The Senate historically has been considered the "upper chamber" and the more deliberative body given the longevity of service of members and broad swath of constituents each senator represents. In recent years, unfortunately, the Senate has been described in a number of derogatory ways, such as "the place where legislation goes to die." Over the years partisanship and deadlock have increasingly come to characterize Congress. One-third of Senate seats are up for reelection every two years.

> "In the Senate there is the opportunity to be more thoughtful because you have more time. We move slower—on a six-year cycle versus a two-year cycle in the House. The House can move like a freight train. You can start with an idea and shape a bill and move it onto the floor for a vote within a matter of weeks. In the Senate it is months or years to move something through the process. We spent eight years developing No Child Left Behind in the Senate. It is more collaborative, and you have to cross party lines and that takes time." (David Cleary, author interview, September 15, 2022)

Because of election cycles, a new Congress is seated every two years. For example, after the elections in November 2020, a new Congress—the 117th—was seated in January 2021. The 117th Congress runs from January 2021 to January 2023, the 118th Congress will span January 2023 to January 2025, and so on.

When an old Congress ends, all legislation that has been introduced or considered in that Congress dies. To be considered in the new Congress, a bill from a prior Congress must be reintroduced. New committee assignments are made, and new leadership elections are held. The process of determining who is on which committees includes considerations such as seniority, interest, and the scope of influence of the committee (*About the committee system*, n.d.). The number of members from both the majority and the minority parties on each committee is determined by the proportion of members from each political party in each congressional body (*House committees*, n.d.). For example, if the House were to comprise 335 Republicans and 100 Democrats, the ratio on committees would be quite different than if the House comprised 225 Republicans and 210 Democrats.

The power of a member of Congress is often measured by their seniority (e.g., how long he or she has served in the body or on a committee), the role they are playing (e.g., Speaker of the House, chair of a committee), how vulnerable they are electorally (e.g., they won the last election by a landslide versus squeaking by), and their relationships with peers. The status of a member of Congress is significant as it confers their sphere of influence. The Speaker of the House has considerably more influence than a freshman member who is just learning the ropes.

CONGRESSIONAL STAFF AND CONGRESSIONAL COMMITTEES

Congressional staff are the engine that makes the legislative process move (Petersen, 2021). Each of the 100 senators and 435 members of the House of Representatives has a personal office in Washington. Each member also has offices back in their state or district with local staff based there. In addition, most members of Congress belong to one or more committees or subcommittees, each of which has their own staff. Committee or subcommittee staff are generally considered to work for the chairperson or ranking minority member of the committee or subcommittee.

> "I was on the education committee staff in the House and the Senate. On both, the staff are looked to by other members of the caucus as the experts on the issues of jurisdiction of the committee. I spent a lot of time talking to other Republican offices about ideas they had for a particular bill and how we could shape them into something that might move. A lot of my time was spent lobbying within Congress—explaining a bill the committee had developed and providing rationales for why certain provisions were included and why others were not." (Lindsay Fryer, author interview, September 22, 2022)

Much of the business of Congress is done through its subcommittee and committee structures. While there are at least three types of congressional committees, the most significant policy making ones are called standing committees (Congressional Research Service, 2017). See table 3.1 for a list of standing committees in the Senate and the House of Representatives. Each standing committee has a particular jurisdiction with responsibilities for a certain set of laws—monitoring their implementation, providing oversight of their implementation and the federal agencies that administer them, and rewriting them when the time comes. Committee websites explain their jurisdiction and their functions.[2] These subunits of the Congress often serve as the experts for the rest of the members of the body. For example, the education staff of the Committee on Education and Labor in the House of Representatives may serve as advisors and resources to all 435 members of the House, in addition to carrying out the committee's responsibilities.

Usually created at the discretion of the full committee, subcommittees come and go. My experience working on the Subcommittee on the Handicapped (subsequently renamed the Subcommittee on Disability Policy) is described in textbox 1.1. Originated in 1969 as the Special Subcommittee on Handicapped Workers, the subcommittee was eliminated in 2009 with its jurisdiction absorbed by the full committee.

TEXTBOX 1.1. **MY EXPERIENCE AS A CONGRESSIONAL STAFFER**

I first came to the U.S. Senate as an intern in January 1983. My six-month internship was part of my doctoral program in special education at the University of Maryland. My placement was on what was at the time the Subcommittee on the Handicapped, which was part of what is now the Committee on Health, Education, Labor and Pensions—the HELP Committee. Sen. Orrin Hatch (R-UT) was the chairman, and I was working for Sen. Lowell Weicker (R-CT), who chaired the subcommittee. I quickly learned that this would be a sink-or-swim experience, as I was expected to learn the ropes and pull my weight. I went to meetings with other congressional staff to discuss "state grants" and "funding formulas"—concepts and terms that were new to me. While I had learned a lot from my experience as a special education teacher and administrator and from my master's and doctoral studies, I had no conception of what public policy really meant. I knew about the federal law governing the education of students with disabilities—IDEA—but from the point of view of a practitioner. I witnessed what seemed like intense and blunt arguments between Republican and Democratic staff about matters I had never considered, such as the use of public funds in private schools. I was used to people talking in a far more circumspect and "polite" manner. These dialogues were blunt and to the point. I later came to appreciate that the pressure of finding compromises and making decisions about difficult issues on a timetable that often changed with little notice necessitated such interaction. With great mentorship and support from my colleagues, my perspective and skill set broadened. After six months my internship ended and I was hired as a legislative assistant. I eventually become the staff director of the subcommittee, leaving the Senate in 1986. My experience left me with great respect for hardworking Hill staffers.

While committee staff serve as experts with deep content knowledge in a particular issue area, staff who work in personal offices of members of Congress have

2. For example, see the Senate HELP (Health, Education, Labor and Pensions) Committee at https://www.help.senate.gov/about.

broad portfolios encompassing a range of issues from transportation to foreign relations to agriculture to national security to climate change to racial justice. In addition, they must regularly monitor the legislative schedule on the floor as well as in relevant committees in order to advise and prepare the member for whom they work. Members of Congress also have district office staff who are based in the member's district or state (in the case of senators) and are generally primarily concerned with case work rather than policy making. For example, they may assist a veteran in securing their benefits or help a Social Security recipient rectify a problem with their payment. They also assist in scheduling meetings and events for the member when they are at home.

Other congressional staff work in congressional support agencies such as the Congressional Research Service, the Congressional Budget Office, and the Government Accountability Office (Brudnick, 2020). Recent estimates indicate that there are about thirty-four thousand congressional staff working in all areas of the legislative branch (Cioffi & Saksa, 2022).

A new development among congressional staff unfolded in 2021—a push to unionize (Manríquez, 2022). Spurred into action because of safety concerns after the January 6, 2021, events in the Capitol and long-standing concerns about working conditions and access barriers to staff positions for people of color, congressional staff organized anonymously and created a revealing Instagram account: @Dear_White_Staffers (DWS). Growing to a following of ninety-one thousand, the account posted numerous anonymous complaints about abusive bosses, low pay, long hours, safety, and more. Prior to the creation of DWS, some congressional staff had begun to organize in groups like the Congressional Progressive Staff Association.[3] The momentum led to the May 2022 passage of a House resolution protecting workers' rights to organize in the House—including personal office staff, committee staff, and some other groups of staff—adopted with only Democratic support. House staffers created the Congressional Workers Union,[4] which began organizing individual House offices to apply to the Office of Congressional Workplace Rights to create unions. Staff from multiple Democratic offices have submitted applications as of July 2022, and more are expected (Schnell, 2022). The Senate may follow suit as Majority Leader Chuck Schumer expressed support for the unionization of staff (Cioffi & Saksa, 2022). Multiple complexities remain in terms of how such unions would work, particularly on committees that include staff from both Democratic and Republican offices.

RELATIONSHIPS ARE EVERYTHING

The policy making world in DC is not unlike any other human endeavor in that relationships matter tremendously. They can be the difference between success and failure, progress and deadlock, good policy and bad policy, winning and losing. The most important advice I ever received when I was first starting out as

---

3. For more information, see https://www.cpsadc.org/.

4. For more information, see https://www.congressionalworkersunion.org/.

a staffer in the Senate was "There is nothing more important than the relationships you build." In fact, I often heard the statement, "All you have up here is your word." I took this to mean that once you don't keep your word, your credibility is shot. And getting that back may be impossible.

> "The time to make relationships is before you need them. You build relationships so that when something challenging comes up, you can rely on those relationships." (Kuna Tavalin, author interview, August 17, 2022)

Policy making has an odd rhythm of poking along for years and suddenly taking off in a split second. Important policy decisions may be made quickly—sometimes in the middle of the night when the pressure is on to meet a deadline. In such high-pressure circumstances and with a lot at stake, trust is paramount.

Because of the ongoing turnover of members of Congress and the relatively low pay for staff,[5] congressional staff frequently change (Glassman, 2018). As most staff work at the pleasure of the member of Congress who was elected, and elections can be lost, staff may lose their jobs when the member they work for loses an election. A newly elected member may bring in new staff, sometimes those who worked on the campaign to help them get elected or longtime allies from back in the district or state. Other times, newly elected members may seek out experienced Hill staffers and recruit them to work in their offices. Often a newly elected member will have a mix of staff new to Congress as well as experienced hands.

Committee staff are less likely to turn over as quickly as personal office staff, as they tend to have significant content expertise in the policy area where they work, which is needed to carry out the work of the committee, and they are generally paid more than personal staff, unless the personal staff are in leadership roles, such as chief of staff. Thus, some committee staff may have worked for several different chairs or ranking members over time. Whether staff are new or experienced, it is critical for advocates to make ongoing efforts to retain existing relationships and build new relationships with new staff. It is not uncommon for Hill staff to eventually work for each of the three sectors represented in the iron triangle. When a new president is elected, some congressional staff with allegiance to the same party may leave Capitol Hill to gain executive agency experience. A relationship with a Hill staffer could evolve over time to encompass multiple roles and activities.

The media would lead us to believe that Republicans and Democrats are at each other's throats nonstop. While this may often be the case, it is also most often

---

5. In May 2022, House Speaker Nancy Pelosi raised the minimum salary for House staff to $45,000—still an amount that can be difficult to live on in an expensive city like Washington, DC. Rep. Alexandria-Cortez has a pay floor of over $50,000 for her staff. In addition she pays interns, who are usually unpaid, $15 per hour (Manríquez, 2022).

the case that staff of Republicans and Democrats work well together and form close friendships. In the many years I have worked with and come to know Hill staffers, I have never encountered bitter relationships based on politics. Policy disagreements may be significant, but to get the work of Congress done, staff must work together. If there is a particular allegiance to be noted, it is often to the legislative body where they work—House staff are allied with other House staff and Senate staff with other Senate staff.

"I worked on committee staff in both the House and the Senate between 2016 and 2021. In the early days relationships between Republican and Democratic committee staff were very strong. Today relationships are not as strong, and it is harder to negotiate policy. We used to go on committee retreats—with staff from both sides of the aisle. We would talk about policy implementation and big policy topics with good speakers. In the evening we would get together to socialize, and a lot of relationship building went on there." (Kim Knackstedt, author interview, August 12, 2022)

The Executive Branch

The White House and the many federal agencies that make up the executive branch are vital to the policy making process, with the essential functions of carrying out and enforcing laws. In addition, the president holds a megaphone unlike any other. The impact of the bully pulpit cannot be overstated. President Trump exponentially enlarged the presidential platform when he took this pulpit into the world of social media. He tweeted approximately 340,000 times between the time he announced his candidacy in June 2015 and through the four years of his presidency—for an average of thirty-four tweets a day with a record of two hundred tweets and retweets on one day. With so much media coverage, President Trump's tweets were often boosted, invigorating both his supporters and his opponents. His tweets announced new policy decisions, announced hirings and firings, praised and derided friends and foes, amplified falsehoods and fanned the flames of insurgency—until the president was blocked by Twitter in the final days of his presidency because of his incitement to violence. The influence of the presidency has always been extensive. But the vastly expanded impact of that influence by social media is yet to be fully understood.

The president is the only term-limited position in all three branches of government, allowed to serve a maximum of two four-year terms. The president serves as CEO, commander in chief, head of state, and lead policy maker for the nation. While Congress has the ultimate authority to create laws, the president wields considerable policy authority through the ability to galvanize public opinion and set a policy agenda.

The president can hire and fire political appointees across the government and holds the power to veto legislation passed by Congress. As one individual, the president can speak with a unitary voice and promote a unitary agenda, whereas Congress often appears to have 535 individual policy agendas.

The role the Office of the President plays in policy making is circumscribed by whether or not the president's political party controls the House or the Senate. Members of the president's party often defer to the president's agenda and may introduce legislation requested by the White House. When the same party controls the White House and both legislative bodies, agreed on priorities will often set the stage so progress can be made. When the margins of control are close in the House or Senate, success is challenging and bipartisan support is often needed.

Executive agencies of the president that are critical to policy making include the Office of Management and Budget (OMB)[6] and the Domestic Policy Council (DPC).[7] OMB organizes and manages the publication of the all-important budget proposal every year, serving as a clearinghouse for agency priorities to ensure they are in line with the president's priorities. It provides oversight of agency performance, regulatory policy, legislative clearance, and support for development of executive orders and presidential memoranda. Staff of the DPC work closely with political appointees in the various agencies, ensuring that the president's goals are prioritized and often preventing agencies from veering off in divergent directions.

With just over two million employees (excluding the postal service and the armed forces), the federal government is the largest employer in the nation. The congressional workforce is a shadow of this behemoth. The federal government has a vast hierarchical structure, organized by fifteen executive agencies and multiple non-Cabinet-level independent agencies.[8] Each Cabinet-level agency, and most non-Cabinet-level independent agencies, are led by a political appointee, chosen by the president and confirmed by the Senate. Multiple additional political appointees (who may not have to be confirmed by the Senate) fill hundreds of additional positions in agencies. Civil service positions are filled by career agency staff, sometimes referred to (unfortunately in a derogatory manner) as bureaucrats. Career agency staff often have deep knowledge about how federal programs work and how government works. While the political appointees turn over, generally every four years, career staff often remain for their entire careers.

Small independent federal agencies can sometimes play a critical policy making role. For example, the National Council on Disability[9]—a group of fifteen political appointees and eight or so staff—drafted the original Americans with Disabilities Act beginning in 1983. They were involved throughout the legislative process, working with both the White House and Congress, to the culmination of the signing of the law by President George H. W. Bush in 1990 (*ADA history*, n.d.).

6. For more information, see https://www.whitehouse.gov/omb/.

7. For more information, see https://www.whitehouse.gov/briefing-room/presidential-actions/2021/05/06/domestic-policy-presidential-directive-1-dppd-1/.

8. For more information, see https://www.usa.gov/federal-agencies/d#current-letter.

9. For more information, see https://ncd.gov/.

The chair of NCD, Sandra Parrino, stood alongside the president on the podium at the White House celebratory signing event (Young & National Council on Disability, 1997).[10]

> "Congress has stopped working. This leaves a void and executive action takes over. The executive branch sucks up all the space. This happened with Obama and Trump, and now Biden. And now we have the judiciary weighing in in a partisan way. The judicial branch used to stay away from partisan fisticuffs. But now they are fully embroiled. This arises from Congress's inability to pass laws. Congress is not checking the executive or judicial branches." (Jonathan Fansmith, author interview, August 16, 2022)

While Congress is the legislative branch of government with the core function of writing and revising our nation's laws, the executive branch is not a silent bystander when laws are under development. Since it is the executive branch that must interpret and implement the laws passed by Congress, they have much to say about how laws are drafted and implemented. In recent years, many argue that the balance of power has shifted from Congress to executive agencies and the judiciary. When Congress is unable to act, it leaves a void and the other two branches of government move in to fill it. Chapter 3 reviews policy making processes that involve both the legislative and executive branches of government.

> "The Congress is a lot of fiefdoms—535 personal offices and multiple committees. The White House is one big machine with many moving parts. You are representing the policies and priorities of the president, but also the chief of staff, the head of the Domestic Policy Council, the First Lady, the vice president, the Second Gentleman, etc. I set six-month goals based on campaign promises and the president's priorities." (Kim Knackstedt, author interview, August 12, 2022)

Interest Groups

There is a vast literature on interest groups (see, for example, Birkland, 2016; Holyoke, 2021; Kingdon, 2010). In general, an interest group is a collection of people or organizations united for multiple purposes, including influencing policy

---

10. For more information, see https://www.whitehousehistory.org/photos/americans-with-disabilities-act-signing.

toward their desired outcome. Individuals and organizations join interest groups to amplify their voices and perspectives, particularly at the national level, in a manner that an individual acting solo cannot. John Kingdon (2010) astutely notes that "organized interests are heard more in politics than unorganized interests" (p. 53). Examples abound, with most located in, or at least focused on, the nation's capital or state capitals across the country. A report from the Congressional Research Service captures numerous sources that catalogue the thousands of interest groups with lobbying functions (Watkins, 2008).

Interest groups are generally considered to fall into at least four categories: professional and trade associations, organizations composed of businesses or corporations, public interest groups, and think tanks.

PROFESSIONAL AND TRADE ASSOCIATIONS

Professional and trade associations comprise members of the same profession or trade, such as the American Bar Association for attorneys or the American Association of Colleges for Teacher Education, to which deans of colleges and schools of education in institutions of higher education belong. Such organizations generally promote their economic self-interest as well as what they believe to be in the best interest of the public. In addition to offering policy and advocacy services, they may provide their members a range of professional benefits, such as annual conferences, professional learning opportunities, and more. They are generally nonprofit entities, even if their members may be for-profit entities. Multiple associations in the education sector fall into this category.

BUSINESS OR CORPORATION ASSOCIATIONS

Business or corporation associations are composed of the members of an industry in the business sector and seek to promote policy that will secure and expand their interests, as well as improving business conditions. Examples include the National Association of Manufacturers, the National Restaurant Association, and the American Booksellers Association. While such entities are generally nonprofit organizations, their members may all be for-profit entities. The line between a professional association and a business association is not always clear. For example, the association known as Career Education Colleges and Universities is composed of for-profit colleges and universities and promotes their business perspective as well as serving their members.

PUBLIC INTEREST GROUPS

Public interest groups are organizations formed to promote what they believe is in the interest of the broader public. They may or may not be membership organizations. High-profile public interest groups include Common Cause, created to bring about reform in the financing of elections; Sierra Club, dedicated to preserving the environment; and the American Civil Liberties Union, dedicated to preserving the rights and freedoms provided to Americans through the Constitution and by law. The definition of exactly what is in the public interest is often debated and is generally defined by the organization itself. There is considerable gray area, exemplified by the National Rifle Association. Dedicated to promoting gun rights, some argue that it is defending the public interest of safety and general welfare. Others argue that the NRA is more of a faction whose ideology may infringe on the rights of others (Cost, 2018).

Public interest groups may serve as a counterpoint to business interest groups. While business interest groups seek to preserve and expand their private business interests, public interest groups may see those interests as undermining the greater good. For example, while the fossil fuel industry may seek to expand, organizations seeking to address climate change may seek to reduce their success in influencing policy.

THINK TANKS

A fourth type of interest group is think tanks. In general, think tanks are described as nonpartisan nonprofit policy entities that conduct research and provide information to inform policy. However, think tanks often have a political leaning, one way or the other. For example, the Center for American Progress (CAP), founded by former Obama administration staff and allies, describes itself as an "independent non-partisan policy institute . . . for progressives who want to change the country." CAP is considered a liberal think tank. On the other side of the ledger is the Heritage Foundation, which describes itself as a "conservative think tank" intended to build and promote conservative policy.

Think tanks and public interest groups are not membership organizations. Their funding comes from foundations, corporations, and other donors rather than membership fees. They may receive funds to pursue a particular approach to a broad range of policy areas, or they may circumscribe their work to one policy domain. For example, the Cato Institute inserts a libertarian approach to a range of policy matters—both domestic and international. On the other hand, the Learning Policy Institute's work is solely focused on creating a stronger, more equitable education system. Their work is circumscribed to the education sector. Another important characteristic of think tanks is that they do not engage lobbyists who directly seek to influence policy makers and would be required to register with Congress. In general, they are behind the scenes, offering technical assistance and information to inform policy. The line is gray and at times hard to discern (*Some think tanks blur line*, 2016). Over the years think tanks have proliferated and become increasingly influential in policy making, outside of the compliance requirements for lobbying.

WHAT DO INTEREST GROUPS DO IN RELATION TO POLICY AND ADVOCACY?

Interest groups engage in numerous activities in relation to their mission and toward achieving the goals of the organization. Their work may be considered in five general categories: (1) general awareness education about the policy problem and possible solutions; (2) building support and momentum for the policy problem and preferred solution; (3) targeting programs or sectors for increases in funding; (4) amending or developing new policy; and (5) preventing the progress of proposals and positions that run counter to their interests. They target their work to a range of audiences, from the general public to other interest groups, to specific members of Congress, to executive agency officials. The effort that interest groups may put forth to stop "bad" policy from taking hold may be considerable. This includes actively opposing bills introduced in Congress, developing and providing information and arguments to policy makers that would deter the progress of a policy proposal, actively generating opposition to a policy by developing allies, and undertaking strategic initiatives that may involve constituents of the policy maker and other influencers.

> "The American Council on Education is an umbrella organization for the entire higher education enterprise. We are involved at the federal level with every issue that touches colleges and universities—environmental issues, justice, transportation, sustainability, and more. So much of what we do as advocates is to build relationships. For example, when the White House announces an initiative, we usually have had background conversations with them. The public things you see are often the result of days and weeks and years of work—so that what emerges takes into account our members' views." (Jonathan Fansmith, author interview, August 16, 2022)

Interest groups may or may not have a significant influence on policy. In his groundbreaking research analyzing how members of Congress make decisions, Kingdon (2010) found that the degree of influence an interest group has on policy is to some extent dependent on the sector in which it works. For example, they are much more likely to be persuasive in the transportation sector than the health sector. Kingdon concludes: "Generally, then, the lower the partisanship, ideological cast, and campaign visibility of the issues in a policy domain, the greater the importance of interest groups" (p. 47).

> "Effective interest groups include federal policy experts; experts from the field with knowledge and experience; and grassroots people, communities, and organizations. You can't do this work alone." (Ashley White, author interview, September 23, 2022)

POLITICAL ACTION COMMITTEES AND 501(C)(4)S

Most interest groups have nonprofit status as described by section 501(c)(3) of the tax code, meaning they are exempt from paying taxes and have a charitable or educational purpose. As such, they are not allowed to provide resources for electoral politics or make campaign contributions to candidates pursuing election or reelection or to political parties. Many nonprofits create spin-off entities, such as political action committees, or 501(c)(4)s, which do engage in political activities, both promoting and opposing candidates. Think tanks may do that as well as membership organizations. Both teachers' unions, the American Federation of Teachers and the National Education Association, are examples of nonprofit membership interest groups with spin-off entities that engage directly in political campaigns.

COALITIONS

A number of interest groups in a similar sector or with a similar goal often join together to create a coalition. As policy voices on Capitol Hill have proliferated over the years, coalitions have become increasingly significant strategies for influence. Coalitions enable small interest groups to band together with larger, better resourced, and more powerful interest groups to speak with one voice. While policy makers may not be influenced by one organization, they may pay attention when one hundred national organizations take the same position. The more unity there is by interest groups, the easier it is for policy makers to act in cohesion. Organizations with vastly disparate viewpoints on some policy issues in a sector may unite around a broader policy goal in the sector. A good example is the Committee for Education Funding.[11]

> "Coalitions unite organizations. When organizations disagree on solutions, it makes Congress less likely to act. Congress doesn't want to get in the middle of stakeholder arguments. They want to see a united front in support of a solution." (Kuna Tavalin, author interview, August 17, 2022)

Founded in 1969 and composed of more than one hundred national education organizations, Committee for Education Funding has as a unifying mission to secure an adequate federal financial investment in education. Membership in the coalition spans "early childhood education, elementary and secondary education, higher education, adult and career education, and educational enhancements such as libraries and museums—including students, teachers and faculty, parents, administrators, counselors and other school employees, and school board

---

11. For more information, see https://cef.org/about/.

members." Organizations that disagree about other education policy matters—such as the role of charter schools in public education—all agree that the federal government should invest more in the education system as whole.

Another example of a long-established coalition is the Leadership Conference on Civil and Human Rights (LCCHR).[12] Founded in 1950, LCCHR now comprises more than two hundred national organizations with a unified mission of full equality for all. Promoting equal opportunity and social justice, LCCHR works in the areas of democracy, justice, inclusion, and opportunity. Advocacy at the national level is a significant aspect of their work, where they weigh in on policy matters, offer testimony, and issue reports.

GOVERNMENT RELATIONS/LOBBYING FIRMS

Washington, as are state capitals, is filled with government relations firms, which are hired by interest groups or by individual institutions or organizations to promote their interests with policy makers through lobbying, advocacy, and strategic advice. Those who work for government relations firms often have significant experience working on Capitol Hill or in the executive branch. Their connections with policy makers are significant, and their knowledge of the players involved, the politics at hand, the legislative and executive processes available, and the policy issues under consideration is deep.

An interest group may seek to weigh in on a policy matter that affects their members; however, it may be outside of their general sphere of influence, or the policy makers who are key are not well known to them—or may have been their opponents on previous policy matters. In such circumstances they may seek to hire an outside firm with a lobbyist who fits the bill. Some interest groups hire firms that specialize in a certain sector to extend their reach and amplify the work of a limited staff within the interest group. Some interest groups contract out all of their government relations work to government relations firms. In the education sector, there are numerous government relations firms that are hired by interest groups, including Penn Hill Group,[13] Bose Public Affairs Group,[14] and the Raben Group.[15]

LOBBYING

The Lobbying Disclosure Act outlines the legal parameters of lobbying (*The Lobbying Disclosure Act at 20*, 2015). It defines a lobbyist as one who is "employed or retained by a client for financial or other compensation for services that include more than one lobbying contact, other than an individual whose lobbying activities constitute less than 20% of the time engaged in the services provided by such individual to that client over a 3-month period." All three criteria must be met for

---

12. For more information, see https://civilrights.org/about/the-coalition/.
13. For more information, see https://pennhillgroup.com/.
14. For more information, see https://bosepublicaffairs.com/.
15. For more information, see https://rabengroup.com/about/.

a person to meet the definition of lobbyist—more than one lobbying contact within three months, receipt of compensation, and spending 20 percent or more of their time lobbying. Such individuals must register with the House and the Senate and make regular reports describing their work. This information is a matter of public record.[16] In addition, the Internal Revenue Service places limitations on how much lobbying an organization with a nonprofit designation may conduct (*Lobbying*, n.d.). Nonprofit organizations may engage in some lobbying so long as it is not a substantial portion of their activity.

Over the last two decades the number of registered lobbyists in Washington has ranged from eleven thousand to almost fifteen thousand (*Number of registered active lobbyists*, 2022). However, the universe of those who do not meet the threshold to register but are involved in lobbying, or advocacy and policy activities, is significantly greater than fifteen thousand. The activities of advocacy and policy influencing are similar whether one is registered as a lobbyist or not. Those who hold titles as disparate as director of government relations, chief advocacy officer, policy advisor, legislative counsel, director for congressional and federal affairs, legislative representative, director of federal relations and policy analysis, and director of lobbying and federal relations are generally engaged in the same activities, perhaps with a slightly different focus depending on the organization and the size of the team. In small organizations, it is not uncommon for a staff person to carry out multiple functions that may include membership, communications, and government relations all in one role. In larger organizations, the policy and advocacy team may be five or six people or more.

BEYOND THE IRON TRIANGLE

Multiple entities and sectors beyond the iron triangle influence the policy making process, increasing its complexity and density. These include courts, social media and the press, public opinion, constituents, grassroots movements and organizations, and experts.

The Courts

The third branch of government, the judiciary, plays the essential role of interpreting fundamental policy declarations, including statutory language, regulations from executive agencies, executive orders issued by the president, and prior court decisions. A court decision may invalidate a statute all together. The federal court system is the final arbiter in interpreting the Constitution—deciding whether a particular provision of law or its application violates the Constitution. Federal courts are comprised of the Supreme Court, thirteen circuit courts, and ninety-four district courts, as well as multiple other specialized courts, such as bankruptcy courts.

---

16. Lobbying forms submitted to the House of Representatives can be searched at https://lobbying disclosure.house.gov/, while the forms submitted to the Senate can be searched at https://lda.senate .gov/system/public/.

While courts only deliver opinions on cases that are brought before them, they may have a significant and far-reaching impact on policy implementation. *Brown v. the Board of Education*, which declared that separate is not equal in education—is a landmark example of the broad reach court decisions can have. As court opinions are generated over time, they form a body of "case law" that is considered part of the law. These decisions establish "precedent," which informs future decision making by the judiciary.

Statutes often are crafted with language that is general rather than specific, as they are the result of negotiations of those holding varying opinions. The more detailed a policy becomes, the less likely compromise can be reached. In addition, statutes are written to be applied to a range of situations and circumstances. Knowing that circumstances are multiple and varied—and that some may develop that were not envisioned (for example, the provision of education during a pandemic)—lawmakers may choose broad wording, leaving specific interpretation to both the executive branch via rule making and the judicial branch via the rendering of court decisions.

Congress can play a significant role in responding to court decisions by determining that they are a misinterpretation of congressional intent. My dissertation examined legislation that overturned a Supreme Court decision and provided clarification on the provisions of concern. See textbox 1.2 for a description of my dissertation.

TEXTBOX 1.2. **LEGISLATION OVERTURNING A SUPREME COURT DECISION: A CASE STUDY**

My dissertation was a case study of how a bill becomes a law. I analyzed the Handicapped Children's Protection Act of 1986, a law that was enacted in direct response to the Supreme Court decision *Smith v. Robinson* in 1984. The court decision held that parents were not entitled to recoup attorneys' fees for administrative proceedings or court actions when utilizing the due process system under the Education of All Handicapped Children Act (EAHCA, which is now IDEA). The court reasoned that if Congress had intended the award of attorneys' fees under EAHCA, it would have specifically authorized such reimbursement. Congress immediately responded by introducing bills in both the House and the Senate to reverse the decision. The next two years were spent negotiating and refining the legislative language. Enactment of the Handicapped Children's Protection Act of 1986 reversed the decision, allowing for the reimbursement of fees for prevailing parties or in situations where the parents are substantially justified in rejecting a settlement offer.

In recent years the courts have increasingly played a strong role in policy making, at times overshadowing both Congress and the executive branch. As political polarization has expanded, as appointments to the Supreme Court have become increasingly political, and as Congress has appeared gridlocked, the courts have flexed their muscles, making decisions on hot-button issues as far reaching as abortion, gun rights, climate change, separation of church and state (Liptak & Kao, 2022), and the ability of federal agencies to regulate (Rainey & Ramsey, 2022). The historical check and balance that the courts provide to Congress and the administration may be leaning toward a lopsided configuration where the courts increasingly exercise authority over policy making. In addition, Supreme Court decisions may increasingly return authority to states to determine matters that were once primarily determined by federal law.

Social Media and the Press

Reinforcing the notion that the government is accountable to the people, the press plays a role of both providing information and holding government officials and entities accountable. One need only watch a White House press conference to see both roles exemplified. Historically, the press has been represented by newspapers and major television news outlets and targeted to the general public. With the advent of cable TV and social media, the boundaries of "the press" are not so clear.

The growth of social media—Twitter, Facebook, Instagram, YouTube, and more—offers both advantages and disadvantages beyond the traditional press. Social media provides instant communication in real time and with great frequency. Communication can reach a wider audience than traditional press, spreading or amplifying a message astronomically and instantly. The consumer is empowered to access a broad range of sources. Social media allows for two-way communication between the sender and the receiver, thus reinforcing transparency and the democratic notion of elected officials being in touch with constituents and the public at large. With functions such as retweeting and "likes," the consumer becomes part of the story. These functions are appealing to policy makers and the policy making apparatus.

Disadvantages of the use of social media in the policy realm include the lack of established rules of the game, such as traditions or requirements for checking sources or verifying stories. Members of the traditional press are professionals, trained journalists, whereas social media communication is available to anyone and everyone with minimal parameters. Those parameters are being increasingly tested with the proliferation of "fake news" and conspiracy theories.

Members of Congress are enthusiastic users of social media to spread their perspective and share their accomplishments. Virtually every member of Congress has a twitter account, and most congressional offices monitor their twitter accounts, just as they do phone calls and emails, particularly from constituents.

One analysis pointed out that while there was a proliferation of use of social media by members of Congress in 2020, there was a notable decline of legislative activity (*Congress on social media 2020*, n.d.). Consider the following data points, covering the time period November 1–30, 2020:

- Members of Congress posted across Twitter, Facebook, Instagram and YouTube 784,614 times in 2020 compared to 715,124 time in 2019.

- Meanwhile, of the 5,117 bills introduced in Congress in 2020, only twenty-eight were enacted, compared to 169 in 2019 when 8,364 bills introduced were introduced.
- While members of Congress tweeted fifty times per bill introduced in 2019, they tweeted ninety-eight times per bill introduced in 2020.

The report concludes that "Twitter replaced floor debates in 2020."

Of the four platforms considered (Twitter, Facebook, Instagram, and You-Tube), Twitter was used the most by members of Congress, with 500,366 posts during 2020, for an average of 1,604 posts per day. As a group, Democrats out-posted Republicans. Democrats were more prolific on Twitter than Republicans, with 313,739 posts compared to 186,627. However, individual Republican members of Congress were the highest users of Twitter during 2020, with Sen. Ted Cruz (R-TX) holding the record in the Senate at 5,282 tweets and Rep. Chip Roy (R-TX) holding the record in the House at 7,928 tweets. It is clear that the use of Twitter is a bipartisan enterprise.

> "Social media is another powerful tool used at the federal level more fre-quently. Sen. Alexander (R-TN) was a Twitter user. It was a platform for him to communicate and reach people in real time and get feedback from likes and retweets. Members care about how many of their posts are being liked or retweeted. They pay attention to twitter campaigns with hashtags to stop or support bills. Members notice tweets that include their names. You can't ignore thousands of people raising an issue or retweeting you. I believe Twitter is the 'go to' for social media for policy makers." (Lindsay Fryer, author interview, September 22, 2022)

Interest groups utilize social media extensively as well—to promote their messages and accomplishments, to provide information, to persuade others, and to build coalitions, and gain supporters. Being engaged in the policy making process means having a social media presence and using it strategically. Many interest groups, such as Triage Cancer, keep and update lists of social media handles and addresses for members of Congress.[17]

Public Opinion

Public opinion polls offer a broad snapshot of a general view of a topic, an action, or an electoral race at a certain period of time. They are often used by policy makers as one set of information in decision making. Those engaged in the policy making process are likely to cite public opinion polls that bolster their case

---

17. For more information, see https://triagecancer.org/congressional-social-media.

and ignore those that do not. There are multiple examples where public opinion and public policy are not in alignment, such as gun control. There is also evidence that public opinion may constrain policy options by setting parameters on options that appear to be unpalatable to the general public. Public opinion polls can also facilitate understanding of where constituents stand on particular issues. Some organizations, such as Data for Progress,[18] provide data tied to a particular set of issues they prioritize.

Constituents

TEXTBOX 1.3. THE INFLUENCE OF A CONSTITUENT

When I worked on the U.S. Senate Subcommittee on Disability Policy, Sen. Lowell Weicker (R-CT) was the chair. Our staff director, John Doyle, routinely went to Connecticut to check in with constituents. On one such visit he met with a parent of a child with speech therapy needs. The parent reported being very concerned when they were told that the federal law allowed only a small number of sessions of speech therapy for students per year—and that their child had hit the maximum allotment. Being intimately knowledgeable about the governing federal law, the Individuals with Disabilities Education Act (IDEA), the staff director told the parent that there was no such provision in federal law. The parent was astounded. The staff director returned to Washington and began to develop a program that would provide support to parents around the country to understand the requirements of the law. That program remains today, decades later, as the $27 million Parent Training and Information Centers.[1] It funds parent-run centers in every state that provide information and support to parents of students across the country who receive services under IDEA.

---

1. For more information, see https://www2.ed.gov/programs/oseppic/index.html.

Constituents are those who live within the jurisdiction each member of Congress is elected to represent. Constituents may be considered the "employers" of elected representatives in that they have the ability to "hire" (vote into office) and to "fire" (vote out of office) their congressional delegation. The voice of constituents, depending on the issue, may or may not send a clear message. The more accord there is, the more likely the elected representative is to clearly reflect constituent preferences in their legislative actions. One area where this is clearly seen is in the extent to which a particular employment sector is prevalent in a member of Congress's state or district. For example, if agriculture is a major employer in a member's district, it is very likely that the member will support initiatives related to the agriculture sector. Furthermore, the member is likely to seek membership on a committee or subcommittee that has jurisdiction over agricultural issues, thus giving them a greater opportunity to shape policy.

---

18. For more information, see https://www.dataforprogress.org/.

"Constituents can make a huge difference. In Tennessee there are many songwriters—it is a very large industry. We knew them for some time and met with them a lot. They explained to us how they got compensated— that they were paid pennies on the dollar for their work. Performers and radio stations made a lot of money, while they did not. They would have to write thirty to forty hits to make essentially minimum wage. They were living on a subsistence level. Out of those meetings we developed the Music Modernization Act, which transformed how they get compensated. It was a two- to three-year process of negotiating. After the law was enacted, a songwriter met with us and brought his first check from after the bill was passed, and a check he had gotten before the bill was passed. One was $2,500 and the other was $15,000—for the same work. His life was changed. We turned a hobby into a career." (David Cleary, author interview, September 15, 2022)

In his research as reported in *Congressmen's Voting Decisions*, John Kingdon (1989) interviewed multiple members of the House of Representatives and analyzed how they came to make decisions about voting on a particular piece of legislation. Because members of Congress must vote on a wide range of issues with great frequency and minimal time to fully examine each, he determined that members developed a set of decision rules to enable them to respond in a timely manner. He noted that the voice of constituents matters most when the intensity is robust. "Constituents' intensities count for as much as their numbers," he said (p. xii). He further concluded that interest groups gain influence when they involve constituents who are mobilized.

Constituents may become increasingly influential as a member of Congress approaches reelection. Since members are motivated to win the votes of constituents, openness to listening and being influenced may be at its peak during the election cycle.

Direct communication with elected representatives is critical in developing influence. The volume of direct communication to a policy maker (such as emails and phone calls) is often considered a proxy for significance. Congressional offices keep tabs on how many phone calls or emails they receive on a particular issue and what the opinions are. Often those tallies are connected to constituents. They are routinely reported to the member in order to inform their decision making. The old adage "the squeaky wheel gets the grease" remains a truism on Capitol Hill.

In addition to volume, ongoing relationships with constituents developed over time make a difference. To the extent a constituent becomes a trusted informant connecting salient national policy matters to the circumstances in the district or state, they become a go-to advisor. Offices may begin to reach out proactively and request opinions from trusted informants on matters such as whether or not to cosponsor a piece of legislation, to get suggestions for amendments, and for recommendations regarding funding priorities. Such relationships require ongoing cultivation and attentiveness and represent the pinnacle for an influential constituent.

Grassroots Movements and Organizations

Policy priorities and opinions are often shifted by grassroots movements and the grassroots organizations attached to them. The civil rights movement of the 1960s, today's Black Lives Matter movement, and the movement against school shootings are salient examples of how demands for change begin to grow at the local level as a result of events. Grassroots movements often develop to include specific funded initiatives to amplify their voice and perspective nationally, becoming grassroots organizations.

> "Grassroots movements are so important for public policy—to raise awareness and build momentum. It takes time. For example, while violence by police against Black people goes back generations, George Floyd's murder galvanized much of the country. The video of his death transformed the dialogue so much that racial equity became a cornerstone of Joe Biden's policy platform." (Michael Yudin, author interview, August 12, 2022)

The enactment of the Americans with Disabilities Act (ADA)[19] in 1990 represents a landmark example of the significant role of grassroots activism in influencing policy. In reflecting on lessons learned from the enactment of the ADA, Pat Wright (often referred to as the "general" of the ADA advocacy work) noted the following in relation to the mobilization of the grass roots:

> One of the great hallmarks of the passage of the ADA is that the grassroots came to "own" the legislation. They were mobilized and activated to vociferously fight for the legislation and tell their stories of why the legislation was needed. People came to Washington from all over the country to communicate with their Representatives and press for passage of the law. (Wright & West, 2000)

Experts

Those with high-visibility knowledge and experience in a particular area may serve as policy elites (Kingdon, 1989, p. 33) connecting their expertise with policy makers or intermediate vehicles (such as interest groups) that amplify their voices

---

19. For more information, see https://www.ada.gov/ada_intro.htm.

in policy making—perhaps through serving as expert witnesses at hearings or "go to" influencers with congressional offices, congressional committees, or administration officials.

When researchers serve as policy elites, they bring their research to bear on a particular policy challenge. However, research alone is not a ticket to the policy table. Since research is often long-term (and the policy making process is so often quick-turnaround, short-term) and may be too specific to be helpful in determining a policy position, it may be considered ancillary to policy making. Policy makers may look for research that bolsters a predetermined position rather than informing a position. Researchers may play more of a role in uncovering problems and informing the policy agenda than by offering solutions to policy problems.

Those who are both constituents and experts can be powerful voices at the policy table, as they offer the policy maker both a view from back home and a broader view informed by experience and knowledge. When such an individual is also aligned with an interest group with a national presence, the impact is further elevated. In all cases, building the bridge to have access to the policy maker's office and communicating in such a way that the message is heard and is useful are critical.

THE CULTURE OF POLICY MAKING VERSUS THE CULTURES OF OTHER SECTORS

Most of my career has involved working with interest groups in the education and disability arenas. A key aspect of my role, no matter what the organization, has been to develop and maintain relationships with key players in Congress, the administration, and other interest groups. In so doing, I view my role as being a bridge, or a connector, between members of the interest groups and the policy world in Washington. A portion of this role involves translating—or tour-guiding. It is as if one is entering another country and needs to become familiar with the culture and norms in order to engage successfully.

> "More than 50 percent of the work is education—educating those we work with about how it works inside the Beltway and educating legislators and executive branch staff about what is happening on the ground. It is a translation from the real world into the policy world and vice versa." (Kuna Tavalin, author interview, August 17, 2022)

A useful way to consider differences between the Washington policy making culture and cultures in other sectors is to analyze various dimensions of those cultures and how they differ. Table 1.1 offers eight dimensions and compares the culture in Congress with that of higher education and disability rights.

TABLE 1.1. The Culture of Policy Making versus the Cultures of Other Sectors

Dimension	Higher Education	Disability Rights	Policy Makers
Currency	Knowledge, expertise	Lived experience	Power
Tenure of members	Long-term	Long-term	Election cycle—2–6 years
Timing	Long-term	Long-term	Immediate
Communication	Elaborate, detailed	Direct impact, urgent	Brief, talking points, persuasive
Information sources	Scholarship, professionals, published books and articles in professional journals	Lived experience, peers	Media, constituents, mass influencers, party leaders, colleagues, public opinion, funders
Institutional incentives	Contributions to scholarship, research for tenure	Empowerment, choice, inclusion, access, impact on individual lives	Influence among peers, reelection
Key audiences	Peers, research funders	Public opinion, policy makers	Constituents, funders
Key activities	Research, publish, teach	Advocacy, activism	Vote, craft laws, run for office

Note: Adapted from McLaughlin et al., 2016.

The first dimension to consider is *currency*, or the medium of exchange. For each of the sectors, what is the most salient aspect of interaction that is essential in the functioning of the culture? For the policy maker it is generally developing, maintaining, or expanding power, as power broadens the influence of the policy maker, enabling them to intensify their impact. A freshman member of Congress may seek support from leadership in order to secure a coveted position on an influential committee. For those in higher education, knowledge and expertise represent the most potent currency. Researching, publishing, and teaching all contribute to developing the expertise that is highly valued in that setting. For disability rights organizations, bringing the lived experiences of their members to the table is paramount.

The second dimension of consideration involves the *tenure* of people in each of the sectors. For policy makers, the tenure is dependent on election cycles—every two years for House members and every six years for senators. Compared to higher education faculty, this is a short horizon. While the notion of tenure is changing in higher education, securing a tenured position is coveted as it represents long-term stability for the pursuit of research and scholarship. Most faculty members enter higher education intent on a long-term career. This may or may not be the case with policy makers, who are vulnerable every election cycle. For people with disabilities, they are in it for life. The experience of living with a disability in society changes over time and needs repeated sharing in order to educate the public and to influence policy makers.

The third dimension is *timing*. Driven by election cycles, policy makers are always eager to deliver results while they are in office. In contrast, academics are used to having plenty of time—for their research, their lectures, their books, and scholarly inquiry. Academic endeavors are generally a long game—over years and decades. Researchers are often challenged by the policy appetite for immediate bite-sized determinative pieces of information that will support or undermine a particular policy position. Laurence Lynn reflected that policy making generally takes place in the framework of an adversary process, which is not the scientific process that characterizes research. He notes that the various stages of policy making generally do not wait for relevant knowledge to become available, and often the "systematic accumulation of knowledge may not begin until policies and programs are enacted" (Lynn, 1978, pp. 16–17). This disconnect has at times given higher education a poor reputation with policy makers. As one Capitol Hill staffer once told me, "Higher education is more interested in admiring the problem rather than solving it." A 1971 National Research Council report noted that "research producers are sometimes viewed as being more interested in furthering their academic disciplines than providing operational help" (Lynn, 1978, p. 3). For researchers to become successful advocates, an awareness of this potential disconnect is critical.

Disability rights organizations are motivated by both short-term and long-term horizons. Many people with disabilities face urgent life-or-death situations that motivate them to engage with policy makers intensely and for immediate results. The organized voice of disabled people can have a significant and immediate impact when a targeted policy decision is on the horizon—for example, in the multiple efforts to scale back the Affordable Care Act (Nichols, 2017).

Communication is the fourth dimension. In the policy maker's world, shorter is better. Writing and conversation need to be in the vernacular and to the point. As policy makers must have passing knowledge on the broad set of public policy issues; there is little time to read detailed reports or study scientific journals. In addition, the nature of the communication is often persuasive, framed as why one particular solution is preferable to another or how the data about a situation leads directly to a particular policy solution. The best communication for policy makers involves persuasive data, compelling stories or anecdotes, and recommendations for solutions. In higher education nuance, conditional propositions, deep scrutiny, and limitations of conclusions are valued and considered at length. With little time for such deliberation and the pressure of making decisions about policy solutions in the short term, policy makers need communication that will meet their needs. If it does not, it will be discarded. Ensuring that advocacy messages meet the test for consumption by policy makers is critical to being heard and being successful in influencing policy.

Disability rights organizations have often communicated by engaging in direct action. For example, during various debates about health care, they have swarmed the halls of Congress with signs and chants, risking arrest (Nichols, 2017). During consideration of the ADA, one thousand disabled people rallied at the White House, eventually making their way to the Capitol, where what is now called the "Capitol Crawl" occurred (Nichols, 2017). Sixty disability activists left their wheelchairs to climb the Capitol steps and demonstrate the impact of inaccessibility. It was a direct communication about the impact of policy choices on their daily lives.

The fifth dimension of comparison is *information sources*. Policy makers receive information from multiple sources—some with more resonance than others. Experts, researchers, academics, and public interest advocates represent one set of sources. Depending on a number of factors, interest groups and experts may be outflanked by others, including constituents, political party leaders, and campaign donors. Being aware of the range of information sources available to policy makers assists advocates in making their voice unique and persuasive. For example, when disability advocates share how a particular health care policy provision has directly affected their well-being, a connection is made between policy and daily life. This can be a unique and significant perspective in advocacy and may be more persuasive than organizations whose positions are grounded in research or ideology. However, multiple factors determine the resonance of a particular perspective with policy makers.

The sixth dimension is the *institutional incentives* at play for different cultures. In general, policy makers want to be in a position to be reelected when the time comes. They will be keeping an eye on public opinion polls and social media posts on various issues as well as messages from powerful constituents in their district or state and potential challengers in their next election. They will seek to gain popularity among political leaders of their party and other influencers, such as campaign funders. Those in interest groups will reflect the institutional incentives of their sector. In higher education, faculty are incentivized to perform in three areas: teaching, research, and service. Matching those incentives with the incentives in a policy making environment can be challenging. Incentives at work for disabled people are often measured by changes in their quality of life in terms of access, inclusion, and independence.

The seventh dimension of consideration is *key audiences*. Constituents, political party leaders, and campaign funders are key audiences for policy makers. All are essential in sustaining and continuing in elected office. In higher education, faculty generally target other scholars in their field. Sharing knowledge and building a research base are essential. In addition, potential funders for research are important to many faculty to sustain their work. For disability rights organizations, policy makers are a significant target audience. A corollary is public opinion, which can influence policy makers.

Finally, the eighth dimension is *key activities*. The role of lawmakers is to act—on policy, oversight, nominee confirmation, and more. Public positions must be taken and defended. Facing accountability through elections is ongoing. Higher education faculty prioritize researching, publishing, and teaching. Disability rights organizations prioritize advocacy and activism as essential activities.

Considering the differences in cultures between interest group sectors and the policy making world will inform how and when advocates engage with policy making.

REPRESENTATION MATTERS

Those who are at the heart of the policy making apparatus in our nation's capital do not reflect the demographic makeup of our nation.[20] As with elites in many sectors, they are disproportionately White, male, and older. In most of the coalitions I have belonged to over the years, as well as in the organizations I have been affiliated with, people of color, people with disabilities, and LGBTQI individuals are underrepresented. This is the case, even though my work is in a sector with a core belief in equity. Certainly, things are changing, and diversity, equity, and inclusion now appear as priorities for virtually all national associations. But there is a long way to go, and political challenges to these concepts are surging.

> "Working in the House as a Black and African American woman was extremely isolating. Ironically, I thought the Hill would be more sophisticated. I thought the Hill was where big thinkers worked. But the presence of racism, even at this level, illustrates how structural it is and how deeply racism and other isms are ingrained in society. And little attention was paid to it. As prevalent as DEI [diversity, equity, and inclusion] conversations are these days, not once was there a convening of staff for such a discussion. One way I was able to navigate this was to find other Black women who understood these issues and just how debilitating they could be. We could discuss what in academia we call 'the hidden curriculum.'" (Ashley White, author interview, September 23, 2022)

---

20. For more on the makeup of Congress, see https://www.govtrack.us/congress/members.

The votes of people of color, particularly Black Americans, were pivotal in handing victory to Democrats in the 2020 election—in the White House, the Senate, and the House of Representatives. Thus, the stage was set for a more diverse Congress and a more diverse set of administration officials, representing slow but steady change.

The 117th Congress, which was seated in January 2021, represents the most racially and ethnically diverse Congress in history (Schaeffer, 2021). Almost a quarter (23%) of members of the House and Senate are racial and ethnic minorities. A total of 124 senators and representatives describe themselves as Black, Hispanic, Asian/Pacific Islander, or Native American. This represents a 97 percent increase over the Congress of 2001–2003, which included only sixty-three members who were racial or ethnic minorities. Democrats account for 83 percent of racial and ethnic minority members, while Republicans account for 17 percent. Despite this shift, the makeup of Congress remains out of sync with the population of America, where 60 percent of the U.S. population is White while 77 percent of voting members of Congress are White. While women represent 50.8 percent of the population, they are only 38 percent of members of Congress. The average age of members of Congress is fifty-nine, with half of senators being over age sixty-five and 141 members of the House of Representatives over age sixty-five (*How old is Congress?*, 2017). While estimates reveal that about 25 percent of Americans have a disability (*CDC: 1 in 4 US adults*, 2018), very few members of Congress have a disability or identify as having a disability. Likewise, few members of Congress identify with the LGBTQI community, though there are more now than in past years. State legislatures also reflect this disproportionality. Every state legislature in the nation is disproportionately White, with the exception of Hawaii (Zoch, 2020).

"More member diversity can get more people excited about participating in politics and policy making. When you see someone at the national level who looks like and is like you, you might feel a connection—in the same way that students of color can be more successful when they have teachers of color. We need to have candidates who are reflective of America's demographics." (Lindsay Fryer, personal correspondence, September 22, 2022)

Congressional staff generally reflect the demographics of members of Congress. A 2020 study of racial diversity among Senate staff found that while people of color make up 40 percent of the U.S. population, only 11 percent of top Senate personal office staff are people of color (Brenson, 2020). Seventy-two Senate offices, including those representing states with large minority populations like Texas and Georgia, did not employ a single person of color in top jobs. While the overall percentage of personal office top staff of color increased from 7.1 to 11 percent between 2015 and 2020, numbers for Asian American/Pacific Islander and Native American staff declined.

The lack of diversity among congressional staff is tied to access barriers, which the unionization of congressional staff, discussed earlier, is intended to address. In a recent interview, Rep. Alexandra Ocasio-Cortez said,

> The moment I got here, I saw how privileged this place was, from the very top to interns; and the reason for that is the only type of people that can afford to send their child on an unpaid internship are people who are wealthy enough to pay extra rent to let their kid live in Washington. From the interns to legislative assistants to chiefs of staff . . . a pay floor allows diversity of class, diversity of geography, diversity of race and culture to be able to be represented on the Hill, and it allows interns to be able to have the financial possibility of having this experience. (Manríquez, 2022)

TEXTBOX 1.5. EXPERIENCE OF A BLACK HILL STAFFER ON JANUARY 6, 2021

Josh Delaney, a Black man and former deputy legislative director for Sen. Elizabeth Warren (D-MA), penned an op-ed for the *Boston Globe* shortly after the January 6, 2021 storming of the Capitol Building. While he was working virtually that day and not in the building, he watched in shock as intruders brazenly waived the Confederate flag in the Rotunda of the Capitol. He feared for the safety of his staff colleagues who were in the complex as well as the many Black and Brown support workers who keep the Capitol complex functioning daily. The presence of the Confederate flag shook him. Seeing the photo of that flag made him realize he was not safe. Josh went on to serve as legislative director for Sen. Raphael Warnock (D-GA).

President Biden set out to ensure that the political appointees in his administration would reflect the demographics of the nation. Data indicate that he has made considerable progress toward his goal, with two high-profile appointees being Secretary of Transportation Pete Buttigieg, a gay man, and Secretary of the Interior Deb Haaland, a Native American (Zweigenhaft, 2021). President Biden created a new position in the Domestic Policy Council for disability policy and appointed Dr. Kim Knackstedt (Abrams, 2021), an exceptional leader whom I first met when she was a doctoral student in my class.

The underrepresentation of so many groups of Americans in policy making and policy influencing positions makes a difference in how policy problems are framed and the solutions developed to address those problems. The lived experience of people of color, people with disabilities, and others who have been marginalized as they interact within every sector of society—education, criminal justice, employment—is different from those of us who are White. People in policy making roles are deeply informed by their lived experience. Representation makes a difference in policy decisions that are made.

TAKEAWAYS: PEOPLE

1. The iron triangle (Congress, executive agencies, and interest groups) represents the core sectors that interact to generate policy.
2. Beyond the iron triangle, there are multiple influences on the policy making process, including courts, social media and the press, public opinion, constituents, grassroots movements and organizations, and experts.
3. While Congress creates laws, the executive branch has considerable policy latitude to implement and further define statutory requirements, though recent Supreme Court decisions may curtail that authority.
4. Developing relationships with the key policy actors in your advocacy sphere is essential.
5. Understanding the differences between the sector you are in (e.g., higher education) and the policy making world provides insights in how to proceed with advocacy.
6. The lack of representation of racial and ethnic minorities, people with disabilities, the LGBTQI community, and other marginalized peoples among those involved in policy making impacts the policy results.

CHAPTER 2

Politics

· ·

You may not be thinking about politics, but politics is thinking about you.

—Kerry Washington (Spiering, 2012)

Kerry Washington reminds us that as much as we may want to ignore politics, we do so at our own peril, for politics is not ignoring us (Spiering, 2012). How much better for us to be a conscious part of the political process rather than a passive recipient of its outcomes. While most professionals are interested in public policy, they often express a lack of interest or a disparagement for politics. There is a sense that the political aspect of the work somehow degrades the policy work—that being involved in politics means getting your hands dirty or cutting backroom deals, leaving the intellectual and substantive policy work tainted. The desire to stay true to research or to hold on solidly to a pure position based solely on the merits is admirable. But those who hold on to this view will deal themselves out of the policy making process. Their seat at the table will remain empty, until it is quickly filled by others. As all policy is the result of compromise, of give and take, it is always deeply influenced by politics. There simply is no policy without politics. One does not exist without the other. Without policy there is little purpose for politics beyond power.

> "Politics and policy are completely intertwined. While there have always been political factors influencing policy, politics is now the driving factor." (Kim Knackstedt, personal correspondence, August 12, 2022)

Lawrence Mead (2018) makes a persuasive case pleading with academia to integrate the study of public policy with the study of politics. He argues that research on policy is increasingly remote from actual government and how it works, and this weakens both sides of the equation. Policy and politics are two sides of the same coin, he notes, with each shaping the other. He urges us to consider that policy solutions that are simply unachievable politically may require us to think first about what is politically feasible and then develop policy solutions, rather than the other way around. This is not to imply that walking away from the

· ·

table is always a mistake. When the only available options are in direct opposition to the nonnegotiables of the policy positions held, walking away may be the right move. Finding a good balance between policy positions and political achievability is a key task for successful advocates and calls for sophisticated strategy and ongoing adjustments and realignments.

At the center of politics are the two major political parties and the elected officials who belong to them—Democrats and Republicans—in terms of power differentials. The following political dimensions are important to consider in engagement in the policy making process.

MAJORITIES AND MINORITIES IN CONGRESS

The significance of which political party holds the majority (the party with the most members elected to the body) in the House and the Senate cannot be overstated. The advantages of the majority party include the chair of every committee and subcommittee, a greater proportion of resources (including staff), the leadership of the body (speaker in the House and majority leader in the Senate), potentially winning every vote, and the all-important ability to control the agenda—what is considered, when it is considered, and how it is considered, as well as what is not considered.

> "It is always better to be working in the majority. You can determine priorities, set the agenda, and schedule the calendar. In the Senate, the minority has a very relevant role, as individual senators can block bills and votes. You have to negotiate. In the House, it is awesome working in the majority. You rule the roost and don't listen to the minority until conference comes. The worst position to be in is the minority in the House. You are just putting up roadblocks and waiting around to be in the majority." (David Cleary, author interview, September 15, 2022)

The minority party is the party with fewer elected members than the majority. Minority parties elect their leader for the House and the Senate, just as majority parties do. These leaders are called minority leader in both the House and the Senate. Every committee and subcommittee in both the House and Senate has a "ranking member"—the most senior member of the minority party on the committee. At times, the chair of the committee and the ranking member will work together to create bipartisan initiatives or hearings. At other times, the ranking member will hold little authority other than speaking out, while the committee chair holds the reins on hearing topics, witnesses, and the legislative agenda.

> "While you predominately work with the majority party to impact change, you have to work with the minority too—to prevent roadblocks if nothing else." (Kuna Tavalin, author interview, August 17, 2022)

The privileges conferred to the majority party remain intact no matter how small the margin of control might be. In other words, if Democrats hold 432 seats in the House and the Republicans hold three, that does not change the privileges conferred if the Democrats held 220 seats and the Republicans held 215. However, larger and smaller margins will be reflected in committee makeup and resource allocation. The smaller the margin, the more difficult it will likely be for the party to hold together on every vote and defeat the minority. With a small margin, there is little room for losing votes to the other side.

The rules for determining the chair and the ranking member of committees are complex, frequently change, and differ for the House and the Senate. Each body creates and changes its own set of rules that governs the choosing of these leaders. The Congressional Research Service (Hudiburg, 2019) offers a detailed look at an example of the complexity of House rules related to committees for the 116th Congress (2019–2020).[1] The rules address issues from the creation of new committees to the jurisdiction of committees to time lines for notifications about committee action. One interesting change that was made in the 116th Congress was the removal of term limits on chairs of committees, which had been in effect for the prior twenty-three years. Other changes of note include the creation of two new select committees, a requirement that any member who has been indicted or charged with certain felonies refrain from committee business, and a change to the names of two committees, including changing the Committee on Education and the Workforce to the Committee on Education and Labor—clearly a reflection of the control of Democrats in the House.

Seniority in Congress

Seniority is a key factor in determining leadership roles in both the House and the Senate. In general, the longer the member has served in Congress, the more access they will have to positions of leadership. There are no term limits on members of Congress; one may serve for as long a period of time as they can be reelected. The majority of members of the House and the Senate seek reelection rather than stepping down or retiring, enabling them to climb up the seniority ladder. For example, in the 2018 midterms, 87 percent of incumbents who were up for reelection—or 408 members of Congress—sought reelection. Of those only thirty-nine, or less than 10 percent, lost (*Incumbents defeated in 2018*, n.d.). Historically,

---

1. Every Congress lasts for two years. For example, the 117th Congress spans 2021 and 2022. Year 2021 is called the first session of the 117th Congress, and 2022 is referred to as the second session of the 117th Congress.

this is a high percentage of incumbent losses. As a general rule, incumbents hold advantages over challengers, in that they are in a position to demonstrate past accomplishments for constituents, have broad name recognition, and have more direct access to campaign financing, having utilized it previously.

The average number of years of service for members of the 117th Congress as of January 3, 2021, was 8.9 years in the House and 11.0 years in the Senate. In the early 1880s the average number of years of service was three years (*Congressional careers*, 2021). The tenure averages may disguise the significant number of members of Congress who serve for decades. One analysis reports 115 members of Congress who have each served thirty-six years or longer, including individual service in both bodies (List of members, n.d.). Former representative John Dingell (D-IL) holds the record for service at fifty-nine years and twenty-one days. As of early 2021, Rep. Don Young (R-AK) is the longest serving member of the House of Representatives, having served for forty-eight years. Sen. Patrick Leahy (D-VT) was the longest serving senator of the 117th Congress, having served for forty-six years.

Seniority also influences office location, the position of a senator's desk in the chamber, and committee memberships. Seniority on committees is also determined by the length of service on individual committees. Those who have served the longest on committees are generally considered to be next in line to be the chair or ranking member, should such an opening occur. Committee chairs may become quite powerful if they serve in that role for some time.

Knowledge of seniority and the roles of members of Congress—whether the Speaker of the House or the chair or ranking member of a committee, how vulnerable they are electorally, when they are up for reelection or may be retiring—inform policy advocacy. Approaching the Speaker of the House is different from approaching a freshman member who does not serve on any committees of interest, as their sphere of influence will be quite different. Chairs and ranking members of the committees are always key policy players in the policy areas under their jurisdiction.

THE WHITE HOUSE

As the single most powerful policy making role in the nation, and perhaps the world, the president of the United States is unparalleled in their influence on public policy. When the party of the president is the same party that controls the House and the Senate, an alignment occurs that confers significant favor to the party in charge. The minority party is often relegated to a role of opposition, with occasional bursts of bipartisan cooperation. Likewise, when the reverse is true and the House and Senate are controlled by the party opposite to that of the president, the president's policy goals are curtailed. When one party controls the White House and either the House or Senate, political maneuvering, often utilizing legislative processes that favor the controlling party and limit the influence of the minority party, may be utilized. Success in carrying out a presidential agenda will have its limitations.

Chairs of committees in the House and the Senate will generally coordinate their policy agendas with the White House if they are of the same party, or at a minimum they are unlikely to pursue a policy direction in contradiction to that of the president. Deference will be shown to the White House and accommodations will be made. However, deference and accommodation only go so far. Members of Congress may act out of a sense of loyalty and party unity to ensure a White House priority is on the agenda, but without the needed support of other members legislative progress may be stalled.

ELECTION CYCLES

Every two years, all 435 seats in the House of Representatives are up for reelection as well as one-third of the one hundred Senate seats. The presidential election cycle is every four years. Candidates pursuing election or reelection will be seeking support and optimizing their interaction with voters, providing unique opportunities for direct engagement.

Members of the House of Representatives may be in office for only two years, or for many years through multiple election cycles. A member of Congress may be quite senior, perhaps having served for decades, or quite junior, having just been elected. The vast majority of members of Congress want to be reelected, so as early as the first day after their election, they may begin planning a strategy for reelection. Understanding what they may be facing in reelection helps to plan an advocacy strategy. For example, if a Republican was just elected by a slim margin for the first time and knows they are likely to face a more conservative Republican opponent in the next election (sometimes referred to as "being primaried"), this may shape the positions they are willing to take. On the other hand, a member who has served a long time and is retiring may be looking to consolidate their legacy, and thus may be open to a bold policy move.

When a senator has just been reelected to a six-year term, knowing that their term is just beginning, they may be in the best position to move forward with a policy proposal that is considered large and perhaps controversial, especially if it was a component of their campaign platform. Members of Congress will be eager to demonstrate their accomplishments to their constituents when it comes time for reelection, so assisting them in achieving such accomplishments will be viewed as helpful to their reelection campaigns. Policy making interacts with election cycles, providing timing opportunities or obstacles. Considering a message and a request that will resonate with a policy maker in relation to their election cycle status is good strategy.

"Senators are most attentive to what is happening in the state during the two years before they are up for reelection. Advocates can take advantage of this by inviting them to events in the state on your issues. If media outlets will be present, that means free media for the member, which is a great advantage as media is very expensive for candidates. It is good strategy to invite them far in advance and highlight how they will get attention for speaking. Candidates are always looking for positive media attention." (David Cleary, author interview, September 15, 2022)

PARTICIPATING IN ELECTION CAMPAIGNS

As citizens, we make our voices heard through the ballot box. We are routinely called on to show support or displeasure for elected officials and the policy positions they represent. In this way, citizens serve as the employers and elected officials as the employees. In other words, "We hire 'em and we fire 'em." An election campaign is analogous to a job interview. What do we want to know about the candidate? Are they qualified? How would they handle matters important to us? What is their track record? This is the opening offered to advocates during an election.

In exchange for your vote, you are entitled to understand the aspiring official's thoughts about the issues you advocate for. There are multiple opportunities to do this. Rallies and town halls (both in person and virtual) offer opportunities to listen and ask questions. You can inquire directly whether the candidate supports your position. For example, "If elected, would you work to establish a public option for health insurance?"

The websites of candidates will explain why they are running and what they seek to accomplish. There may be a way to email questions directly to the candidate through the website. Candidates often issue newsletters, which you can review to learn more about their views and aspirations. Perhaps you will learn that you personally know someone who is in the orbit of the candidate—a family member, staff member, former colleague, or neighbor. These people might serve as surrogates for the candidate.

Advocates can also be involved in campaigns directly—as supporters, volunteers, or even campaign staffers. The most common way of participating is to donate funds. Most of us have been barraged by campaign ads, emails, and phone calls during an election; candidates make it easy to donate—five dollars, ten dollars, or more. Some supporters host get-togethers in their homes to introduce candidates to other potential supporters. Volunteers may work the phones, urging people to vote for the candidate, or drive people to the polls to vote. Campaign staffers sign up for a short but grueling season of endless activities racing toward election day hoping for a win. People may take a leave of absence from their job for such an experience, sometimes hoping to be rewarded by a full-time position on the candidate's staff if they are elected. Participating in a campaign, as a volunteer or paid staff member, is an excellent way to build a relationship with a potential public official as well as their potential staff.

Campaign and political work should be undertaken as individual citizens rather than under the auspices of a professional role. For example, a teacher or higher education doctoral student should volunteer on personal time, not on work time. Most public employees are prohibited from engaging in political work during work time. Yet all citizens are free to engage in campaign efforts on their own time. Donations to campaigns should be made from personal funds, not organizational funds.

While as policy advocates our focus is on working with those currently serving as policy makers, we also need to participate in the electoral process, as this is the ultimate opportunity to provide feedback to those who were elected to represent us.

TRANSITION TO OFFICE AFTER WINNING AN ELECTION

The period of time after a public official is elected and before that official takes office is considered a transition period. For members of Congress, that period is between the time they win the election in November (always the Tuesday after the first Monday in November, as set out in the Constitution) and January 3 of the following year, when they are sworn into office. Even after they are sworn in, there will be a period of time of settling in—determining the location of an office, moving in, being trained in their roles and responsibilities and the rules of the chamber, figuring out committee assignments, and hiring staff. It may take until March before a new Congress is fully up and running with all its members settled in.

For the president and vice president, the transition begins with the appointment of a transition team shortly after the election. That team will likely work with the president to lay out the overarching goals or policy areas where the president will work and begin to vet potential candidates for high-level political appointments—particularly Cabinet members. For example, the Biden team laid out four immediate priority areas (Barlow, 2021) for his administration shortly after his election: the COVID-19 pandemic, the economy, racial equity, and climate change.

Transition teams for each of the federal agencies (sometimes called landing teams) will also be appointed. These teams focus on one agency and are responsible for conferring with those in the agency to better understand the key issues and perhaps the policy changes implemented by the previous administration, which the new administration may want to change. It is common that political appointees from previous administrations of the same party who served in the department under consideration will be appointed to the transition landing team, as they will have a deep understanding of how the agency works. In addition, staff from entities that were key to the success of the president's election may be represented on these teams. For example, incoming president Biden chose representatives of teachers' unions to be on the education landing team. Landing team members also talk to interest groups and other advocates to better understand particular issues and perspectives. The transition landing teams finish their work by completing materials that they leave for the new administration to use as a starting point when they take office in January. Being in touch with a member of the transition team enables an advocate to press their case early on as well as to get to know people who may continue to play a key role in the administration. Sometimes members of landing teams are appointed by the president to serve in their administration.

"The purpose of the transition team is to set the stage for the new administration so they can hit the ground running on day one. Campaign promises were our road map. We wanted to honor the campaign promises and create a path for keeping those promises. We had to prioritize and propose a time line for implementation—for the first one hundred days, for the first six months, and for the first year. And we had to do that with multiple unknowns, including not knowing who the appointees would be to lead the agency.

"In addition, the certification of the president was delayed and COVID required us to do all of our work virtually. Because of a contested election in the Senate, it wasn't until January that we knew that the Democrats would control the Senate. We had to think about the best vehicles to carry out campaign commitments—the budget proposal, new regulations, executive action, etc.—and all in the political context of the time." (Anonymous, author interview, September 1, 2022)

After the inauguration on January 20, the president takes office and begins to make political appointments. The highest-level positions—Cabinet positions in particular—require Senate confirmation. The president and his team will develop a list of possible candidates for each position. Each candidate will go through an extensive vetting process, which will include background checks, review of tax records and investments, and multiple interviews. If the candidate passes the vetting process and is the final choice, the individual will be formally nominated by the president and referred to the Senate for the confirmation process. The committee of jurisdiction in the Senate will likely hold a confirmation hearing, or hearings, and vote on whether or not to support the candidate. Finally, the full Senate will vote on confirming the candidate. If the candidate receives at least fifty-one votes, the candidate is sworn into office by the president or vice president and their term begins in the position for which they were nominated. The House of Representatives plays no role in the confirmation of presidential appointees.

The nomination process and confirmation hearings are important opportunities for advocates to learn and to weigh in on their priorities (*Appointment and confirmation*, 2021). Confirmation hearings, like other committee hearings, are public events and generally may be watched live in person or online. Advocates may request that members of Congress who sit on the committees holding the hearing

"I was nominated by President Obama for the role of assistant secretary for the Office of Special Education and Rehabilitative Services in the Department of Education in 2012. I had already been serving as an Obama appointee as deputy assistant secretary for the Office of Elementary and Secondary Education, so I was a known entity, particularly in the Senate, where I had ten years of staff experience. I had to be confirmed by the Senate in order to serve in this position.

"The Republicans were in charge of the Senate then, and they had made the political decision to block *all* Obama nominations. So I was blocked for two years, with no movement. President Obama had to renominate me twice. I had been serving in an acting capacity since my nomination, and I would be going into my third year without confirmation, which is prohibited by law, so I had to leave the job.

"Because of my relationship with the chief of staff for the committee that was in charge of my confirmation (the Senate HELP Committee), I went to him to see if there was any way they could help. He readily agreed to look into it, as the block on my nomination had nothing to do with me or my qualifications. He proceeded to secure agreement from Republican members of the HELP Committee that my nomination could move forward without objections and by unanimous consent. In addition, he secured an agreement with Sen. McConnell's office, who was the majority leader at the time. And I was finally confirmed by the Senate.

"This story points out the importance of relationships. I had worked with the chief of staff for years, and he knew and respected my skills and experience. In the end he thought it was the right thing for the country to have someone knowledgeable and competent in this role. He used his political capital for me, which is a true mark of a strong bipartisan relationship." (Michael Yudin, personal correspondence, August 12, 2022)

ask the nominee specific questions, thereby establishing a record of commitment or intention that can serve as a reference point moving forward for future interaction. For example, if a candidate commits to a certain course of action during a hearing, members of the committee are likely to follow up to monitor the carrying out of that commitment. Likewise, an advocate may follow up.

Constituents and advocates may also make their voices heard in terms of whether or not they support the nominee, usually via phone calls to senators' offices, leaving messages urging a yea or nay vote and why. The confirmation hearings for President Trump's nominee for secretary of education, Betsy DeVos, generated more phone calls in opposition than any other nominee for secretary of education in history. While she did finally win confirmation, it was because the vice president cast the tie-breaking fifty-first vote—also the first time in history that the secretary of education required a tie-breaking vote. The nominee for secretary of education has never been so controversial (Nelson, 2017).

There are many other political appointees across government who do not require Senate confirmation. As of 2016, there were about four thousand political appointment positions across the federal government that a new administration needs to fill—including 2,800 that do not require Senate confirmation (Rosalsky, 2020). These individuals may be assistant secretaries or deputies in federal agencies. While they play critical policy roles and serve at the pleasure of the president, they are not required to go through the Senate to secure their jobs. These appointments, like Senate confirmation appointments, may take months for a new administration to complete.

BIPARTISANSHIP

Bipartisanship signifies Republicans and Democrats working together. Bipartisanship may mean that one Republican votes with all the Democrats to pass a bill; it could also mean that both parties work together for months and come up with a compromise plan that garners virtually all the votes of the body from both Republicans and Democrats. At times public opinion polls may be used to assert bipartisan support, even when a policy does not have support from both Republicans and Democrats in Congress. Whatever the thresholds used, most agree that bipartisanship is desirable.

> "The events of January 6 hardened partisan lines. Most Democrats view it as a fundamental moment of reckoning. Most Republicans view it as a bad day with bad people and we should move on. You can't really reconcile that. This is a huge divide. But as time passes it is getting better." (David Cleary, author interview, September 15, 2022)

Bipartisanship signals unity of purpose and unity of people. As a nation, unity has great appeal. President Biden ran on a platform of unity, noting if elected he would be the president for all Americans, not just those who voted for him. As Americans, there is a deep impulse to feel like we are on the same team pulling for our nation. We have seen remarkable showings of unity after crises that our nation has encountered, mostly after threats from other nations, such as the destruction of the World Trade Center towers in 2001.

Historically, bipartisanship is more likely under divided party control—when the president is from one party and the other party controls the House, the Senate, or both (Palazzolo, 2021). Because Senate rules currently require a "supermajority," or a vote of sixty out of one hundred members, in order to prevail in passing most legislation, bipartisanship is generally a must. Rarely has a majority party controlled sixty or more seats in the Senate. Bipartisanship is less likely under a unified government—when the same party controls both houses of Congress and the White House. While there are multiple examples of bipartisan accomplishments

(*History of bipartisanship*, 2021), bipartisanship does not necessarily equal a more productive government. The relationship between bipartisanship and productivity is not straightforward. Often measured in terms of legislation enacted, productivity has occurred in both partisan and bipartisan circumstances. While both the 98th Congress and the 112th Congress were instances of divided government, the 98th Congress was far more productive, with 677 bills enacted into law compared to 284 enacted into law in the 112th Congress (GovTrack, 2021). One commentator has argued that "partisanship and productivity have not always been antonyms" (Grumet, 2019).

Bipartisanship support for legislation is usually considered a proxy for policy success and longevity. In other words, the more bipartisan a new law is, the more likely it is to be successful and stand the test of time because of broad support. While this may be the case at times, it is not always so. The No Child Left Behind Act of 2001, considered in chapter 4, provides an example. Despite broad bipartisan support, the law engendered a considerable backlash over time and was amended significantly by the Every Student Succeeds Act in 2015—once again with broad bipartisan support.

> "When I worked in the Senate from 2001 to 2010, virtually all the education bills we worked on were bipartisan, with No Child Left Behind being the flagship. Bipartisanship was the expectation. That has certainly changed. In the past politics did not interfere with policy development at the staff level. Now the politics just takes over at some point." (Michael Yudin, personal correspondence, August 12, 2022)

There is much speculation about why bipartisanship has waned: a stronger commitment to ideology than to compromise; a threat that if a member of Congress compromises, they will be "primaried" by someone to the right or left of that compromise position and may lose their reelection bid; a desire to shrink the federal government so that fewer laws are passed; fewer close, personal relationships across the aisle, leading to less trust; and a belief that governing needs to be about winning—ensuring that one point of view prevails—thus equating compromise with losing.

But evidence of bipartisanship remains—in both policy and relationships. There are a number of bills introduced and passed every year with both Republican and Democratic support. In 2022, Rep. Rosa DeLauro (D-CT) chaired the all-important Labor, Health and Human Services, Education and Related Agencies Subcommittee of the Committee on Appropriations for the House. The ranking Republican on that subcommittee was Rep. Tom Cole (R-OK). They worked together as the two subcommittee leaders since 2015, flipping back and forth as chair and ranking member depending on which party was in charge of the House.

> "The Senate markup of the Every Student Succeeds Act was remarkably bipartisan. Chair Alexander (R-TN) and Ranking Member Patty Murray (D-WA) put aside priorities for the sake of a compromise that would move. Early on Sen. Alexander decided not to include his voucher bill that he was committed to, as he knew it would sink the bill. Sen. Franken (D-MN) agreed to postpone offering an amendment at the committee markup related to discrimination, as he knew it could jeopardize the bill and possibly keep it from making it to the floor. Both sides worked to pull off poison pill amendments before the bill hit the floor. There was a real commitment to bipartisan compromise so that we could actually get the bill over the finish line. And we did." (Lindsay Fryer, author interview, September 22, 2022)

They presented a model of bipartisan decorum and respect.[2] It was rare to hear one speak without referring to the collegiality of the other. They often took opposing positions in votes and disagreed with each other. But the underlying respect and cordiality remained, and finding common ground was a mutual pursuit.

> "A lot of work goes on that people do not see. The partisanship is a little overblown. We still do a lot in a bipartisan way, but the stuff that isn't controversial doesn't get noticed. With Sen. Alexander we did a lot by unanimous consent and the media did not cover it. Only the car crashes and the train wrecks get reported. For the most part Republican and Democratic offices still have pretty good relationships, though certainly not all." (David Cleary, author interview, September 15, 2022)

TAKEAWAYS: POLITICS

1. There is no policy without politics.
2. The majority party holds great advantage over the minority party in policy making, in both Congress and the executive branch.
3. Where a member of Congress is in their election cycle may influence their policy activity.
4. The seniority of a member of Congress confers advantages related to committee assignments, roles, and more.
5. Participating in our electoral process is part of successful advocacy.

---

2. To view hearings from the Labor, Health and Human Services, Education and Related Agencies Subcommittee, visit https://appropriations.house.gov/subcommittees/labor-health-and-human -services-education-and-related-agencies-116th-congress/congress_hearing.

6. The election of a new president is followed by a transition process that sets the stage for four years of policy activity.
7. While bipartisanship may be hard to come by, it is still alive and offers a meaningful message of unity. However, it is not a proxy for productivity, nor does it ensure policy success or longevity.

CHAPTER 3

Process

....

This chapter is markedly different from the others in this book. It will read more like a textbook or a reference book; this is my intention. My goal is to have an integrated set of information—both the scholarly and the practical—for you to reference as needed. Knowing the scholarly thinking over the decades on policy making is illuminating and helps in understanding what goes on in real time. The practical information about the workings of Congress and the executive branch may be more than you will ever need to know—but just in case, you have a one-stop resource. And as you do your advocacy work, you will be aware that behind the curtains there are a lot of complex bells and whistles that may on occasion take center stage.

Policy and process are inextricably linked. Rules and procedures affect policy outcomes. The nature of a policy can determine what process or procedure should be utilized in moving it forward. Conversely, particular processes will circumscribe policy options. For members of Congress, having a keen grasp of procedures and processes is essential to being successful in moving legislation. Senate or House rules about scheduling, debate time, amendment requirements, and more all have significant effects on processes—which in turn affect policy. Some congressional offices have a staff member whose key responsibility is mastering floor and committee rules and procedures. Former representative John Dingell, reflecting that process trumps policy, offered: "If you let me write the procedure and I let you write the substance, I'll [beat] you every time" (Oleszek et al., 2020).

> "Most people have a prime-time TV vision of how policy is made in Washington. They are often surprised at what really goes into making a bill become a law. Understanding the process means knowing when the right time is to weigh in. This strengthens advocates' ability to make an impact."
> (Kuna Tavalin, personal correspondence, August 17, 2022)

Having a grasp on the various processes that constitute the making of public policy is essential for successful advocacy for at least four reasons. The first is related to *timing*. Awareness of cycles in policy making processes enables identification of reliable opportunities for advocacy work and avoidance of the pitfalls of

....

proceeding at an inopportune time. For example, when the president issues a budget request, which occurs every year around February, this is a signal to engage in a campaign targeting Congress to promote a particular level of funding for a program of interest. Likewise, just after completion of the annual appropriations process in Congress, which is scheduled to be completed September 30 of every year (though it is often postponed or delayed), would not be the best time to begin an advocacy campaign for a particular level of funding for a targeted program.

The second reason advocates want to understand basic policy making processes is to understand a range of **options** for progress. For example, when a bill is being developed and after it is introduced, sponsors will be eager for other members to cosponsor the bill. Understanding what cosponsorship means and whom to target as cosponsors will enhance advocacy work. Likewise, if a bill of interest is scheduled for a markup in a committee, knowing that may trigger advocates to develop and pursue the introduction of an amendment during the markup and garner support for its adoption. Finally, when advocates are aware of a bill coming to the floor of the House or the Senate for a full vote, they may want to launch a campaign promoting either a "yes" or a "no" vote on the bill.

Third, a working knowledge of policy processes and procedures is critical to *anticipating, planning, and strategizing*. With a broad view of the cycles of budgeting, appropriations, and authorizing, advocates can look ahead and identify a number of opportunities for participation. For example, if one is advocating for a program in the Higher Education Act and that law is in the process of being reauthorized, or revised, by Congress, there is an opportunity to provide suggestions on how the law should be changed. These opportunities will occur in both the House and the Senate during the initial drafting of a bill, during committee consideration of the bill, and during full floor consideration. Advocacy efforts can be strategically developed for each body and at each juncture. If the legislation has been recently enacted and signed into law by the president, advocates might want to target the rule-making process of the Department of Education and anticipate opportunities to provide public comment or possibly participate on a rule-making committee.

Finally, policy making process knowledge enables advocates to *initiate* policy proposals. For example, if a member of Congress gives a speech about the importance of addressing the shortage of fully prepared teachers, an advocate may follow up and highlight an opportunity to request funding in an upcoming appropriations bill for a program on the books that addresses that challenge but is underfunded. It is impossible for each of the 535 offices of members of Congress to fully grasp all of the policy developments in every policy area. Working as experts in their area, advocates become reliable resources pointing out opportunities that arise during committee hearings and markups and more. Textbox 3.1 provides a summary of the four reasons why understanding policy processes empowers advocacy.

Part I of this chapter briefly considers some well-established frameworks of the public policy making process offered by the political science and public policy literatures. Part II of the chapter offers an overview of the processes and

> **TEXTBOX 3.1. HOW UNDERSTANDING POLICY PROCESSES PROMOTES EFFECTIVE ADVOCACY**
>
> - *Timing*—Predictable cycles of policy making enable the identification of advocacy opportunities for policy change and avoidance of proceeding at the wrong time.
> - *Options*—Knowing policy processes enables identification of advocacy options, such as promoting a "yes" or "no" vote at a markup, securing a cosponsor for a bill, promoting the adoption of an amendment, and utilizing House and Senate procedures for strategic advantage.
> - *Anticipating, planning, and strategizing*—A broad view of routine cycles of budgeting, appropriations, and authorizing promotes planning ahead and strategizing as there may be numerous entry points to change policy, including executive agency processes such as rule making.
> - *Initiating*—Knowledge of policy making processes offers access to opportunities to initiate policy engagement; for example, hearing a member of Congress question a potential secretary of education about a matter may lead to follow-up with that member to develop a bill or a "Dear Colleague" letter.

procedures utilized in Congress—the number-one policy making component of the federal government. The chapter concludes with Part III, a review of key executive agency processes, including executive orders, rule making, and guidance.

PART I: SUMMARY OF THE LITERATURE ON PUBLIC POLICY MAKING PROCESSES

The policy making process is a problem-solving endeavor, with multiple actors at the table weighing in, arguing, compromising, and moving forward—toward a solution or toward stalemate. The process is a long game, sometimes with short-term solutions but more often with ongoing reconsideration of persistent public problems being redefined and revisited as society changes, circumstances evolve, and political winds shift. Much of the public policy literature offers a cyclical or a stage model conception of the policy making process (see, for example, Birkland, 2016; Fowler, 2013; Jones, 1984; Kraft & Furlong, 2021; May & Wildavsky, 1978). The first discussion below relies heavily on Fowler's (2013) conception of the cyclical framework, is informed by the work of many public policy scholars, and considers each phase in turn. The second notion of the policy process put forward below examines John Kingdon's (2010) concept of policy streams. This approach stands in contrast to the rational-sequential cyclical approach, highlighting dynamism and ongoing flux. Both frameworks provide insight for advocates. These overviews are intended to provide research-based foundations for what follows—a nitty-gritty examination of congressional and executive branch processes and procedures.

Framework # 1: The Cyclical Framework

The traditional notion of the public policy framework as a cycle is described below with six distinct phases: problem definition, agenda setting, policy formulation, policy adoption, policy implementation, and policy evaluation.

PROBLEM DEFINITION

Kingdon (2010) points out the difference between a condition and a problem. While there are many unpleasant conditions people face, not all of them are suitable for government problem solving. A condition, or a situation, may become a public policy problem when there is a decision that it is something government could or should address. While many social problems face the public and may be considered worthy of the consideration of public policy, many never reach the agenda. Reasons include cost and a lack of political will. Poverty is a prime example. It is complex, with multiple views on why it exists and what can be done to remedy it. Poverty might be addressed through income support, education, housing, childcare, or all of these and more. Some might believe that poverty is a matter of individual circumstances and that government does not have a role in addressing it. Often such significant and long-standing public problems will be defined in limited or bite-sized ways so that the policy making apparatus might be

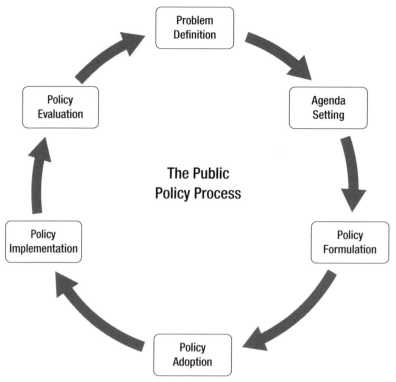

FIGURE 3.1. The Public Policy Process: A Cyclical Framework
Adapted from Fowler (2013, p. 16).

able to find a solution that is politically obtainable, timely, and not too expensive, such as ensuring that students in low-income schools have access to free lunches. While such Band-Aid-sized solutions to gaping wounds do not succeed in offering a full-fledged remedy for the problem, they can provide incremental progress and a sense of moving forward to solve problems; however, they may also leave the impression that a problem has been addressed when it really has not. The political appetite for sustained focus is limited.

Problem definition is fraught with values and political overtones. Categorizing problems into established issue areas can determine what solutions might be offered. For example, if lack of access to public transportation is a transportation issue, that leads to one set of solutions. However, if lack of access to public transportation is defined as a civil rights issue, that leads to a different set of solutions. It is important for advocates to carefully consider exactly what problem they are trying to solve. The difference between ensuring that every child has access to a high-quality education and ensuring that schools offer high-quality education is significant and leads to different policy strategies and solutions.

AGENDA SETTING

Agenda setting is the process by which a problem secures a spot on the public policy agenda. Few public problems actually manage to do this—and even fewer survive the policy making process to actually enact policy. There are numerous determinants that influence agenda setting, including data reports and studies, systemic procedural occurrences, Supreme Court decisions, crises, and election results. We will consider each of these briefly.

Data Reports and Studies. Data reports and studies include the routine issuance of information related to the ongoing monitoring of a number of issues across the federal government, including unemployment, disease rates, highway deaths, airplane safety, changes in climate, immunization rates, infant mortality rates, health insurance trends, graduation rates, college debt, changes in consumer prices, the usage and cost of entitlement programs, and more. In addition, the government and interest groups may issue reports highlighting a challenge that needs attention. The Congressional Budget Office or the Office of Management and Budget may issue a report on the status of the national debt, which might trigger Congress to institute spending controls. Many laws require annual reports from federal agencies with information about the status of a sector or an ongoing challenge. For example, the Higher Education Act requires an annual report from the secretary of education on the quality of teacher preparation. A finding from that report that few states were reporting low-performing programs, as required by law, triggered a multiyear regulatory effort under the Obama administration, which is analyzed in chapter 4.

In reflecting on indicators that may lead to policy changes, John Kingdon (2010) notes: "The countable problem sometimes acquires a power of its own that is unmatched by problems that are less countable. Mass transit people become fixed on ridership, and find it much more difficult and less rewarding to concentrate on such 'softer' areas as quality of service" (p. 93).

This dynamic is visibly present in education policy, where data points are considered indicators of quality, when in fact they may not be. For example, results of K–12 student standardized test scores have been promoted as a proxy for teacher quality. Teacher quality is a concept that is hard to measure; however, having numbers to attach to it feeds the policy appetite for quantifiability.

Systemic Procedural Occurrences. These are routine policy making mechanisms in Congress and the executive branch that offer predictable opportunities for policy change. Three key processes advocates look out for in Congress are the annual budget process, the annual appropriations process, and the routine reauthorization of laws. In the executive branch, rule making—or the development of regulations—is a systemic procedure where policy change takes place. We will review these more carefully later in this chapter.

Supreme Court Decisions. Supreme Court Decisions may trigger Congress to respond by reversing the decision through the enactment of a new law. For example, in 1991, Congress passed a broad new Civil Rights Act that reversed five Supreme Court decisions that had restricted workers' rights under federal antidiscrimination law. The topic of my dissertation, the Handicapped Children's Protection Act of 1986, is a case study of how Congress passed a law to overrule a Supreme Court decision as described in textbox 1.2. While not a routine occurrence Supreme Court decisions may open the door for an issue to find a place on the legislative agenda.

Crises. Crises of significant proportion can catapult a matter onto the policy agenda. The attack on the World Trade Center on September 11, 2011, generated the creation of the Transportation Safety Administration (TSA), which requires extensive screening before boarding a plane. The rash of random mass shootings in schools and public venues has generated executive action and some policy change, albeit modest in comparison to the magnitude of the events. Deaths of Black Americans at the hands of police have generated a broad national movement for reform and some incremental policy shifts. Changes in climate that have increased flooding, wildfires, and temperatures have likewise produced modest movement in climate policy.

Ongoing and repeating crises like the ones noted above often galvanize public attention and outrage, which gradually fades until the next crisis. The attention span for policy makers is constrained by time, other pressing matters, and influences of politics and the election cycle. This is one reason why routine procedures, such as appropriations, reauthorization, and rule making, offer predicable vehicles to address issues generated by crises.

Election Results. Election results impact agenda setting. A new president will generally set policy goals for the first one hundred days of their presidency and galvanize an agenda around those goals. Newly elected officials have campaigned with platforms that set out their vision and priorities, which may be translated into items on the policy agenda. Even when candidates lose elections, their visibility can catapult an issue and imbue it with staying power. For example, in his run for the presidency in 2020, Sen. Bernie Sanders (I-VT) was successful in sustaining his vision for free community college so that it was initially incorporated into the Biden-Harris agenda and gained support among some congressional colleagues.

POLICY FORMULATION

Policy formulation involves determining plans for addressing the problem. How a policy actor defines the problem greatly circumscribes the type of policy solution that is proposed. Moving back and forth between problem definition and policy formulation is a common occurrence, particularly as new information may come to light while investigating and developing policy solutions.

Government has a number of approaches that are commonly employed as solutions—for example, targeting a specific group of individuals and entitling them to benefits, regulating how people behave or how industries may function, protecting citizens from harm, taxing, sanctioning, subsidizing, offering incentives, rationing, privatizing, capacity building, researching, and educating. Laws and policy proposals may include a range of these strategies. For example, the Individuals with Disabilities Education Act provides for inducements, sanctions, entitlements, specific procedures to regulate behavior of educators, and more. Advocates will want to consider a range of policy tools in formulating proposals, as described in chapter 4.

POLICY ADOPTION

Policy adoption refers to the process of formal embrace of a policy proposal. This is a dance of individual decision making—for example, an individual member of Congress—and collective decision making—for example, the House of Representatives. For the House of Representatives this means a vote from the majority of members (218 of the 435) to pass the bill. In the Senate, for most measures, a vote of sixty of one hundred senators is required to pass the same bill. For the executive branch this could involve the president signing a bill into law and an agency finalizing regulations or guidance.

Anderson (1999) outlines six factors that contribute to gaining approval for a specific policy decision—which he describes as *decision criteria*. While Congress has changed considerably since the 1980s, these factors continue to be on point.

The first factor is *values*, where a determination is made if a particular policy proposal is in line with the values of those who are proposing it as well as those from whom approval is being sought. For example, the Democratic Party would likely be eager to ensure that a health care policy proposal is aligned with the value of expanding health care coverage to more Americans. Republicans might measure a policy proposal against the value of reducing taxes.

A second consideration is *political party affiliation*. Most members of Congress will seek to be loyal to their political party most of the time. There will be pressure from the leaders of the parties to line up behind a particular policy position. Party affiliation is a powerful predictor of how a member of Congress will vote. In the executive branch, allegiance to the proposals of the president will be paramount as decisions are made, particularly if they were campaign promises.

Third, *constituency interests* are weighed. Since voters are the employers of members of Congress, it can be problematic to vote in conflict with constituent views. If there is a conflict between party loyalty and constituent views, it is not uncommon for constituent views to prevail, particularly if a member plans to seek reelection or has made a campaign promise to constituents. At times, constituent views on a policy proposal may be unknown or may conflict. When this is the case, legislators are likely to rely on other factors to make decisions, including their own values. Interest groups and their allied experts have become increasingly influential in recent years as they have proliferated and garnered considerable resources. (See chapter 1 for a discussion of interest groups and others outside of government.)

Fourth, *public opinion* factors into policy adoption. The broader the issue, the more likely there is to be information about public opinion. In addition, public opinion polls may report differing results. The policy maker weighs the source of the information and the consistency of the opinions among polls as they consider support for the proposal. Multiple smaller policy issues may not have penetrated the public's attention or interest in order to generate public opinion information. For example, while climate change or immigration policy proposals will garner the attention of the public, how to evaluate the success of teacher preparation programs may not.

Fifth in consideration of policy adoption is *deference*. In the executive branch, deference is given to superiors in the hierarchical chain, particularly political appointees who are in place to carry forth the president's agenda. Members of Congress may also weigh in with executive agencies, particularly chairs and ranking members of committees of jurisdiction for the policy under consideration. Members of Congress are often in a position where they need to cast a vote on a matter they know little about, that is exceedingly complex, or in which they have little interest. In such situations, they increasingly defer to others—in some instances committee chairs or ranking members on the committee with jurisdiction over the policy, and in other cases the leadership of their party in the body in which they serve. In recent years—particularly as Congress has become polarized with razor-thin margins for the majority—power has increasingly been centralized in the leadership of the parties (Price, 2021). Thus, deference to party leaders is more pervasive than in the past.

The sixth factor influencing policy adoption is *decision rules*. While there is no one set of rules policy makers use in determining policy positions, there may be persuasive factors invoked that regularize the process. A key example is the concept of precedent. If a new policy under consideration has components that have already been adopted in a previous policy, this can be a powerful influencer. Such considerations were key in the deliberations over the Americans with Disabilities Act, which was grounded in precedents set by previous civil rights laws and shored up by decades of implementation and judicial decisions. Measuring the constitutionality of a proposal may also be a decision rule. Some education proposals have been challenged as violating the constitution in that it gives primary authority for education to the states.

In addition to the factors that influence policy adoption, there are several strategies, or styles, of policy adoption that can be identified—all with the goal of garnering enough support from individuals so that the collective decision can be made to cross the finish line. These approaches include *bargaining, persuasion,* and *command* (Anderson, 1999, p. 65–73).

Bargaining is by far the most common strategy used to build a winning collation for policy adoption. In both the legislative and executive branches of government, unilateral policy adoption without the support of others is virtually impossible. Bargaining involves negotiation, give-and-take, horse-trading, and compromise. While the president has the greatest independent authority to change policy, it is rare that they go it alone without the support of key supporters, including interest groups, key members of their party and of Congress, and other leaders in their administration. Policy adoption is an institutional process in both Congress and the executive branch.

The most common form of bargaining is "logrolling," or the mutual exchange of support for two different items. It may be a straightforward tit-for-tat exchange between negotiating parties. For example, a leader in Congress might agree to support an administration proposal if the administration agrees to nominate a particular individual for a judgeship. This would be a high-stakes exchange but not unheard of. Another practice that was once part and parcel of the appropriations process, and has recently returned, is the inclusion of "earmarks." Earmarks are projects requested by members of Congress that target funding in appropriations bills to projects in their districts or states. Historically, these were popular with members of Congress as they gave a clear example of "bringing home the bacon" to constituents. Criticism about the efficacy of the projects led to the end of the practice in 2010; however, as of 2022, they have returned. Many argue that the return of this practice will enable Congress to pass more bills and avoid standoffs that may result in government shutdowns. Earmarks are further described later in this chapter.

A second form of bargaining is *compromise.* Compromise is generally centered on one particular policy provision and involves give-and-take or questions of more or less of something. The old saw "half a loaf is better than none" captures the concept of compromise. Budging for the sake of making it across the finish line was historically part of the art of legislating. The legislative saga of the Americans with Disabilities Act (ADA) offers a powerful strategy for strategic compromise. It is described in chapter 5.

A second strategy for building a winning coalition to adopt a policy is *persuasion.* Persuasion involves convincing others to come around to your point of view on the merits—without modifying your position. Information, including research, policy analysis, and budget estimates, are often featured in persuasive efforts. Persuasion is commonly the first strategy used to secure policy adoption; however, alone it is rarely successful as so many other factors are at play, as noted above.

The third strategy for securing policy adoption is *command*. Command requires hierarchical relationships whereby those in authority seek a particular outcome and simply determine that outcome or utilize sanctions or rewards to remove opposition. The process undertaken every year to develop the president's budget proposal offers an example of command. While each federal agency submits their recommendations for funding of programs in their department to the Office of Management and Budget (OMB), OMB has the final say, issuing a final budget proposal that may or may not be in sync with a department's request. There is no real recourse for the department, except in extraordinary circumstances where the White House may reevaluate the situation. In Congress, party leaders may exercise their authority to withhold perks from members if they stray from the party line.

POLICY IMPLEMENTATION

Policy implementation is the operationalization of an adopted policy. Many experience implementation as commands from above, which must be instituted by willing or unwilling recipients of those commands. While this is but one form of implementation—and not a very effective one in most settings—it grew to dominate the education policy landscape during the Obama years, with years of holdover. The influence of education reformers, philanthropists, and corporate supporters routinely outweighed the influence of actual educators, with a result that command performances often became opportunities for resistance rather than implementation. Such resistance often generates a backlash response to the policy, as described in chapter 4.

Given the unique roles of federal, state, and local government in education, tension about implementation decisions is often in evidence, as state and local levels of governments have important authorities that may not be in line with federal requirements. At times, a new federal policy may involve state legislatures, which may have to change state law in order to receive federal funds. In addition, there are many federal policies affecting any one policy area. Different federal policies may be at odds with each other, making the task of implementation all the more complex and labor intensive. With policy goals sometimes unclear, implementers will often have conflicts about interpretation, which need to be resolved. Policy makers may continue to be involved with implementation as well as interest groups and courts. Research suggests that new policies are often not implemented at all or changed considerably during implementation. Yet implementation is critical, as it is when most Americans actually come into contact with government and form opinions about its effectiveness. These opinions will affect politics and policy making.

The scholarly literature and research on policy implementation is rich (e.g., Anderson, 1999; Birkland, 2016; Fowler, 2013; Jones, 1984; Kraft & Furlong, 2021; May & Wildavsky, 1978; Nakamura & Smallwood, 1980; Pressman & Wildavsky, 1984; Ripley & Franklin, 1986). Jones (1984) suggests three components of implementation: *organization*, *interpretation*, and *application*. *Organization* involves establishing or rearranging resources, structures, and methods in order to put the policy or program into effect. In other words, a federal agency may need to determine which subunit of that agency will be in charge of implementation and what staff will be involved. Collaboration with other federal agencies might be required. More people may need to be hired or roles rearranged. The second component, *interpretation*, is the translation of the policy into acceptable and feasible plans. Federal agencies need to determine their actual authority under the statute. Some statutes are quite prescriptive in how a policy is to be implemented and others are not. For example, negotiated rule making on a particular issue may be required by law. Concepts in law may need further clarity, such as the definition of "high quality" or what entities are eligible for funding under a newly created program. Time lines might need to be established as well as processes and requirements for grant application submission. The third aspect of implementation, *application*, is simply doing the job, for example, providing the goods and services required or monitoring the utilization of a particular standard, such as ensuring minimal levels of toxins in water or time lines for compliance.

Fowler (2013) maintains that successful policy implementation depends on two factors: will and capacity. If those involved in implementation have neither the motivation nor the capacity to make the required changes, chances of success are slim. Policies are too often developed without knowledge or consideration of the culture into which they are being inserted. It is often said in the education world that "culture eats policy for lunch any day of the week." Resistance to new policies may be generated when the self-interest of those required to carry them out is threatened—for example, job security or status. If new policies conflict with professional values of those required to carry them out, resistance will result that may generate policy failure, organized movements of opposition, exit of those required to carry out the policy, or out-and-out refusal to carry out the policy.

Research on policy implementation can be considered in three phases (Fowler, 2013). The first generation of policy implementation research focused on why policies fail and found key causes to be that implementers do not understand the policy and intermediaries do not have the knowledge, skill, or resources (e.g., time, money, materials) to implement the policy. Despite this knowledge generated in the 1970s, the same implementation mistakes continue today.

The second generation of implementation research involved analysis of success and failure in policy implementation. Miles and Huberman (1984) studied implementation of various school improvement policies in twelve schools and determined factors related to success and failure. A Rand study of the implementation of 293 federal projects in eighteen states found limited success in implementation but determined that successful implementation was not a mechanical cookbook process but rather one of "mutual adaptation," where both implementers' behavior and the details of policy design were adapted to fit local circumstances (Berman & McLaughlin, 1976).

The third generation of research, according to Fowler, focuses on implementing complex policies. Education policy has become increasingly complex and ambitious over time, often requiring significant changes to practice. This implementation research focused on implementing policy that requires major changes in practice and how to spread successful implementation from a few sites to many sites. Key lessons from this third generation of research include considering implementers as learners who need professional development and opportunities to grow. Third-generation research suggests that strong social infrastructure for implementation is critical. This might include joint planning time, conferences, and workshops. The "sink or swim" approach is ill advised.

My experience in policy making has led me to conclude that policy design can have a significant effect on policy implementation. This is why it is critical for those with knowledge about how things really work at the implementation level to be at the table when policy is designed and to offer feedback about how a policy might or might not be implemented. Those who live in the culture where the policy is implemented can identify both pitfalls and opportunities that policy makers may be unaware of. Likewise, the research affirms that if people are charged with implementing a policy for which there is neither the will nor the resources, it will falter.

In 2017, I worked with the National Network of State Teachers of the Year[1] to design an innovative bill intended to promote successful policy implementation—the Teachers and Parents at the Table Act (2017). The bill established a teacher advisory committee that would bring accomplished teachers together to advise policy makers on the implementation and impact of the Every Student Succeeds Act—the nation's key federal law related to elementary and secondary education. While introduced in several Congresses, it never gained the traction to garner the broad support needed for enactment; however, it stands as an example for future consideration.

POLICY EVALUATION

Policy evaluation is intended to determine the impact of a policy. In the last few decades policy evaluation has grown into a full-fledged enterprise—an academic field with professional associations, journals, research, and scholars; an industry sector supported by federal and private funds; and government entities with missions to evaluate the impact of policy and make recommendations, such as the Institute for Education Sciences,[2] which conducts large-scale evaluations of federal education programs and policies. (For more information about policy evaluation, see Anderson, 1999; Fowler, 2013; Jones, 1984; May & Wildavsky, 1978; Nakamura & Smallwood, 1980.)

The goal of policy evaluation is to determine if the policy (or programs) are working as intended. Ideally the results of evaluation complete a feedback loop, infusing information about results into a revision or updating of policy. The reauthorization process in Congress—whereby laws are routinely examined and altered—is an institutionalized process that exemplifies this intention. Results are

---

1. For more information, see https://www.nnstoy.org/.
2. For more information, see https://ies.ed.gov/aboutus/.

intended to inform both implementation activities as well as policy change. As government investment in addressing challenging societal problems has grown over the years and as research methodologies have evolved, the desire for accountability and justification of government spending and functions has ballooned. Yet the results of evaluation studies and assessments do not necessarily lead to change. The reasons are many.

First, policy evaluation is a political endeavor. While it is tempting to believe that it takes place outside the realm of politics, that simply is not the case. Certainly, well-established scientific norms and protocols are utilized in policy evaluation; however, this does not isolate the work from its political context. Anderson (1999) outlines three reasons for this: (1) the policy being assessed is the product of a political process, (2) evaluation reports influence the political arena, and (3) there is much on the line, including careers, reputations, resources, and more. The parties involved in policy evaluation often include those involved in policy making—those who may have either supported or opposed the policy—or simply hold strong beliefs about the rightness or wrongness of the policy. These may include policy makers, policy implementers, the intended beneficiaries of the policy, interest groups, and the evaluators themselves.

A second challenge for policy evaluators is determining the actual goal or purpose of the policy and how to measure its impact. Policy goals may be broad. For example, the purpose of Title I of the Every Student Succeeds Act is "to provide all children significant opportunity to receive a fair, equitable, and high-quality education, and to close educational achievement gaps" (2015). In order to evaluate this sixteen-billion-dollar-plus policy investment, evaluators would need to decide on indicators that would reveal the extent to which the purpose of the title was being achieved. These might include implementation factors, such as mechanisms and procedures for distributing funds to states and districts or the utilization of evidence-based practices in the provision of a "high-quality" education. An impact evaluation might utilize the results of standardized reading or math assessments to determine program success. The options are many, and there is no perfect answer. The efficacy of the indicators must also be considered. For example, are standardized test results of students an accurate measure of a high-quality education? The process of choosing indicators to measure, as well as how to measure them, is bound to be influenced by a range of judgment calls of participants in the evaluation, including funders.

A third challenge encountered by evaluators might be acquisition of data needed for the evaluation. Data desired simply may not be available or might be too costly or time-consuming to acquire. Privacy laws may also present insurmountable challenges.

A fourth challenge could be determining causality. Did the policy actually cause the result being measured? With policies and programs with ambitious goals related to intransigent challenges, such as providing a high-quality education for every child, the factors that influence the success of that policy are multiple, including the skill of education staff, the poverty level of students in a school, and the adequacy of the building itself.

A fifth challenge relates to resource constraints—notably, time and money. Evaluations have time lines that may or may not allow for sufficient time to determine impact. Evaluations are often expensive, and policy makers are sometimes hesitant to dedicate needed funds to evaluation, as they would rather see the funds go directly to intended beneficiaries, such as students and schools. Limits on time and money may require evaluations of implementation rather than impact, or evaluations of limited scope since impact may take decades to unfold. As part of a political process, policy evaluation is influenced by political cycles.

A final challenge relates to resistance. In many evaluations, the results will imply winners and losers. There may be a lot on the line if a program is determined to be unsuccessful. Many federal programs generate a cadre of powerful supporters whose mission is to protect and expand the program. Efforts may be made to alter the nature of the evaluation, delay the evaluation, or bury the results if they appear to be threatening to key players.

While policy evaluation may result in policy termination, the more likely scenario is that it will influence policy change. Functions, organizations, and policies themselves are challenging to end, particularly if they have been around for a long time. However, policies may be replaced, consolidated, split into smaller portions, or defunded (Fowler, 2013). Likewise, implementation protocols may be improved as a result of policy evaluation.

Despite the limited impact of policy evaluation initiatives on substantial policy change, they play a significant role in the policy making process. The appetite of policy makers, interest groups, and the public to understand the impact of government spending only grows over time. Policy makers look to impact data and evaluation reports to justify the continuation of policies and programs; as rationales for limiting, terminating, or increasing funds; and as opportunities for improvement.

Framework #2: Policy Streams

The previous portion of this chapter outlined a standard stage model or cyclical approach to understanding policy making. While helpful in breaking down a complex process, the stage model cyclical approach sometimes leaves one with the impression that policy making is a sequential set of activities. Nothing could be further from the truth. John Kingdon (2010) offers a conception of policy making that highlights the dynamism and eternal flux of policy making that captures its essence.

Kingdon describes three policy streams: problems, policy proposals, and politics. He envisions these streams as flowing independently and circuitously—each with its own geographic characteristics, dynamics, obstacles, and flow pattern. At critical junctures, the three streams come together—and this is when policy change happens. While Kingdon describes it as "coupling," I prefer to think of it as a massive convergence—where the three great branches of a river come together to generate something altogether new—perhaps a lake—or a policy.

The problem stream is seen when problems are brought to the attention of policy makers—for example, mass school shootings. Whether or not the problem will be addressed is often determined by comparisons—for example, asking, Are there some states/localities where this is not a problem? Could we put a new policy in place to have the same outcome? Are other countries more successful at addressing this problem? Perhaps we have this problem in the wrong category—rather than a mass shooting problem, perhaps it is a gun ownership problem. As the problem streams ebb and flow within their banks, so do the policy and political streams.

Kingdon describes the policy stream as a "policy primeval soup" where the process of natural selection occurs to determine what policies rise to the top and survive. Generated by policy players through writing papers, introducing bills, advocacy initiatives, giving speeches, providing testimony, holding forums, and the like, policy proposals float around in the soup and bump into each other—all hungry for survival. Among the criteria that will determine their survival are technical feasibility, fit with dominant values, national mood, cost and budget feasibility, and political support or opposition. The selection process narrows policy options to a short list of those that could be seriously considered.

The third stream, politics, swirls wildly or calmly, influenced by election processes and outcomes, turnover of parties in Congress and the White House, the partisan versus bipartisan sentiments in the country, the national mood, and activities of pressure group campaigns.

When the three streams converge, the policy window opens. This may occur with the appearance of an urgent or compelling problem or shifts in the political stream. Policy entrepreneurs will be in these windows ready to act. Kingdon describes policy entrepreneurs as "people who are willing to invest their resources in pushing their pet proposals or problems, [and] are responsible not only for prompting important people to pay attention, but also for coupling solutions to problems and for coupling both problems and solutions to politics" (p. 20). Kingdon quotes an analyst for an interest group who vividly describes the ongoing preparation and eternal readiness for a policy window to open.

> When you lobby for something, what you have to do is put together your coalition, you have to gear up, you have to get your political forces in line, and then you sit there and wait for the fortuitous event. For example, people who were trying to do something about regulation of railroads tried to ride the environment for a while, but that wave didn't wash them in to shore. So they grabbed their surfboards and they tried to ride something else, but that didn't do the job. The Penn Central collapse was the big wave that brought them in. As I see it, people who are trying to advocate change are like surfers waiting for the big wave. You get out there, you have to be ready to go, you have to be ready to paddle. If you're not ready to paddle when the big wave comes along, you're not going to ride it in. (p. 165)

The analogy I often use is that advocates are like travelers waiting by the track for the train to come—their bags are packed, they know exactly what is in them, and they are ready. But there is no way to tell if any of the trains will actually get to the destination they seek. So they have to jump on every train that comes—hoping that one will arrive at the destination one day. And one thing is for sure—if they don't get on any of the trains, they will never arrive at a destination.

PART II: CONGRESSIONAL PROCEDURES

Laws are like sausages. It is better not to see them being made.

—Otto von Bismarck

Unpacking how Congress actually works can be a lifelong pursuit; however, knowing the basic standard procedures serves as a grounding benchmark from which deviations can be better understood. The traditional notion of "how a bill becomes a law," familiar to many through the iconic Schoolhouse Rock video (Jabbow, 2011), is generally referred to as "regular order." For decades standard procedure prevailed, providing predictability, transparency, and multiple opportunities for input and debate from members of Congress and other stakeholders. In recent years "regular order" has been increasingly sidelined for ever-evolving and often unpredictable "nonregular order." At the core of this shift is the move from a committee-centered legislative process to a leadership-party-centered process (Oleszek, 2020). In other words, it is increasingly common for the Speaker of the House and their team or the Senate majority leader and their team to develop legislative proposals and bring them up directly on the House or Senate floor rather than see them evolve through the committee process. Political polarization is at the heart of this shift, with "party unity" privileged over debate and compromise. The minority party is often left with little motivation to compromise, and considerable risk—the possibility of being ostracized by party leadership and "primaried" by a candidate whose party loyalty credentials outshine the member in question. Sometimes it seems the political parties are more interested in winning than legislating. The result can be dysfunction and stalemate as members of Congress become laser focused on the next election and how their party can continue to consolidate power.

Despite the decline in regular order, many bills continue to proceed through the standard committee process. For example, between 2009 and 2011 more than 40 percent of House bills and 80 percent of Senate bills were deliberated outside of committee (Bendix, 2016), leaving many bills within the committee structure for consideration.

There are multiple obstacles for a piece of legislation to encounter on its way to the finish line. Very few bills that are introduced actually become law. In every Congress since 1973, the percentage of bills introduced that become law has fluctuated from 4 to 9 percent (*Statistics and historical comparison*, n.d.). It is important

"Increasingly what we see is that the only way we get legislation completed is through giant emergency last-minute bills. The idea that you can complete standalone legislation, like the reauthorization of an education law, is almost gone. There is very little deliberative lawmaking. Most changes to higher education now come through other bills, like the COVID relief bills, omnibus appropriations bills, and reconciliation bills. With these vehicles, there is less ability to influence from the outside because there are too many interests involved and they can't let one small provision take the bill down. There is limited opportunity for content-specific deliberation, like what happens when a bill goes through the committee process. Decisions are made totally on politics. It's all about how to get the bill over the finish line, not necessarily about good policy." (Jonathan Fansmith, personal correspondence, August 16, 2022)

to bear in mind that the significance of different bills is highly variable. Some may be renaming a post office. Others may provide for a massive overhaul to our health care system or fund multiple federal agencies for a fiscal year. In general, the more circumscribed and targeted the bill, the more likely it is to pass. However, not all bills that are introduced are intended to become law. Some are intended to send a message and indicate that a member of Congress has particular interest in a policy area. A bill can be used to build support and momentum by accumulating cosponsors and endorsements from interest groups, thus gaining the attention of leadership or committee chairs. Often bills will be introduced that amend portions of laws that may come up for reauthorization at a later date, signaling a desire to have the bill included as part of a large reauthorization package.

While partisanship is on the rise, some degree of bipartisan success is always at play, with Congress motivated to demonstrate it can function and with a common desire to avoid breakdown of the essential functions of government such as the military.

TEXTBOX 3.2. **ONE SENATOR'S PRESCRIPTION FOR FINDING COMMON GROUND**

In December 2020, after serving twenty-four years in the Senate, Sen. Mike Enzi (R-WY) delivered his farewell address on the Senate floor, offering advice for how members of Congress can find common ground. He developed what he called the "80 percent tool." Generally speaking, people can talk civilly on 80 percent of the issues. It's only about 20 percent of issues where you will find real contention. Now even on the individual issues you might find disagreement, but once again you need to focus on the 80 percent of that issue that you can agree on. It is all about focusing on what you can get done, and not focusing on the points of disagreement . . .". (Office of Sen. Mike Enzi, 2020)

At the level of congressional staff, bipartisanship remains the rule rather than the exception. Most Republican and Democratic legislative staffers continue to be cordial and develop good working relationships. While disagreements and political challenges are generally acknowledged and understood, congressional staffers work hard to keep the legislative process moving as best they can. Students who have visited congressional staff with me are generally surprised by the reasonableness and cordiality they witness among staff from different political parties, as it does not comport with the predominant partisan polarization that is the drumbeat of press coverage. But stressors do emerge. For example, during the COVID pandemic, congressional offices differed in terms of mask and vaccination requirements, generally reflecting the different views of the political parties. Since staffers encounter each other for meetings, meals, in elevators, and in restrooms, these differences were at times stressful.

How a Bill Becomes a Law: The Seven Steps of Regular Order

Even when violated or adapted, the core processes to enact legislation remain intact, solidified by historical precedent and the appeal of predictability. Committee functions—oversight, hearings, markups, and investigations—for years have been the heart and soul of the deliberative role of Congress, providing opportunities for deep policy dialogue, a range of opinions, scrutiny related to policy functioning and effectiveness, examination of innovative solutions to societal challenges, and of course political grandstanding. Committees have specific jurisdictions for which they are responsible, enabling the members of the committee and the committee staff to develop a level of expertise that is not otherwise possible for offices that are covering every issue that comes before Congress. Members of Congress seek membership on particular committees because they are knowledgeable about the issues in the jurisdiction of the committee, because they are passionate about particular issues, because they want to become experts on the issues, or because there is a keen interest among their constituents in the issues. Committee membership provides members of Congress with important platforms to speak to stakeholders and their constituents and to advance policy in an ongoing manner. Committee chairs and ranking members generally serve as the expert voice for their caucus on matters in the committee's jurisdiction.[3]

Figure 3.2 provides a summary of the traditional steps involved in how a bill becomes a law. The Congressional Research Service provides additional detail on the process, which holds for both bills and the three types of resolutions, though these two categories of legislation are used for different purposes (*Introduction to the legislative process*, 2020). Textbox 3.3 provides a description of the four types of legislation. The discussion below focuses on bills rather than resolutions, as they represent most of Congress's policy work. The basic steps of regular order in legislative development are outlined.

---

3. In reviewing this section, it may be helpful to consult a glossary of legislative terms, which can be found at https://www.congress.gov/help/legislative-glossary.

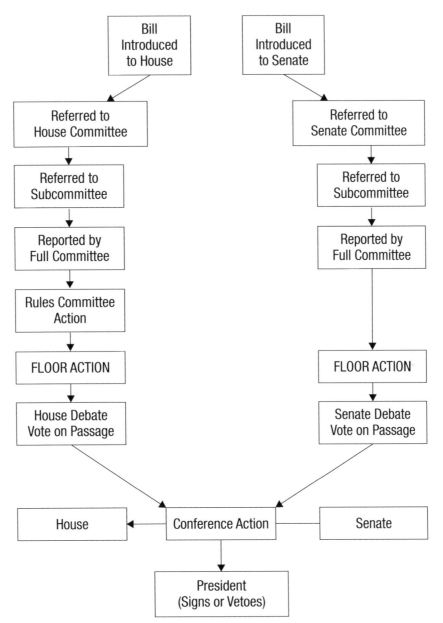

FIGURE 3.2. How a Bill Becomes a Law Flowchart

Reprinted from Hartranft (n.d.).

BILL INTRODUCTION

Any member of Congress may introduce a bill about any topic at any time. That bill is given a bill number (H.R. XXXX in the House and S. XXXX in the Senate) and then referred to the standing committee (or committees) of jurisdiction. (See table 3.1 for a list of standing committees.) For example, the Keeping All Students Safe Act, S. 1858 (2021b), was introduced in the 117th Congress by Sen. Murphy (D-CT). In the House the bill, H.R. 3474 (2021a), was introduced by Rep. Byer (D-VA). This bill addresses the practice of seclusion and restraint in schools; thus, it is in the jurisdiction of the HELP Committee in the Senate and the Education and Labor Committee in the House. The bills were referred to those two committees for further consideration. Note that bills are only referred to committees in the body in which they were introduced. In other words, if only Rep. Byer had introduced the bill in the House and there was no companion bill in the Senate, the bill would only be referred to the House Committee on Education and Labor. Also, some bills are referred to multiple committees for consideration. This occurs when there is overlap in committee jurisdiction. For example, both the Senate Committee on Finance and the Senate Committee on HELP have jurisdiction over health matters. When a member of Congress introduces a bill, they are likely to send a "Dear Colleague" letter urging other members of Congress to support it, as described in textbox 3.4.

TEXTBOX 3.4. "DEAR COLLEAGUE" LETTERS IN THE HOUSE AND SENATE

"Dear Colleague" letters (Straus, 2017) are official correspondence signed by members of Congress and distributed to their colleagues. "Dear Colleague" is the salutation in the letters and has become their moniker. Letters may be sent by a member of Congress, a committee, or an officer of the House or Senate. Most commonly the letters are used to encourage other members to cosponsor, support, or oppose legislation. Such a letter often includes an overview of the legislation, a rationale for why members of Congress should consider supporting it, and a list of others who support it. "Dear Colleague" letters may be used to gather support for a certain level of funding for a particular program in an appropriations bill. "Dear Colleague" letters are also used to urge other members to cosign letters to executive branch officials, congressional leadership, or committee chairs. Advocates may be invited by congressional offices to spread awareness about a "Dear Colleague" letter or to participate in soliciting the sign-on of members of Congress.

Any member of the House of Representatives may cosponsor any bill introduced by another member of the House. The same is true in the Senate. Cosponsorship is significant as it shows the level of support for the bill. The act of cosponsorship is a relatively easy and straightforward gesture a member can make to take a policy position and further a policy solution. Textbox 3.5 provides an overview of cosponsorship.

THE COMMITTEE RECEIVES THE BILL

The vast majority of bills—as many as 90 percent—die in committee. In other words, after the bills are referred to committee, no other consideration is taken. This is not necessarily bad, as many bills are introduced to send a message, to stake a claim on a particular aspect of a larger bill that will be considered at another time (for example, addressing student loan debt), or because of promises to constituents or other stakeholders. Thus, introduction of a bill can serve many purposes in addition to beginning the legislative process. Table 3.1 provides a list of standing committees where bills could be referred for further consideration.

The member of the House or Senate who introduces a bill or resolution is the sponsor of the bill. When additional members of Congress sign on to support the bill, they are called cosponsors. A bill may have only one sponsor but multiple cosponsors. When a cosponsor signs on to a bill at the time of introduction, that member may be called an "original cosponsor." Information about bill sponsors and cosponsors is available to the public.[1] When a bill gains a large number of cosponsors, a message is sent to congressional leaders and the public about its popularity and broad appeal. A bill with both Republican and Democratic cosponsors is viewed as bipartisan, which often enhances its appeal. Cosponsorship can build momentum, which raises the level of awareness and interest in a policy area, and may enhance chances of enactment. Advocates routinely ask their congressional delegation to cosponsor bills as a show of support for the policy solution they are seeking.[2]

---

1. For more information, see https://www.congress.gov/.

2. For more information, see *Sponsorship and cosponsorship of Senate bills* (2021) and *Sponsorship and cosponsorship of House bills* (2019).

TABLE 3.1. Standing Committees in the U.S. House of Representatives and the U.S. Senate

House	Senate
Standing Committees	
• Agriculture	• Agriculture, Nutrition, and Forestry
• Appropriations	• Appropriations
• Armed Services	• Armed Services
• Budget	• Banking, Housing, and Urban Affairs
• Education and Labor	• Budget
• Energy and Commerce	• Commerce, Science, and Transportation
• Ethics	• Energy and Natural Resources
• Financial Services	• Environment and Public Works
• Foreign Affairs	• Finance
• Homeland Security	• Foreign Relations
• House Administration	• Health, Education, Labor, and Pensions
• Judiciary	• Homeland Security and Governmental Affairs
• Natural Resources	• Judiciary
• Oversight and Reform	• Rules and Administration
• Rules	• Small Business and Entrepreneurship
• Science, Space, and Technology	• Veterans' Affairs
• Small Business	
• Transportation and Infrastructure	
• Veterans' Affairs	
• Ways and Means	

Note: From *Committees of the U.S. Congress* (n.d.).

POSSIBLE REFERRAL TO SUBCOMMITTEE

Some committees have a number of subcommittees; others have none. When I worked in the Senate, I worked on the Subcommittee on the Handicapped, a subcommittee of what is now the Committee on Health, Education, Labor and Pensions. Along the way, the committee made the decision to eliminate the subcommittee and to address all the issues in its jurisdiction at the full-committee level. However, when the subcommittee was active, all bills related to the education of people with disabilities—including the Individuals with Disabilities Education Act, the Vocational Rehabilitation Act, and more—were referred to the subcommittee, which would then proceed with the process of hearings, markups, and reporting out as described below.

HEARINGS AND MARKUPS

If a committee or subcommittee decides to act on a bill, the first step is to schedule one or more hearings. These are public events whereby both Democrats and Republicans on the committee may call witnesses to testify before the committee. Witnesses will include experts, state and local officials, representatives of stakeholder groups, family members, representatives of the administration, and public citizens. All are open to the public, and most are recorded and can be viewed on committee websites.[4] These are an excellent resource for learning about the history of a bill or how an issue was being viewed at a particular time.

Markups are convenings of the committee or subcommittee to consider, amend, and vote on a bill. Markups are generally open to the public. Members may offer amendments and debate them, or an entire substitute bill may be offered and considered. Votes are taken, and if a majority concurs, the bill is passed on favorably to either the full committee (in the case of a subcommittee acting) or the floor of the full body (in the case of a full committee acting). Rarely is a bill defeated at a markup, as the committee chair would not likely have scheduled the markup if that was the anticipated outcome. When a bill is reported out of committee, it will likely be accompanied by a committee report, which includes the text of the bill, an explanation of the bill, and other legislative history.

FLOOR CONSIDERATION

After the committee reports the bill to the floor, it is up to the leadership in the House and the Senate, respectively, to determine when and if the bill will be scheduled for a vote. Sometimes that never occurs, as legislative schedules are precious real estate with intense competition for space and time. If the bill is thought to be controversial and time-consuming, it may be sidelined. The procedures for considering a bill on the floor are different in the House and Senate. Most notably, the House usually (unless there is a determination for expedited

---

4. For example, see the Committee on Education and Labor at https://edlabor.house.gov/hearings-and-events.

"Markups can mean long demanding hours for staff. Sometimes they last multiple days. There is no time limit. It goes on as long as it takes. All committee members have the opportunity to share their ideas and offer amendments to the bill under consideration, with passage as the goal for the majority party (or both majority and minority if it is bipartisan) so it will go to the floor so all members of a chamber can vote on it. If the bill is partisan, the minority may try to stop the bill from passing committee, by offering tough amendments, for example. In the House, markups can be especially challenging because there is no requirement to prefile amendments before the markup. Staff may see amendment text at the markup for the first time right before an amendment is considered, and it's a scramble to digest it and make vote recommendations in the moment. Members must speak on the amendment in real time. In the Senate amendments are prefiled, so staff can be prepared with talking points and recommendations for a senator." (Lindsay Fryer, personal correspondence, September 22, 2022)

procedure, or "suspension of the rules") requires a "rule" to be established by the Committee on Rules before a bill appears on the legislative calendar. The Committee on Rules meets and creates a rule for the individual bill under consideration, which addresses matters such as how long debate will last and the number of amendments that can be offered on the floor. At times only specific predetermined amendments will be allowed, or amendments may be precluded all together. When the rule is determined by the Committee on Rules, it must be adopted by vote by the House prior to proceeding to the actual bill. Consideration of the bill follows adoption of the rule.

In the Senate a vote must first occur whereby there is agreement to consider the bill. This may be via "unanimous consent" or a "motion to proceed" to the bill. A unanimous consent agreement indicates that all members of the Senate agree as to how to proceed in terms of time allotted, number of amendments, and so on. Such an agreement can only be changed by another unanimous consent agreement. If a "motion to proceed" is utilized, there are no limits on debating that proposal. It is subject to endless debate, or filibuster. Senators must vote to end debate by at least sixty votes (called a cloture vote). Amendments to a bill may not be considered until the Senate has agreed to "proceed" to the actual bill. Amendments may also be filibustered, again requiring sixty votes to end the debate. The Senate rules, unlike the House rules, are tailored to provide significant authority to individual senators. (See sections later in this chapter on Committee on Rules and filibuster and cloture in the Senate for more information.)

If the bills proceed in both the House and the Senate through floor passage, they are ready for a conference committee.

CONFERENCE COMMITTEE

Unless both chambers pass identical versions of a piece of legislation, a conference committee must be appointed to iron out the differences between the two versions. The committee is made up of members from both the House and the Senate, usually many of them members of the committees that reported the bills. Conference committees hammer out the differences between the two bills, seeking an agreement that will later be endorsed by both the full House and the full Senate. When that agreement is complete, a conference report is issued, which includes the text of the final legislation. The conference report can then be considered by both the House and the Senate. A conference report cannot be amended in either body. For the legislation to become law, both bodies must pass the conference agreement and send it to the president for his signature. Increasingly, Congress bypasses the conference committee step in lieu of "preconference." In this situation the House and Senate negotiate an agreement in advance of floor passage, so that each body passes the exact same bill, thus avoiding the need for conference.

PRESIDENT'S SIGNATURE

When the president receives a bill from Congress, they have ten days (excluding Sundays) to sign it or veto it. If the bill is signed, it becomes law. If the president does nothing—neither signs nor vetoes—it will still become law but without their signature. (There are some circumstances related to congressional adjournment where this is not the case.) When the president signs a bill, he will often issue a statement, which may become an important part of the legislative history. (See, for example, textbox 3.6 on President Ford's statement when he signed IDEA into law in 1975.)

The president may also veto a bill, returning it to Congress for a possible veto override. In order to be successful, both the House and Senate must endorse an override with two-thirds of those voting affirming the override. Overrides of a presidential veto are rare. Presidents often issue veto messages along with their veto, explaining their reason for vetoing the bill.

Enacted bills are assigned a Public Law number and incorporated into the body of law of the United States. The first two digits of a public law number reflect the number of the Congress that enacted them, and the last three digits reflect the order of signature by the president. For example, P.L. 94-142 was the 142nd bill signed into law during the 94th Congress.

Chapter 5 provides an overview of multiple artifacts of policy making processes that are rich resources for researchers and advocates.

Three Core Legislative Processes: Budget, Appropriations, Authorization

Each of the three basic lawmaking operations of Congress—the budget process, the appropriations process, and the authorization process—involves distinct sets of purposes and procedures; however, they are intertwined in significant ways. Together these processes make up the vast majority of policy work conducted by Congress. The dance between the three processes provides numerous opportunities for advocacy.

BUDGET PROCESS

Derived from a number of statutory requirements and sets of rules and procedures, the budget cycle begins annually with the president's submission of a budget request to Congress on the first Monday in February. While that time line often slips to days or months later (particularly when a new president has just been seated in January), it is the official kickoff of the process. The proposal includes descriptions of federal programs and specific line-item suggested funding amounts for each program in the federal budget. Often there will be budget summaries and justifications from the federal agencies that provide supplemental information. It is not uncommon for budget proposals to recommend program eliminations, new programs, or significant policy shifts, in addition to addressing existing programs. When Betsy DeVos was secretary of education during the

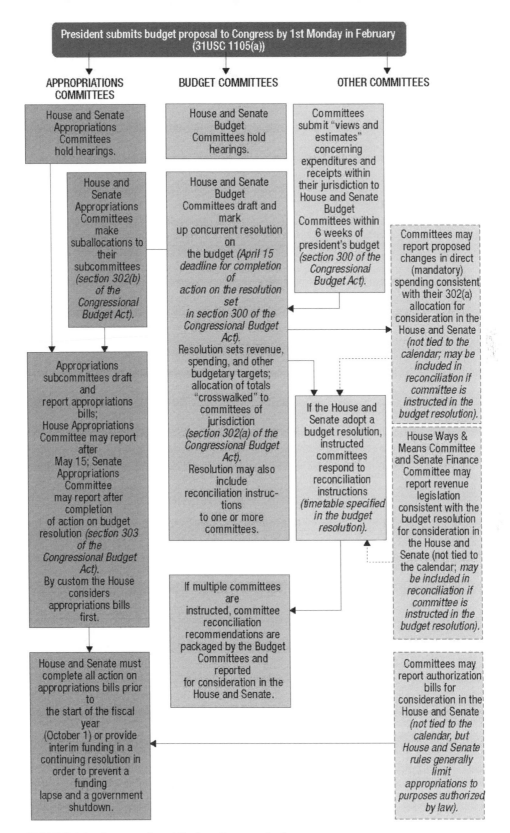

FIGURE 3.3. Congressional Budget Process Actions

From Saturno (2020b).

Trump presidency, a number of voucher programs were recommended in the budget proposals that would have resulted in new federal support for private schools with decreasing support for public schools (*U.S. department of education*, n.d.). While Congress never adopted these proposals, they became signature efforts of the Trump administration. President Biden's first budget proposal included significant new spending targeted to his priorities (*Fact sheet*, 2022). For example, in education he recommended a 41 percent increase in funding—the largest ever recommended by a president. Thus, the budget request often serves as a road map of an administration's priorities for the year.

Every budget proposal is developed with extensive input from each of the federal agencies involved in implementing laws and carrying out programs. The Office of Management and Budget, under the guidance of the White House, makes final decisions about what will be in the budget request.

Informed by the president's request, Congress begins a complex set of steps that are intended to result in funding for the upcoming fiscal year as well as managing the receipts, borrowing, and debt of the federal government. While amended many times, the Congressional Budget Act of 1974 remains the fundamental authority for the budget process, establishing the federal fiscal year as October 1 through September 30, House and Senate Budget Committees, the Congressional Budget Office, and the requirement that Congress annually adopt a concurrent resolution that sets overall fiscal policy. The time line for the budget process is outlined in law.

The first task for Congress, after receiving the president's budget request, is to develop a concurrent budget resolution. The resolution sets budget policy and priorities for the upcoming year and multiple additional years. It determines spending levels for different functions of the budget. Most importantly, it assigns an overall spending figure for the upcoming fiscal year (in Washington parlance, the "302(a)," referring to the section of the Congressional Budget Act that includes the requirement) to the all-powerful Committees on Appropriations in the House and Senate. It does not allocate specific funds for specific programs, as this comes later under the authority of the appropriations subcommittees.

The House and Senate Committees on the Budget are responsible for drafting the budget resolution and marking it up. It must be passed by each body. The resolution is not signed by the president; however, it is considered binding on Congress and the appropriations process that follows.

As the Committees on the Budget pursue their work on the resolution, they may receive input from the Congressional Budget Office as well as information from other committees, called "views and estimates." "Views and estimates" enable committees of jurisdiction, such as the Senate Committee on Health, Education, Labor and Pensions, to provide information about the preferences of the committee and upcoming legislative plans, which may influence what appears in the budget resolution.

The Committees on the Budget report their resolutions out for consideration by the full membership of the House and the Senate. Each body must pass the resolution, based on the rules of the body and the statutory requirements of the

Congressional Budget Act. Notably, in the Senate only fifty-one votes, a simple majority, are required to pass the resolution. If the budget resolutions in the House and Senate are different, they must be merged into one agreed-upon resolution by a conference committee. That final compromise bill must be adopted by both the House and the Senate. When the final concurrent budget resolution has been adopted by each body, the work moves to the Committees on Appropriations to determine spending for the next fiscal year (Saturno, 2020b).

RECONCILIATION

An optional component of the budget resolution is called reconciliation. Increasingly utilized as Congress has become more polarized, this process enables passage of significant legislative changes by a simple majority of fifty-one votes in the Senate. When finding the usually required sixty votes for passage of a bill in the Senate becomes virtually impossible due to partisanship, the majority party may resort to this mechanism. For example, in the early days of his presidency, facing the slimmest of majorities in the Senate (only fifty Democratic senators—and with the addition of the vice president making fifty-one votes), President Biden knew he would not be able to find enough Republican senators to support his massive bill to address the COVID pandemic, so he urged Congress to use the reconciliation procedure in order to pass the $1.9 trillion spending bill, the American Rescue Plan Act (2021).

If using the reconciliation process, the budget resolution must provide "reconciliation instructions" to specified committees of jurisdiction directing them to draft and report legislation to change laws related to spending, revenues, or the debt limit. For example, in 2007, reconciliation instructions directed the House and Senate committees with jurisdiction over education policy to craft new student financial aid legislation to recruit high-achieving individuals into teacher preparation programs to meet the demand for teachers in low-income schools. This program, called TEACH grants, was enacted as part of the College Cost Reduction and Access Act of 2007, a statute enacted via the reconciliation procedure (Zota, 2019). All committees of jurisdiction submit their legislative proposals to the Committee on the Budget, which then compiles them and turns them into another bill, a reconciliation bill, that must be enacted into law separately and signed by the president.

DEEMING RESOLUTION

In recent years Congress has frequently been unable to agree on a budget resolution. The alternative utilized is called a "deeming resolution." This resolution establishes the all-important budget levels for the upcoming fiscal year, and sometimes beyond, enabling Congress to move on to the appropriations process without a budget resolution. They are "deemed" to serve in place of the budget resolution. The House and Senate may pass deeming resolutions with different budget levels, requiring future action to come to agreement on one budget level for the funding cap for the upcoming fiscal year.

APPROPRIATIONS PROCESS

After the budget is determined, or increasingly more often even when there is no budget resolution, Congress moves to the appropriations process. This is the annual determination of funding for federal programs, and a key opportunity for advocacy (*Appropriations 101*, 2022). If regular order is followed, the budget resolution will have determined the overall spending level for the fiscal year (called the "302(a)"). Next, the chairs of the Committees on Appropriations in the House and the Senate divvy up the funding between the twelve appropriations subcommittees. These subcommittee allocations are fondly called "302(b)s" (also a reference to the section of the Congressional Budget Act that requires them). They set the all-important spending caps for each of the twelve appropriations subcommittees. These ceilings for spending are critical and are watched carefully by Washington insiders, as they represent the total amount available for each subcommittee, which will then need to be divided between multiple federal agencies and individual programs. For example, the Subcommittee on Labor, Health and Human Services, Education, and Related Agencies must provide funding for three large federal agencies and each of the programs they administer—the Departments of Labor, Health and Human Services, and Education. Thus, the larger the allocation given to the subcommittee, the better the chance for advocates to see increases in the individual programs they have targeted. Table 3.2 lists the twelve appropriations subcommittees along with the total amount each funded in FY 2021. Note that the subcommittee where education resides is the second largest of the twelve subcommittees, with only the Subcommittee on Defense being larger.

When each of the twelve subcommittees of the Committee on Appropriations have received their allocation for the fiscal year, they begin the process of writing an annual appropriations bill. Generally beginning in the spring, this is an excellent time for advocates to be engaged. The subcommittees may hold hearings and

TABLE 3.2. The Twelve Appropriations Subcommittees in the House and Senate with FY 2021 Spending Totals

Appropriations Subcommittee	FY 2021 Appropriation
Agriculture	$23.4 billion
Commerce, Justice, Science	$71.1 billion
Defense	$627.3 billion
Energy and Water	$49.5 billion
Financial Services and General Government	$24.4 billion
Homeland Security	$51.9 billion
Interior and Environment	$36.1 billion
Labor, HHS, Education, Related Agencies	$174.1 billion
Legislative Branch	$5.3 billion
Military Construction and VA	$112.8 billion
State, Foreign Operations	$47.5 billion
Transportation, Housing and Urban Development	$74.7 billion
TOTAL	**$1.298 trillion**

Note: Adapted from *Appropriations 101* (2022).

accept written testimony from the public about the need for funding for particular programs. Secretaries from relevant federal agencies may testify to defend the president's budget proposal. Most national associations write letters to the subcommittees urging a particular level of funding for programs they champion. The case must be made as to the need for the increase in funding. This is often done by providing a combination of data and stories—about the needs that remain unaddressed, the impact of the program, and the difference an increase in funding would make. A good formula is to present the problem and then how the federal government can, or can better, address it. For example, in the education arena, the Committee for Education Funding[5] routinely assembles information about programs, the need for additional funding, and the impact of existing funds. They are a "go-to" resource for Congress.

TEXTBOX 3.7. **MY EXPERIENCE TESTIFYING BEFORE AN APPROPRIATIONS SUBCOMMITTEE**

In the spring of 2022, the staff of Rep. Rosa DeLauro (D-CT) emailed me about the possibility of my testifying before the Labor, Health and Human Services, and Education Appropriations Subcommittee regarding the shortages of teachers. The subcommittee was following the multiple and troubling reports across the country about teacher shortages—with the field indisputably hit hardest being special education. My priority area of expertise for many years has been teacher preparation and the federal role in standards with a focus on special educators. I had a long-standing relationship with the offices of both Chair DeLauro and Ranking Member Cole (R-OK). On behalf of several national associations, I had regularly provided them with information about both the need for special educators and the efficacy of key federal programs that made a difference, urging an increased investment. The hearing was held in part in preparation for the subcommittee to write their FY 2023 funding bill, where they would recommend funding levels for various programs, including those that affect teacher shortages.

I was invited to testify in early May, with the due date for my testimony being May 20 and the hearing scheduled for May 25. The only problem was I was scheduled to be out of the country for most of the month, returning May 19! With incredible assistance from amazing colleagues around the country, I pulled together my testimony and was able to submit it on time (Tackling teacher shortages, House Subcommittee on Labor/HHS/Education Appropriations, 2022). I listened to a couple of hearings the subcommittee had recently held to prepare myself for possible questions and the style of questioning of the various subcommittee members. Despite having planned and attended numerous hearings over the years and having prepared multiple witnesses, I had never actually testified myself. It felt different being in the hot seat! What I prepared for the most was questions that were challenging but tangential, enabling members to explicate their perspective on a particular controversial matter, such as vouchers.

Much to my relief, the hearing went well (*Tackling teacher shortages*, 2022), and I felt that I was able to make my key points. When the subcommittee's proposal for FY 2023 was released in June 2022, there was a increase in funding for each of the three programs I had recommended (House Committee on Appropriations, 2022).

---

5. For more information, see https://cef.org/cef-budget-book/.

The next step is for each subcommittee to introduce their bill and hold a markup on that bill. The bill will include individual funding levels for every program in the jurisdiction of the subcommittee. Traditionally, the House goes before the Senate in marking up its twelve subcommittee bills. This often happens in the spring/early summer. The House and the Senate will most often have different spending levels for individual programs. Advocates are active in weighing in with Congress in support of the higher number for the programs they champion. Eventually, if regular order is followed, each of the twelve bills must pass both the House and the Senate, be conferenced to resolve differences, and be passed again by each body. Thus twelve separate funding bills would go to the president's desk for signature. This should be accomplished by the end of the fiscal year, September 30.

In recent years, the process has rarely unfolded in regular order as described above. The last time Congress passed all twelve appropriations bills on time was 1996. If no action is taken, a government shutdown is the result. Government shutdowns, where some or all federal agencies cease operations, have occurred at least as far back as 1976 (Infoplease Staff, 2020). They may last from a few days to several weeks, as pressure grows on politicians to act to reopen the government.

More commonly, Congress resorts to the passage of some portion of the twelve appropriations bills and a "continuing resolution." For example, if Congress has adopted three of the twelve funding bills on time, they may be packaged into one bill, called an "omnibus" or a "minibus," and be enacted as a group. The other bills may be covered by a "continuing resolution," or a continuation of the existing funding level (perhaps somewhat modified) for a certain period of time. The continuing resolution may apply to the entire government if none of the twelve bills have been enacted, or to portions of the government if some of the bills have been enacted. A continuing resolution may extend for a few days, often to enable further negotiation by members of Congress on a bill, or they may last for the rest of the fiscal year, indicating that Congress has reached an impasse on agreeing to new funding levels. At times, controversial unresolved issues, such as funding clinics that provide abortions, may stop the process in its tracks, requiring a continuing resolution to avoid a government shutdown.

Appropriations bills are intended to fund only programs that have been authorized previously by Congress (see description of authorization process below). In other words, a law, created by a different committee (an authorizing committee), should already be on the books before it is funded. However, programs that have been authorized will not necessarily be funded in the appropriations bills. For example, all programs in the Higher Education Act are eligible for funding in appropriations bills; however, just because they are authorized does not necessarily mean they will be funded. Appropriations bills are not supposed to create new programs to fund or to change statutory requirements for programs already in law. However, Congress does not always follow these rules, and if objections are not raised or do not prevail, such provisions may be included in appropriations bills. These provisions are referred to as "unauthorized appropriations," which are legally binding.

In addition, appropriations bills often include "riders" or policy changes that hitch a ride on the appropriations vehicle, though technically they belong in an authorization bill. For example, in 2012 an appropriations bill added a provision to override a court decision and change the definition of "highly qualified teacher" contained in the No Child Left Behind Act. Instead of the previously agreed upon policy that a teacher would have had to finish their preparation program before being considered "highly qualified," the rider changed the provision to indicate that an individual could be in the midst of their training for up to three years and still be considered "highly qualified."[6]

In addition to passing annual appropriations bills, Congress may also enact "supplemental" appropriations bills to provide additional funds for a particular fiscal year. These bills generally address urgent or emergency situations, such as military operations or natural disasters. When they are considered emergencies, they are not subject to budget caps.

Neither the budget nor the appropriations bills address the totality of the federal budget. Off-budget items, such as receipts and disbursements from the Social Security trust funds and spending for the postal service fund are separate from the budget. In addition, transactions related to government-sponsored enterprises, as well as the Federal Reserve System, are not part of the budget and appropriations processes.

MANDATORY AND DISCRETIONARY SPENDING

There are three types of spending in the federal government: discretionary, mandatory, and interest on the federal debt.[7] Discretionary spending is the type of annual allocation over which the Committees on Appropriations must make determinations, as described above. Mandatory or direct spending is determined on an ongoing basis through statute and generally applies to entitlement programs, such as Social Security or Medicare. When a program is funded by mandatory spending, the money flows without Congress taking any annual action. The only way to end or change mandatory spending is to change the authorization statutes, such as the Social Security Act, which authorizes it. This is rarely done. Some programs are a combination of mandatory and discretionary spending, such as Pell Grants, a

---

6. For a full explanation, see Schuster (2013).

7. While the federal government is allowed to borrow money to run the government, the amount it is allowed to borrow is subject to a cap, called the debt limit. The U.S. Department of the Treasury (n.d.) defines the debt limit as follows: "The debt limit is the total amount of money that the United States government is authorized to borrow to meet its existing legal obligations, including Social Security and Medicare benefits, military salaries, interest on the national debt, tax refunds, and other payments." Congress routinely sets the debt limit and must routinely raise it as debts mount and exceed the limit. As the debt limit is raised and borrowing grows, so does interest on the debt—though how much depends on the interest rate. For FY 2020, the federal deficit was estimated to be $3.1 trillion dollars. Servicing the debt cost $345 billion, or 5 percent of federal spending (*Federal net interest costs*, 2020). The debt ceiling has been raised seventy-eight times since 1960, and it has become an increasingly polarizing and politically partisan act, as politicians use the opportunity to hold the debt limit bill hostage to bargain for limits on spending or other provisions they have been unable to successfully pursue otherwise. Raising the debt ceiling, when the time comes, is considered essential, as without the needed increase, the federal government would default on its legal obligations, causing a financial crisis.

form of student financial aid. Mandatory spending is coveted by education advocates and others, as it represents funds that can be counted on from year to year outside of the annual appropriations process.

The vast majority of funds expended each year—between 60 and 70 percent—are mandatory funds. The portion of mandatory spending in the federal budget has grown steadily in recent years. The proportion of discretionary funding subject to the annual appropriations process is about 30 percent or less. The remaining funds include a small though growing portion of the budget—currently about 5 percent—to service the federal debt (*Federal net interest costs*, 2020). As depicted in figure 3.4, in FY 2020 the federal government spent $4.6 trillion in mandatory funds and $1.6 trillion in discretionary funds (*Discretionary spending in fiscal year 2020*, 2021).

Out of the discretionary portion of funds must come both defense and nondefense spending. In FY 2020, discretionary spending by the federal government totaled $1.6 trillion, of which $714 billion was for national defense and $914 billion was for nondefense expenses (*Discretionary spending in fiscal year 2020*, 2021). Education spending comes from the nondefense discretionary portion of funds. Over the years, funding for social programs, such as education, research, and housing, have been squeezed into an increasingly smaller portion of the federal budget. Education advocates estimate that the portion of the federal budget that is targeted to education spending is usually about 2 percent of the federal budget. This led the Committee for Education Funding to the creation of a campaign slogan to increase the federal investment in education to 5 cents of every dollar—thus the rallying cry "5 cents makes sense" (Committee for Education Funding, 2017).

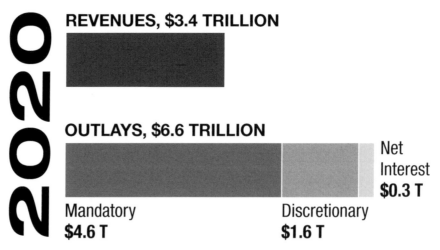

FIGURE 3.4. Federal Budget for FY 2020
Reprinted from The federal budget in fiscal year 2020 *(2021).*

Often described as "congressionally directed spending," earmarks were a part of the appropriations process for years—before challenges related to poor spending decisions and transparency arose (Lynch, 2020). Earmarks enable individual members of Congress to direct federal funding to specific projects and entities in their districts or states. Some analysts believe that the moratorium, or prohibition, of earmarks that began in 2011–2012 contributed to gridlock in Congress. When members of Congress had earmarks in spending bills, they were often motivated to support a bill, which they otherwise might object to. Many believed earmarks "greased the wheels" of the appropriations machinery, promoting the passage of the twelve bills. Earmarks enabled members of Congress to be directly responsible to their constituents, showing concrete results back home. But criticisms of earmarks as wasteful pork barrel spending took hold, and the earmark ban followed.

With the FY 2022 appropriations process and the Democrats in charge in both the House and Senate, earmarks made a return. There were new requirements related to transparency, limits on certain types of earmarks, limits on the amount of earmark spending, and more. What used to be a process that took place behind closed doors, with little to no public visibility, became a public process. All requests made by each individual member of the House could be viewed by the public on the website of the House Committee on Appropriations.[8] For Senators, earmark requests could be viewed on the Senate Committee on Appropriations website.[9] The final $1.5 trillion FY 2022 appropriations bill included five thousand earmarks totaling $9 billion. Democrats claimed 3,682 earmarks for a total of $5 billion; Republicans landed 1,014 earmarks totaling $3.4 billion, and bipartisan earmarks accounted for $609 million. Sen. Lisa Murkowski (R-AK) noted that earmarks were returning Alaskan taxpayer dollars to the state. She said, "There are still some for whom 'earmark' is a four-letter word. I think it's important, again, to recognize that there is a level of transparency now in this process that simply didn't exist" (Broadwater et al., 2022). It will be interesting to see if earmarks persist over time.

AUTHORIZATION PROCESS

The authorization process is predominantly what we think of in considering how a bill becomes a law. While the budget and appropriations processes unfold annually, the authorization process is not on a particular timetable. New authorization statutes may be enacted at any time.

Authorization legislation provides statutory authority for the government to act (Saturno, 2020a). It may create a federal agency or design a program or activity. It may develop policies and restrictions related to organizational, administrative, or programmatic matters. Authorization legislation often recommends a level of

---

8. For more information, see https://appropriations.house.gov/transparency.

9. For more information, see https://www.appropriations.senate.gov/congressionally-directed -spending-requests.

discretionary funding for a government program—called "authorization of appropriations." However, unless the appropriations process results in an allocation of funds, the authorized program will remain unfunded and thus not implemented. There are many authorized programs that have never been funded. However, recall that if mandatory, or direct spending, is called for in an authorization bill, those funds automatically flow and are not subject to the annual appropriations process. In addition, a lack of sufficient funds to carry out legal requirements, such as enforcement of a law, does not excuse the government from that obligation. The implementation of IDEA is a key example of this. While never funded at the authorized level (40 percent of the national average per pupil expenditure), all mandates of the law remain in full force. In FY 2021, IDEA was funded at $12.94 billion, an estimated 14 percent of the authorized level.

In the education arena, there are multiple authorization laws. The Higher Education Act, the Every Student Succeeds Act, and the Individuals with Disabilities Education Act are a few. In general, these laws and many others are only authorized for a set period of time; five years is typical. At the end of the authorization period, laws are intended to be "reauthorized," or revised and renewed in order for the program or activities to be updated and to continue. Congress has increasingly missed reauthorization deadlines as reauthorizations have become more complex and partisanship expanded. Rather than allow laws to expire, Congress generally utilizes an extension mechanism that enables the law to continue as is for a period of time. Examples of laws that are significantly past their reauthorization deadlines include the discretionary programs of IDEA (last reauthorized in 2004) and the Higher Education Act (last reauthorized in 2008). Nonetheless, the policy discussions that surround the contemplation of reauthorization are significant in raising issues and possible solutions, such as how to address the cost of college. This dialogue often results in changes in practice, additional studies and reports, changes in guidance or regulations in federal agencies, or policy "riders" on appropriations bills.

One law that stands in unique contrast to the lagging reauthorization schedule is the Defense Reauthorization Act. This law is required to be reauthorized every year, and it has been since 1961. While controversial issues, such as gays in the military and sexual assault in the military, have temporarily delayed the reauthorization, it has managed to proceed annually (Oleszek et al., 2020).

Some authorization laws are permanently authorized, meaning they do not have to be reauthorized and remain intact indefinitely. Congress can act to change them, but there is no time line set in statute. Examples of permanently authorized laws include civil rights laws, such as the Civil Rights Act of 1964 and the American with Disabilities Act of 1990, as well as most of the core components of the Individuals with Disabilities Education Act. Permanently authorized laws also include the creation of government entities, such as the Library of Congress. Permanent authorization sends a message of stability and commitment on the part of the federal government. Some have noted that civil rights laws are so fundamental that they should never be up for reconsideration. Until the 1950s, most laws were permanently authorized. However, the shift since then has been to more temporary authorizations, giving authorization committees greater control and oversight, particularly of executive agencies and the implementation of programs and requirements (Oleszek et al., 2020).

Every law that is authorized, and every policy area, is under the jurisdiction of a particular committee—in both the House and the Senate. Sometimes a law may be under the jurisdiction of multiple committees. Textbox 3.8 provides a list of areas of jurisdiction for the Senate Committee on Health, Education, Labor and Pensions as of 2022 as an example.

TEXTBOX 3.8. **JURISDICTION OF THE U.S. SENATE COMMITTEE ON HEALTH, EDUCATION, LABOR AND PENSIONS**

Rule 25 of the Standing Rules of the Senate states the jurisdiction of the Committee on Health, Education, Labor and Pensions[1] to be the following: all proposed legislation, messages, petitions, memorials, and other matters relating to the following subjects:

1. Measures relating to education, labor, health, and public welfare
2. Aging
3. Agricultural colleges
4. Arts and humanities
5. Biomedical research and development
6. Child labor
7. Convict labor and the entry of goods made by convicts into interstate commerce
8. Domestic activities of the American National Red Cross
9. Equal employment opportunity
10. Gallaudet University, Howard University, and Saint Elizabeth hospital
11. Individuals with disabilities
12. Labor standards and labor statistics
13. Mediation and arbitration of labor disputes
14. Occupational safety and health, including the welfare of miners
15. Private pension plans
16. Public health
17. Railway labor and retirement
18. Regulation of foreign laborers
19. Student loans
20. Wages and hours of labor

The committee also must study and review, on a comprehensive basis, matters relating to health, education and training, and public welfare, and report thereon from time to time.

---

1. For more information, see https://www.help.senate.gov/about.

Other Congressional Processes

OVERSIGHT AND INVESTIGATIONS

There is no official practice or procedure for conducting oversight and investigation in Congress, though both are generally carried out through the committee structure and are subject to committee rules and procedures. The three core policy making processes described above—budget, appropriations, and authorization—may all be used as oversight and investigation tools; however, more intensive and targeted oversight activities are often conducted by Congress, utilizing the broad authority to examine the activities of both public and private entities in consideration of whether current public policy is effective and whether new policies are needed.

> "Oversight over executive branch actions can be used by both the majority and minority parties. Letters can be sent to the administration asking them to explain or justify a position, action, or decision about how a law will be implemented. This raises the profile of an issue, and if there are a lot of letter signatures the issue might get more attention in the press, for example. An oversight letter can raise public awareness of an issue or increase pressure to receive a response or some action." (Lindsay Fryer, personal correspondence, September 22, 2022)

Congressional oversight serves as a check and balance on the executive branch. As executive authority has expanded over the years, and as Congress has become increasingly gridlocked in its ability to enact legislation, oversight functions have expanded. Oversight can be a relatively straightforward bipartisan fact-finding endeavor, such as the Senate Committee on Intelligence's investigation into Russian interference in the 2016 presidential election (Gazis & Becket, 2020), or it can be adversarial and undertaken with stark partisan overtones, such as the House Select Committee on Benghazi's investigation related to the 2012 attacks in Libya and the role of then secretary of state Hillary Clinton (Herszenhorn, 2016), or it can be an amalgam of the two. When different political parties control the executive branch and either the House or the Senate, oversight functions can serve as an opportunity for the opposition party to challenge the performance of administration officials and their implementation of laws. Congressional oversight also serves the important function of informing the public. Individual members of Congress may hold "field hearings"—usually hearings in their district or state—as a means of oversight where they gather information from constituents about a program or policy issue, while securing local visibility.

Congress routinely receives reports from two key offices that serve important oversight and investigation functions: the Government Accountability Office (GAO) and Inspector General reports (IG reports). Often called the "congressional watchdog," the GAO is a part of the legislative branch (*About*, n.d.). Its function is to watch over how taxpayers' dollars are spent and provide information to Congress and federal agencies about how the government can function more efficiently. GAO reports often point out inefficiencies in the operation of federal agencies and the implementation of programs.

Most offices of Inspector Generals (IGs) are created by statute and all are part of the executive branch (Wilhelm, 2022). A total of seventy-four IG offices across a wide range of federal agencies are mandated by law. The IG's role is to oversee agency operations, root out fraud and abuse, and routinely report to Congress. This is a unique role in the executive branch, as the IG reports directly to Congress and not to the head of the agency where it is housed. Furthermore, IG investigations and findings are not vetted, changed, or approved by the head of the federal agency where the IG is located. The role of the IG is to keep Congress fully informed in a timely fashion.

Congress may utilize a number of legal tools as part of the oversight and investigation function, including issuing subpoenas to witnesses for hearings, taking depositions, granting congressional immunity, and holding witnesses in contempt of Congress. In addition, field investigators may be dispatched to gather information for the investigation. There is no limit to how much oversight and investigation Congress may conduct; however, investigations, in particular, are generally labor intensive and may or may not lead to policy outcomes. Stretching resources to engage in extensive oversight and investigations may be a deterrent to committees that already hold robust agendas and responsibilities.

CONFIRMATIONS

One of the Senate's responsibilities is to confirm a set of political appointees that a president recommends (Rybicki, 2021). These positions include secretaries of executive agencies, which make up the president's cabinet, as well as judges, including those on the Supreme Court, and lower-level special assistants in federal agencies. The president appoints about four thousand individuals to civilian political roles throughout federal agencies. Of the four thousand, approximately 1,200 require Senate confirmation or approval. Multiple Senate committees are involved in the confirmation process, holding hearings and gathering information about nominees who come before them who are relevant to their legislative jurisdiction (*Presidential appointee positions*, 2017). For example, nominees for judgeships are processed through the Committee on the Judiciary. Many nominees are confirmed by the Senate without going through the committee process. For example, most of the sixty-five thousand military appointments that must go through Congress every two years are routinely confirmed en bloc outside of the committee process.

Nominees are extensively vetted by the administration prior to their nomination. Disclosure information about the nominee is often provided to the committee members prior to hearings. In addition, the committee may collect its own information or conduct an investigation about the nominee. Individual committee members may request additional information from the nominee. It is common for nominees to meet with committee members and their staff prior to a confirmation hearing. The House does not play a role in the confirmation of presidential nominees.

> "Before a nomination hearing even happens, in the Senate, committees of jurisdiction over specific agencies vet nominees which the administration puts forward. In the Senate we had an oversight team which would lead the vetting. Staff on the committee from the Republicans and Democrats could question the nominee. The nominee would also meet with each willing senator on the committee to discuss why he or she is a good fit for the job, his or her priorities, the priorities of the senator, etc. Then, there would be a public hearing held where members of the committee could publicly question the nominees to consider whether to vote for them to move to the Senate floor to receive full Senate confirmation. It used to be that many senators would vote for nominees from the other party. There was a common belief that when a candidate wins the presidency, he or she is entitled to pick appointees so long as they are qualified. Sen. Alexander (R-TN) used to say 'elections have consequences.' Now it is more partisan and sometimes the nominees are more polarizing than they used to be." (Lindsay Fryer, personal correspondence, September 22, 2022)

Confirmation hearings are important venues for understanding policy priorities and directions—for both the nominee and the committee members who question the nominee. Listening to a hearing (most are open to the public, available to watch online, and recorded for future viewing), an advocate might learn that a committee member shares the priorities of the advocate, offering an opportunity to follow up and build a champion for your cause. With high-level nominees, such as secretaries of executive agencies, committee members might spar with them, indicating their opposition to the priorities of the proposed secretary and setting up future follow-up for additional information. By the end of a hearing, an observer can usually know which members of the committee will support the nominee, which will oppose, and whether the nominee is likely to be favorably reported to the full Senate for a vote.

After vetting the nominee, the committee has four options: to report to the full Senate favorably, to report unfavorably, to report without recommendation, or to take no action. The vast majority of nominees move to the Senate floor with a favorable recommendation, as it is generally agreed that the president, being duly elected by the people, should be able to have their team in place to carry out their policy agenda. In addition, the extensive vetting process prior to the nomination is likely to screen out individuals who raise red flags and may face stringent objections from members of the Senate. Even when members, particularly of the opposite party, do not agree with the policy priorities of the nominee, they may support the individual.

Since 2011 the Senate has reinterpreted its rules for voting on nominees, making them significantly different from those generally required to pass legislation. The most significant change is that rather than the usual sixty votes required for adoption, only a simple majority—fifty-one—is required to confirm a nominee. This change—the so-called nuclear option—was the result of the minority repeatedly blocking nominees in the Senate, particularly judicial nominees. The section below on filibuster and cloture in the Senate provides additional information.

Senate and House Rules

The House and the Senate develop and routinely amend their procedural rules independent of each other.[10] Thus, rules and traditions that apply in the Senate may or may not apply in the House, or they may apply differently. Rules provide stability and predictability, enabling each body to function. Rules can be used to expedite, slow down, or stop legislation. Changes in rules are motivated by politics, with the majority generally looking to advantage its position over the minority in the legislative process.

Differences in rules are grounded in the key differences in the two bodies. With 435 members and the constant turnover of elections every two years, the House needs more structure to organize its functions and expedite business. With only one hundred members and with six-year terms, the Senate has less structure and a longer-term perspective. The House is designed for simple majority rule. While still acknowledging minority rights in the body, the House rules privilege expediting business over minority rights. In the Senate, where sixty votes are needed for most laws to pass and where extended deliberation is prized, rules enable more of a role for the minority and for individual senators.

Rules for each body can be found in multiple documents (Oleszek et al., 2020, pp. 6–7). These include the Standing Rules for the House[11] and the Senate.[12] Each chamber prints their rules biennially. In addition, each chamber has precedents, which are accepted practices though not formal rules. Some statutes, such as the Congressional Review Act of 1996, include provisions related to congressional rules of procedure. In addition, each of the political parties has a set of rules in each chamber. These rules have addressed matters such as how long an individual may serve as a committee chair. Finally, there are informal practices and customs that are generally acknowledged within the bodies. In addition, committees may set up rules on their own about how they will operate, so long as those rules do not violate the rules of the chamber.

Both the House and the Senate have offices of the parliamentarian (*The Office of the Parliamentarian*, 2018). The role of the parliamentarian's office is to provide expert advice and assistance on questions related to the meaning and application of the body's rules, precedents, and practices. The parliamentarian's office plays a

---

10. For further information on congressional procedures, rules, and norms, see https://www.gov track.us/congressional-procedures.

11. For more information, see https://rules.house.gov/rules-house-representatives.

12. For more information, see https://www.rules.senate.gov/rules-of-the-senate.

critical role in advising the member of Congress who is presiding over the chamber when the body is in session. The office of the parliamentarian is available to every member of Congress for advice and consultation on a confidential basis. Because of the complexity and significance of the rules, precedents, and customs of each body, many individual offices of members of Congress also include a staff member whose job is to stay up to date on rules and precedents and be the internal office resource.

While a full review of House and Senate rules and precedents is well beyond the scope of this book, two that are critical to the policy making process in Congress are worthy of review: the House Committee on Rules and the use of the filibuster and cloture in the Senate.

COMMITTEE ON RULES OF THE HOUSE OF REPRESENTATIVES

The House, but not the Senate, utilizes a specific committee to determine the conditions for considering legislation on the House floor prior to a vote on the legislation, including what amendments may be offered, in what order, and how much debate will be allowed. This committee, the Committee on Rules,[13] is often considered the most powerful committee in the House and the right arm of the speaker of the House. Unlike the ratios of minority to majority members on other committees, the Committee on Rules is definitively tilted to the majority. Composed of twice as many plus one members of the majority party, the committee is highly influenced by the leadership of the majority party, with little influence by the minority party.

When a piece of legislation has proceeded through the committee of jurisdiction and is ready for consideration on the floor, the committee chair contacts the Committee on Rules and requests the determination of a rule. (In addition, the speaker of the House may directly refer a bill to the Committee on Rules without the involvement of any committees of jurisdiction.) The Committee on Rules may hold a hearing where only members of the House testify and urge a particular outcome for the rule. The Committee on Rules then proceeds to mark up and report the rule to the floor.

The committee has three options: the open rule, the closed rule, and the modified closed rule. The open rule allows amendments without restriction; however, under House rules all amendments must be germane to the bill being considered. A closed rule stipulates that no amendments will be offered. There would simply be a vote on the bill as presented. A modified closed rule limits amendments that can be offered to those specifically identified. Most often, the Committee on Rules issues modified closed rules. The Committee on Rules may also decide to delay or deny action on a rule, thus preventing a bill from coming to the House floor.

Before the actual legislation can be taken up by the House, a vote must occur on the rule issued by the Committee on Rules. The rule may be debated for no

---

13. For more information, see https://rules.house.gov/.

"Before a bill goes to the floor for a final vote in the House, it must go through the Rules Committee. The committee determines all the procedures that will be used to consider the bill—how many amendments will be allowed, which amendments, and conditions for debate on the bill overall, etc. The committee is stacked with members from the majority party—a different ratio than on other committees. Some members seeking to offer amendments speak before the committee to make their case as to why their amendment should be allowed. There is always back-and-forth behind-the-scenes-negotiating, too. When a committee is seeking to move a bill to the floor—like a reauthorization bill—the chair and ranking member present the bill to the Rules Committee together and either defend it together if it is bipartisan or the minority party lays out arguments against the chair's bill. When Chairman Kline (R-MN) presented the Student Success Act to reauthorize ESEA, he had to defend certain provisions to members of his own party." (Lindsay Fryer, personal correspondence, September 22, 2022)

more than one hour and is rarely amended. It is unusual for a rule to be defeated; if it is, that signals the death of the bill to be considered.

For measures that are uncontroversial, a unanimous consent process may be used, alleviating the need for a Committee on the Rules determination. If the party leaders agree to unanimous consent, the measure will go directly for floor consideration. However, any member of the House may object, thereby stopping the process. Much routine business of the House is conducted by unanimous consent.

FILIBUSTER AND CLOTURE IN THE SENATE

The filibuster is a political strategy whereby any senator may be recognized to speak on the Senate floor and continue indefinitely without being interrupted. It is generally used to delay a vote on a bill. Even the threat of a filibuster may delay consideration of a bill or a nominee. The filibuster offers unique leverage to the minority party and to individual senators. As the Senate has grown increasingly polarized, threats of filibusters have multiplied, serving to stall the business of the Senate (*Filibusters and cloture in the Senate*, 2017). A senator may use the threat of a filibuster as leverage to negotiate the provisions of a pending bill. There is no filibuster option in the House of Representatives.

The most famous filibuster occurred in 1957 when Sen. Strom Thurmond (R-SC)—well supplied with throat lozenges and malted milk balls—spoke for twenty-four hours and eighteen minutes, stalling the passage of the Civil Rights Act of 1957. His filibuster performance included reading the Declaration of Independence, the U.S. Criminal Code, and the voting laws of forty-eight states.

The only way to end a filibuster, is by a vote to "invoke cloture." However, to be successful a cloture vote requires at least three-fifths of all senators (usually sixty votes) voting yes. This is often a challenging hurdle, particularly in recent years, as the majority party rarely holds sixty seats in the Senate. Thus, a successful cloture vote would require support from members of both parties, which is often hard to garner.

In 2013, frustrated by the obstruction of Senate Republicans in blocking President Obama's nominees for cabinet posts and judgeships, Majority Leader Harry Reid (D-NV), urged the use of the "nuclear option," referring to changing the number of votes needed to invoke cloture—or end a filibuster—so that only a simple majority, or fifty-one votes, is required. By a vote of 52–48 on party lines, the Senate established that Cabinet appointments and judicial nominations could prevail with only fifty-one votes. Supreme Court nominees were an exception, continuing the three-fifths requirement to invoke cloture. However, in 2017, the Senate extended the fifty-one-vote requirement to Supreme Court nominees as well. The 2017 vote, which was also 52–48, took place when Republicans controlled the Senate and President Trump was pursing the nomination of Neil Gorsuch to the Supreme Court. This change has led some commentators to reflect that the Supreme Court has become increasingly politicized, as the minority party may have virtually no say in who is confirmed.

While the fifty-one-vote majority is in place for consideration of nominees, it does not apply to most legislation, with reconciliation being a notable exception (see the portion of this chapter above on reconciliation). The sixty-vote requirement is the general rule. Expansion of the "nuclear option" to the passage of some legislation is under discussion—for example, in the area of voting rights legislation. On the one hand, changing the rule would enable the Senate to be more productive; however, the cost would be a diminishment of the role of the minority party and the minority perspective reflected in policy. Clearly the simple majority requirement favors the party that is in control of the Senate. Thus, it reduces the power of the minority party and can confer either advantages or disadvantages on either party depending on which party is in charge.

PART III: EXECUTIVE BRANCH PROCESSES

While Congress, empowered by the Constitution, makes the laws for the nation, executive agencies play critical roles in further explicating laws and overseeing their implementation. While the judicial branch also plays an important role in policy making, the executive and legislative branches offer the most accessible and routine opportunities for advocates to make their voices heard. However, it is important to bear in mind that the judicial branch has the authority to review legislative and executive action and overturn it based on precedent and interpretation of the Constitution.

The White House and federal executive agencies play multiple roles in influencing federal policy. Several of those functions have been covered in the first two chapters of this book, particularly those that require the president to interact with Congress. Here is a quick recap of those key interactions. The president assembles a yearly budget proposal, which kicks off the critical budget and appropriations processes in Congress. The president must sign legislation in order for it to become law, or the president can veto legislation passed by Congress. The president nominates officials to lead government agencies; however, Congress must confirm many of them. The president has broad authority conferred by the Constitution to issue executive orders, which may address matters as diverse as how to enforce and implement laws and how to manage resources and staff in the federal government. The president also holds unique authority as he serves as the head of state and commander in chief of the armed forces. He also holds particular authorities during times of emergencies and war.

The line between congressional authority and executive authority is one that is frequently challenged and shifts over time. As Congress has become increasingly polarized and gridlocked in recent years, presidents of both parties have claimed increasing executive authority. Knowing Congress will not be able to find the majority needed to challenge or overturn executive decisions can embolden presidents.

> "When Congress is unable to act, they are falling down on the job. We see that in higher education with issues like Title IX regulations and student loans. Because we have not acted, the administrative state takes over. Can Republicans get back to the former mentality held by members like Rep. John Boehner where legislating and leading were the norm rather than just opposing?" (David Cleary, personal correspondence, September 15, 2022)

Executive Orders

The president holds the unique and powerful authority to issue executive orders, which are considered to have the force of law. While there is no legal definition of executive orders, they are generally accepted to be written directives that shape policy. No specific statute grants the president the authority to issue executive orders; that authority is accepted as an inherent aspect of presidential power authorized by either Article II of the Constitution or a specific delegation of power from Congress. In addition to executive orders, the president may issue presidential proclamations and executive memoranda. There is no clear distinction between these three types of presidential actions.

Executive orders generally follow the process outlined in an executive order issued by President John F. Kennedy. That process describes the Office of Management and Budget as receiving comments and suggestions from interested agencies. Draft language is reviewed and sent to the attorney general and the Office of the Federal Register for review, then to the president for final approval. After presidential signature, most executive orders are published in the *Federal Register*. Courts may review executive orders to determine their legality. Executive orders can be amended or rescinded by a different president or by Congress; thus, they may not have the duration afforded to statutes (Gaffney, 2021). Textbox 3.9 provides an example of an executive order.

TEXTBOX 3.9.   **EXECUTIVE ORDER ON ADVANCING RACIAL EQUITY AND SUPPORT FOR UNDERSERVED COMMUNITIES THROUGH THE FEDERAL GOVERNMENT**

On his first day in office, January 20, 2021, President Biden issued an executive order (E.O.) calling for new policy initiatives and rescinding previous executive orders issued by President Trump. E. O. 13985, Executive Order on Advancing Racial Equity and Support for Underserved Communities through the Federal Government, is a set of policy directives aimed at a broad range of federal agencies (Biden, 2021). Key provisions of the E.O. include

- definitions of "equity" and "underserved communities";
- tasking the Domestic Policy Council to coordinate the implementation of the E.O. in order to "imbed equity principles, policies, and approaches across the Federal Government";
- directing the heads of federal agencies to conduct equity assessments examining potential barriers faced by underserved communities and individuals in terms of enrolling in federal programs, utilizing agency procurement and contracting opportunities, and the capacity of offices to advance civil rights where such mandates exist;
- allocation of resources to "address the historic failure to invest sufficiently, justly, and equally in underserved communities";
- establishment of an equitable data working group intended to address the lack of disaggregation of federal data sets in terms of race, ethnicity, gender, disability, income, veteran status, or other key demographic variables needed to measure and advance equity;
- revocation of two E.O.s from the Trump administration: E. O. 13950, Combating Race and Sex Stereotyping, and E. O. 13958, Establishing the President's Advisory 1776 Commission.

Federal Rule Making

The most significant executive process whereby advocates are able to make their voices heard is during the federal rule-making process. Executive agencies create rules, often referred to as regulations, under which a law will be implemented. When new laws are enacted, the regulation writing process is often triggered for the federal agency that will implement the law.

Congress grants the authority to executive agencies, such as the Department of Education, to create regulations to provide details, particularly technical ones, that may require a level of expertise Congress does not have. Rules may interpret policy or describe organizational procedures or practices of an agency (Garvey, 2017). Specific statutes may further circumscribe agency rule making by requiring

"Most people understand the legislative process. Congressional offices do a better job of outreach and explanation than executive agencies. But you can actually make more of an impact on the administrative side—except processes are byzantine so they are dominated by insiders. For example, when a Notice of Proposed Rule Making (NPRM) is issued, it usually invites public comments. This is a real opportunity to influence policy. A thoughtful comment on a proposed regulation can make a big difference, as the agency is required to consider all comments. Some of the comments we have made have been quoted in the final regulation, and some provisions have been altered because of our input. It is much harder to get a provision changed in a bill in Congress." (Jonathan Fansmith, personal correspondence, August 16, 2022)

that rules be developed in relation to a certain provision or prohibiting the promulgation of regulations for another provision. Significantly, final regulations hold the force of law, just like a statute. Congress and the judicial branch retain authority to review, modify, and even reverse regulations, so agencies are mindful of potential challenges as they proceed. Congress has passed several laws, most notably the Administrative Procedures Act (APA), and presidents have issued a number of executive orders that proscribe procedures, parameters, and policies related to rule making. There is broad acknowledgment among policy actors that, next to enacting laws, rule making is a key policy function.

The federal government's regulatory activity is accessible through the website of the *Federal Register*.[14] This website is a gold mine of information about agency activities related to rule making, but also announcements with information such as grant competitions and data collection changes. Anyone can sign up to receive email announcements about developments, tailored to your interests. This is highly recommended as a good strategy for monitoring policy activity.

Below is an outline of the most commonly followed procedures for developing regulations (*A guide to the rulemaking process*, 2011). While there are several exceptions to this process—officially called informal rule making—it is by far the most frequently used.

BEFORE THE PROPOSED RULE

Agencies generally publish a "regulatory plan" annually in the fall and an "agenda of regulatory and deregulatory actions" in the spring and fall. Together these two items are referred to as the "unified agenda." These provide advance notice to the public about upcoming regulatory activities as well as information about completed regulatory action. The unified agenda, as well as other regulation-related information, is posted on Reginfo.gov, on Regulations.gov, and in the *Federal Register*.

---

14. For more information, see https://www.federalregister.gov/.

At times agencies will gather relevant information through formal and informal processes prior to issuing a rule. The agency may publish in the *Federal Register* an "Advance Notice of Proposed Rule Making," which is a formal invitation to provide information that would shape the rule making in advance. Comments can be submitted on the *Federal Register* website.

When regulations are significant, the White House may review them prior to their proposal. The Office of Information and Regulatory Affairs (OIRA), which is part of the Office of Management and Budget (OMB), may provide this review. When regulations are deemed "significant," OIRA must estimate the costs and benefits of the regulation and provide alternatives. OIRA may also estimate the paperwork burden of a proposed rule or its impact on business or state and local government as well as the issue of unfunded mandates.

THE PROPOSED RULE

A Notice of Proposed Rule Making (NPRM) is published in the *Federal Register*, announcing agency plans to address a matter through regulations. The NPRM provides a summary of the issues under consideration, the statutory authority for the rule making, why the rule is necessary, the agency's plan for addressing the issue, the merits of the proposed solution, and supporting data. Interested persons are invited to submit comments; submission requirements are provided, including the time line—which is generally thirty to sixty days from the announcement of the NPRM. Agencies occasionally extend the time line for public comment, and they may hold public hearings to gather further information.

BEFORE THE FINAL RULE

The agency reads and analyzes all public comments submitted in response to the NPRM. All submitted comments are publicly available for review on the *Federal Register* website. The agency must conclude that the final proposal it puts forward will address the issues under consideration, after it has considered alternatives that might be more effective or less costly. The agency may change some aspects of the proposed rule or terminate the rule making and never publish final rules if it is decided that policy arguments or new data pose unsurmountable challenges. While the agency is not permitted to make a final determination based on the number of comments in support or opposition to the proposed rule, the volume and distribution of pro versus con comments is broadly acknowledged as a meaningful measure of public sentiment. For example, if ten thousand comments were received and only one hundred were supportive of the rule, one could assume there is considerable opposition to the rule. Final determinations are intended to reflect expert opinions, scientific data, and facts assembled during the rule-making process.

The White House and OIRA review the proposed final rule if it is significant in terms of policy or cost and provide feedback. Agencies may consult with other agencies, particularly if there is overlap in responsibility related to the topic of the rule.

THE FINAL RULE

After the analysis and review process, the agency publishes the final rule. There is no set timetable for the length of time between the closing of public comments for the NPRM and the publication of the final rule. When it is ready, the final rule is published in the *Federal Register* in total, along with the date the final regulation goes into effect—which is generally no less than thirty days after publication. If a rule is considered significant, the effective date may be sixty days from publication. The publication includes the goals or problems addressed by the rule, the facts and data the department relied on in developing the rule, responses to major criticisms offered in the public comments, and explanations as to why the agency did not choose alternatives. The new regulation is then included in the Code of Federal Regulations (CFR),[15] which is the official compendium of all federal regulations.

In some cases, a final rule may be issued without publishing a proposed rule. This is in situations when the agency has "good cause" to determine that the notice and proposed comment period would be unnecessary or contrary to the public interest. This might include emergency situations, technical amendments with no substantive issues, or rules that affect only federal employees or property. At other times, an agency may publish an interim final rule when it has good cause to not go through the public comment process. In this case, the rule is effective upon publication; however, the public comment period may still be utilized and the rule possibly changed as a result. In general, these exceptions do not include policy implementation issues, which go through the typical process described above, which includes public input.

AFTER THE FINAL RULE

Final rules are sent to Congress and the Government Accountability Office for review prior to their effective dates. The House and Senate may pass legislation disapproving of the rule. If it is signed by the president, or if it is vetoed and then overridden by the Congress, the rule is void and cannot be republished unless Congress approves. The time line and procedures for Congress to disapprove a rule are described in the Congressional Review Act (*The Congressional Review Act*, 2021). While Congress rarely invokes this procedure, they did twice during the 115th Congress (2017–2018) to overturn education regulations related to accountability under the Every Student Succeeds Act (Brown, 2017b) and teacher preparation regulations under the Higher Education Act (Brown, 2017a).

Individuals and entities may challenge a regulation in court, claiming they have been or will be adversely affected by it. The court considers whether the rule is unconstitutional, goes beyond the agency's legal authority, violated the Administrative Procedures Act or other laws, or was arbitrary, capricious, or an abuse of discretion. The court may set aside, or vacate, part or all of the rule. Generally, the court sends it back to the agency for corrections, which may involve beginning the rule-making process over again.

---

15. For more information, see https://www.ecfr.gov/.

Negotiated Rule Making

Fondly referred to by DC advocates as "negreg," negotiated rule making is a process begun in the 1990s to ensure stakeholder input in the development of regulations. An agency may decide, or be directed by statute, to utilize the process. Outlined in the Negotiated Rulemaking Act of 1990 (Carey, 2021), the process must still follow the steps described above. Negreg involves an agency convening a committee of stakeholders with the intention of reaching a consensus on the text of a proposed regulation. When the committee reaches such a consensus, signaling support from a range of stakeholder interests, the rule may be more broadly accepted, easier to implement, and less likely to face a challenge in court.

The first step is for the agency to announce in the *Federal Register* the intention of establishing a negotiated rule-making committee, the subject and scope of the rule to be developed, a proposed agenda and schedule for the committee, a solicitation for comments on the proposed committee, and a description of how a person may apply or nominate another person to be on the committee. At least thirty days must be allowed for comments and application submission to be on the committee. The committee is generally limited to twenty-five members with a facilitator from within or outside the agency. Committee deliberations must be open to the public, and the process must be transparent.

After the committee has convened and deliberated, it transmits a report to the agency, which includes a consensus proposal, if they have reached one, or areas where partial consensus was reached, along with additional information, recommendations, and materials. Individual committee members may also submit materials to the agency. The committee's proposal is not binding on the agency. It may adopt part of it, all of it, or none of it in the published proposed rule. However, if consensus is reached, the agency would be unlikely to publish a different version of the rule, as that could invite criticism from a range of sectors as well as litigation. The agency must still go through the notice and comment period in the *Federal Register* as described above.

In the education arena, both the Higher Education Act (HEA) and the Every Student Succeeds Act (ESSA) require negotiated rule making in a number of policy areas. In HEA rules related to teacher quality enhancement and student financial assistance must utilize negotiated rule making. In ESSA areas related to standards, assessments, some accountability provisions, and federal funds aimed to "supplement, not supplant State and local funds" must utilize negotiated rule making. The opportunity to serve on a negotiated rule-making committee representing the perspective of experts, or of a field, is a significant one for an advocate.

Other Key Federal Agency Functions Related to Policy Making

In addition to developing regulations, federal agencies publish multiple additional documents that can be utilized to enhance advocacy efforts. These include publication of proposed grant priorities seeking public comment, investigations, inspections, adjudication, analysis of the performance of grantees and issuance of reports, compliance requirements, data collection and analysis, withholding of federal funds for violations, creation of commissions and task forces, and reports from the Office of the Inspector General about agency performance and related matters (Natow, 2017). There are multiple publications that routinely monitor and report on federal agency activity—for example, *Politico*, *Ed Week* for K–12 education, and *Inside Higher Ed* for higher education. Most national organizations with government relations components routinely report on federal agency developments on their websites or via their newsletters. In addition, agency websites are rich data sources.

"When I first joined the Department of Education, it was kind of earth shattering to see the many tools available to implement and advance policy. I was used to working in the Senate, and this was a whole different ball game. In the area of discretionary grants, we could shape grant competitions and determine funding levels for specific competitions. We could write policy letters, develop technical assistance, promulgate regulations, provide information via FAQs, issue guidance, and offer 'Dear Colleagues.' We had the pen and the phone. We could call on philanthropy and funders to develop initiatives, like we did with My Brother's Keeper,[1] which targeted the improvement of outcomes for boys and men of color. The administration has far more policy tools than I would have imagined and is more nimble in utilizing them." (Michael Yudin, personal correspondence, August 12, 2022)

---

1. See https://www.obama.org/mbka/.

GUIDANCE

Federal agencies frequently advance policy through subregulatory policy publications, referred to as guidance (*Agency use of guidance documents*, 2021). Guidance may include interpretations of laws or regulations and general statements of policy. Guidance may come forth in a variety of forms, including explanations of how an agency will regulate or enforce a provision of law, clarification of technical details, compliance guides, and training manuals. Materials such as Q&A documents, "Dear Colleague" letters, and handbooks with clarification and resources may also be issued by agencies.

Guidance does not have the force of law as regulations do; however, it is generally considered a directive to grantees or entities addressed by the documents and thus has significant impact on how a law is implemented. Entities to whom the guidance applies generally respond by adopting it as policy. Guidance is not required to follow the processes of public notice and input required by rulemaking procedures. Rather, guidance documents are generated by internal deliberations within an agency, which does not necessarily include public input. The utilization of policy statements and guidance by federal agencies has proliferated in recent years, generating controversy over the line between regulations and policy determinations, which do not go through a public process. Some believe that agencies treat their own guidance as binding, implying it is also binding by regulated parties. For an example of the issuance of guidance from a federal agency, see textbox 3.10.

TEXTBOX 3.10.   **GUIDANCE AND REGULATIONS FROM THE DEPARTMENT OF EDUCATION ON TITLE IX: PROHIBITION OF DISCRIMINATION ON THE BASIS OF SEX**

A striking and controversial example of the use of guidance and regulations to establish new policy is the Department of Education's issuances over two decades related to Title IX (*Title IX and sexual harassment*, 2019). Title IX prohibits recipients of federal funds from discriminating on the basis of sex. It is enforced by the Office of Civil Rights in the Department of Education. Multiple administrations have issued guidance and promulgated regulations over the years related to interpretations of Title IX—many of them controversial and often reversed when a new president takes office. For example, in 2011, the Obama administration issued a "Dear Colleague" letter outlining procedures schools should take in responding to allegations of sexual harassment. In 2014, the Obama administration issued a Q&A providing examples of schools' responsibilities to proactively deter sexual harassment on campus. In 2017, under the Trump administration, both the "Dear Colleague" letter and the Q&A were rescinded, as they "led to the deprivation of rights for many students" (*Title IX and sexual harassment*, 2019). After having gone through the rule-making process and receiving 124,000 comments from the public, the Trump Department of Education issued new regulations on May 19, 2020. The Trump administration argued that those accused of sexual misconduct were not being given a fair hearing under the Obama interpretations. The Trump regulations appeared to critics to provide less protection for the accuser. When President Biden took office, his Department of Education began the process of unraveling the Trump administration's Title IX regulations by holding public hearings on the topic in June 2021 and issuing proposed new regulations in July 2022. By the end of the sixty-day public comment period in mid-September 2022 over 235,000 comments had been received (Knott, 2022). The next step is for the department to review those comments and issue new regulations, which could take a year or more. In addition, in response to a Supreme Court case, the Department of Education issued a new guidance for Title IX holding that it covers discrimination based on gender identity.

Numerous executive orders have been issued, numerous court cases have been brought, and several bills have been introduced in Congress to clarify criteria for an agency utilizing guidance versus regulations, for articulating a process of developing guidance and under what circumstances, and the significance of guidance documents; however, a quick clarification appears unlikely.

TAKEAWAYS: PROCESS

1. The policy making process can be considered as both a sequential cyclical set of events and a collision of multiple streams of activity.
2. Despite what appears to be the loss of regular order in Congress, core and distinct processes of budget, appropriations, and authorization remain central and interrelated.
3. Additional congressional processes, such as investigations and confirmation of nominations, affect policy outcomes.
4. Ever-changing and distinct rules and procedures in the House and the Senate may serve as opportunities or obstacles.
5. Executive branch processes, such as the issuance of executive orders, regulations, and guidance, are central to policy making.

CHAPTER 4

Policy

· ·

> What you always do before you make a decision is consult. The best pub-
> lic policy is made when you are listening to people who are going to be
> impacted. Then, once policy is determined, you call on them to help you
> sell it.
>
> —Elizabeth Dole, former U.S. senator (R-NC)
> and former secretary of transportation

Developed and implemented by government, public policy is
intended to address problems that affect the public. Determining
the dimensions of public policy is fraught with bias, as is the policy making process itself. Beliefs and values are at the core of everyone's engagement in policy making, be they individual advocates, politicians, or national
interest groups. Since beliefs and values diverge, it is no wonder that the notion
of what problems are in the realm of public problems and warrant government
attention, and what problems are not, is an ongoing debate.

The notion of the common good, from which we draw public policy and
which is at the heart of this book, is likewise an unending debate. What is in the
best interest of our common pursuits? What is in the best interest of society as a
whole? How do we balance individual liberties with the common good? What
is the role of the private sector versus the public sector?[1] These questions will be
answered differently at different time periods, for different issues, and by different
policy players. Finding some degree of consensus, even fleeting consensus, is particularly challenging when political polarization is omnipresent. Yet a functioning
government depends on a modicum of consensus.

As we engage in our advocacy work, we will confront challenges to our concept of the common good and our notion of "good policy." Awareness of our own
beliefs and biases is essential as we engage with others who disagree with us.
Wrestling with these differences is at the core of policy making.

As advocates, we are highly motivated to solve the problems that we witness—whether it is students being poorly served in schools, or discrimination and
marginalization of a group of people, or a dire lack of resources to implement
sound solutions. Whatever the problem we want to tackle, our goal is to reach the

---

1. For one insightful perspective on these questions, see Jundt (2010).

· ·

result of a policy—be it a new or changed provision in law, a new regulation, or additional funding.

It is tempting to think in a linear fashion so that one identifies a problem first and then crafts solutions. Indeed, this was my perception as I began my work in the policy world. It is also a framework often presented by policy analysts and scholars (see chapter 3). Over time I have come to believe that the process is not so straightforward.

WHICH COMES FIRST: THE PROBLEM OR THE SOLUTION?

A rational sequential approach would lead us to believe that first we define the problem, and then we find the solution to that problem. In reality, the two are more often deeply intertwined and dance with each other in a process of redefinition and realignment. Naomi Klein (2007) argues persuasively that the solutions often come first—and that they lie in wait for a precipitating event or problem, which catapults them into the limelight. In her book *Shock Doctrine: The Rise of Disaster Capitalism*, Klein explores the intersection of "super profits and mega disasters." She cites Hurricane Katrina as the event that generated "school reform" in New Orleans. Leaning heavily on the work of Milton Friedman, she cites his writing in the *Wall Street Journal* three months after the Hurricane. "Most of New Orleans schools are in ruins, as are the homes of the children who have attended them. The children are now scattered all over the country. This is a tragedy. It is also an opportunity to radically reform the education system" (Klein, 2007, p. 5). Nineteen months after Hurricane Katrina, New Orleans public schools were almost completed replaced by privately run charter schools. The teachers' union contract was virtually null, and all union members were fired. The American Enterprise Institute, a conservative think tank, noted, "Katrina accomplished in a day . . . what Louisiana school reformers couldn't do after years of trying" (Klein, 2007, p. 6).

Friedman further observed that "only a crisis—actual or perceived—produces real change. When that crisis occurs, the actions that are taken depend on the ideas that are lying around. That, I believe, is our basic function: to develop alternatives to existing policies, to keep them alive and available until the politically impossible becomes politically inevitable" (Klein, 2007, p. 7).

Klein's work points out how policy solutions may not grow directly from problems to be solved. I was once told that "Washington is filled with people wandering around with all the answers—if only the right questions would be asked." While as advocates we are all motivated and informed by our beliefs, our experiences, and our convictions, it is important to examine our suppositions about solutions as we take our place at the policy table.

Scholars have written about the "politics of distraction," noting that policy dialogue can be used to frame problems in a manner that reinforces privilege and

> "Lots of bills are solutions looking for problems. This can prevent a deep analysis of the problem. If you don't really know what you are solving for, you don't know where to hold the line in negotiations." (Kim Knackstedt, personal correspondence, August 12, 2022)

diverts attention from unquestioned or deeply challenging aspects of society.[2] Our definitions of problems and solutions can remove us from broader historical contexts and narrow our focus on incremental policies, which may or may not address the real challenges. Ladson-Billings (2013) argues that the policy frames are "at least as significant as the argument we make about [the policies themselves]" (p. 13). Those frames affect how we think about policy solutions and the root causes of problems to be addressed. In 2008 Ladson-Billings argued that the term "achievement gap" should be abandoned as it constructs the differences in performance between students of color and white students as a "gap," with an implication that policy solutions should close the gap—that is, narrow the difference in outcomes between groups of White and Black students. The root causes of this gap—a history of unequal education, lack of access to education, unequal funding for education, and more—are not considered in solutions to the "achievement gap." Rather the focus becomes measuring student performance outcomes, generally with the use of standardized tests, and infusing strategies to close the gap, such as greater curricular focus on reading and math and increased scripted lessons for teachers. Ladson-Billings proposes that inequalities in student performance be defined in terms of an education "debt." Such a rethinking promotes an examination of the causes of the disparities and the genesis of the debt. Others have suggested that "achievement gap" be reconsidered as the "opportunity gap," inviting consideration of inequitable inputs into our education system, such as the disproportionate access to fully credentialed teachers by students in low-income schools and students with disabilities.

> "The lack of representation affects how a policy problem is understood as well as potential solutions that are created by policy teams. As a former teacher and as a Black and African American woman, I think about policy matters through the lens of my experiences—as all people do. But if you can't envision potential consequences of a policy, primarily due to a lack of context and experience, if you can't conceive of them, the preemptive measures to avoid such consequences will not be reflected in the policy." (Ashley White, personal correspondence, September 23, 2022)

---

2. See, for example, Farley et al. (2021).

In 2015, Sen. Jack Reed (D-RI) introduced a bill that reflected the conception of the problem as an opportunity gap. The overriding proposal held that public education should be held accountable for providing equitable opportunities as well as measuring outcomes. Titled the Core Opportunity Resources for Equity and Excellence Act of 2015, S. 37 required states to be assessed on the extent to which equal opportunity was offered to students in terms of provisions such as high-quality instructional teams, school facilities and technology, and specialized instructional support teams as part of a comprehensive program (Core Opportunity Resources for Equity and Excellence Act, 2015). States that failed to make progress toward eliminating such inequities would become ineligible for certain funds. The bill is a marked shift from a measure of the achievement gap to a measure of the opportunity gap.

Carol Bacchi (2012), an Australian scholar, has cautioned us to consider "What's the problem represented to be?" This framework—called WPR—is a policy analysis tool intended to facilitate our examination of our policy work. Manning (2019) calls out three fundamental ideas of the WPR approach:

- Every policy seeks to solve a particular problem.
- The policy represents the problem that it seeks to solve in a specific way.
- The choice of this representation advantages some groups and disadvantages others.

On her website, Bacchi posits that WPR

> challenges the conventional view that public policies are responses or reactions to problems that sit outside the policy process, waiting to be discovered and solved. By contrast, the WPR approach argues that policies contain implicit representations of the "problems" they purport to address. . . . The goal of the WPR approach is to treat these problem representations as problematizations that require critical scrutiny. (Bacchi, n.d.)

Bacchi describes her approach as one with a concern for social justice at the core, presuming that problem representations benefit some at the expense of others. The intention is to intervene to challenge problem representations that would cause harm to some and encourage consideration of issues in alternative ways, so that harm might be avoided, or at least minimized.

Among the six questions the WPR approach proposes are

- What is left unproblematic in this problem representation? Where are the silences? Can the "problem" be thought about differently?
- What effects are produced by this representation of the problem?

The WPR approach reinforces the notion that "If you're not at the table, you're probably on the menu," underscoring the conviction that multiple voices are required for successful policy making. Those who are not at the table are the most likely to be disadvantaged by policy proposals. At a minimum, the likelihood of a policy working as intended is lessened when the voices of those who are experienced with being on the receiving end of policy are not present. Without their voices, their perspectives, their lived experiences, other voices, perspectives, and experiences will prevail, privileging the voices of those who are heard. Coming to the table means coming with humility—knowing that your voice, your perspective, your lived experience are not the only ones. Look around the table. Who is missing? How can you bring them forward? As I noted in chapter 1, the lack of diversity among Capitol Hill staff and among Washington's policy advocates is problematic. This lack of representation will be reflected in policy. How could it not be?

POLICY TOOLS

As advocates launch their work into the consideration of policy problems and policy solutions, knowledge of common policy tools and their strengths and weaknesses is helpful. Many common tools are available at the federal and often at the state level. An understanding of policy tools to utilize will assist in developing possible solutions and in shifting gears if required.

As a first step in choosing a policy tool or set of tools, consideration should be given to whether the policy making body targeted is the legislature—to create or amend a law—the executive branch—to develop or amend a regulation or guidance—or the judicial branch—to interpret a policy provision. It could be that several targets are identified. However, as discussed in earlier chapters, the authorities of the entities targeted will be different. For example, the Department of Education cannot create a new state grant program or refuse to fund a program for which Congress has appropriated funds. The Department of Education can, however, change and issue regulations that interpret a provision related to a state grant program or set priorities for funding certain programs.

Grants

One of the key mechanisms the federal government (and state governments) uses for policy implementation and fund distribution is grants. A grant represents government funds made available to an eligible recipient for a specific purpose. Grants are authorized in statute. In FY 2019 alone, the federal government provided about $750 billion in grants to state and local governments in areas ranging from health care, to transportation, to education, to environmental protection (*Federal grants to state and local governments*, 2019). Additional funds went to other entities, such as nonprofit organizations. The website Grants.gov lists the vast array of federal grants that are available for various purposes to various entities.

When considering the creation of a new grant program or modifications to existing programs, the following questions should be considered:

- Does the grant authorize a program appropriate for the federal government? For example, in the area of education, it would be inappropriate to dictate use of a particular curriculum for local school districts, as that is beyond federal purview.
- What entities are eligible to receive the grants (e.g., for-profit, nonprofit, state government, local school districts, or some combination)?
- What specific activities will be required by grant recipients? Will some be required and some optional?
- Must grant recipients already have certain policies or portfolios in place in order to be eligible, such as a track record of serving disenfranchised groups of people or a state law requiring K–12 standardized student test scores to be used for teacher evaluations?
- Will grant recipients be required to provide a match or an "in-kind" contribution?
- Will specific terms be defined, such as "teacher induction program"?
- How long will the grant period last—for example, for three years or five years?
- How much money will be allocated to the grant program?
- How will the grantee be held accountable for the required activities—for example, via an evaluation, monitoring by federal agencies, submission of reports, or some other method?
- What application process will be used and what information will be required in the application?

Appropriations

As described in chapter 3, the appropriations process takes place annually and determines the amount of money to be available for individual programs. Many advocates spend considerable energy promoting increases for particular programs. Having a policy on paper without sufficient resources to deliver the desired impact is an ongoing challenge. Multiple decisions made by federal agencies regarding the distribution of funds affect policy implementation and impact, such as the criteria set forth for competitions to receive funds.

Civil Rights

Our nation has a strong body of civil rights laws (*Constitutional amendments and major civil rights acts*, n.d.) that prohibit discrimination on the basis of race, color, national origin, sex, disability, age, and religion. Discrimination is prohibited in areas of education, employment, credit, housing, public accommodations, and voting. The Civil Rights Act of 1964, Title IX of the Education Amendments of 1972, and the Americans with Disabilities Act of 1990 are among them, forming a foundation for equity. They are reinterpreted and amended as circumstances and political will shift. Currently the intense debates over the interpretation of Title IX, which guarantees gender equity in education, and the Voting Rights Act, which guarantees full access to voting for all citizens, are at the heart of controversial deliberation over new interpretations and revisions. Statutory changes, regulatory changes, and judicial interpretations are all at play in ongoing considerations of civil rights laws.

Accountability

The appetite for accountability metrics from policy makers and advocates has grown exponentially in recent years. Accountability mechanisms include data collection, analysis of data for purposes of rating programs, mandated research and evaluation studies, and mandated reports to the public and Congress. Accountability serves a number of purposes, including demonstrating the efficacy of a program and ensuring taxpayers that their money is well spent. Policy makers generally want evidence that their decision making is sound.

Of course, accountability is infused with value judgments and political calls. For example, an ideological position (e.g., the belief in the privatization of education) may outweigh the desire for accountability data, as there is a chance the data results may undermine the policy. Or only a certain set of accountability provisions might be adopted, intended to evade uncovering possible policy failures. Likewise, a suspicion that a policy is unsound may be balanced by a requirement for an inordinate set of data, intended to demonstrate the lack of efficacy of the policy. As we will see in the example below about the use of standardized student assessments in policy regimes for accountability, when measurement tools are used for purposes for which they were not designed, results are suspect and unintended side effects are many. Advocates are able to scrutinize accountability measures from these perspectives.

Data Collection

The allure of data to determine impact of policy is a magnet for ensuring accountability. Data can be used to contribute to the evaluation of policy in terms of funds being wisely spent and their impact in achieving the intended goals. But data alone does not point the way to how to improve policy in order to enhance outcomes measured by data collection.

In the area of federal education policy, data collection and its use for accountability have expanded in recent years. Multiple federal data collection efforts are ongoing, some required by statutes and others undertaken via administrative determination. State data related to K–12 student achievement has high visibility. The Institute for Education Sciences routinely collects student achievement data through the National Assessment of Educational Progress (NAEP), an additional measure of K–12 student achievement. The Office of Civil Rights in the Department of Education routinely undertakes the Civil Rights Data Collection (CRDC) to provide a snapshot of a range of civil rights matters, including whether there is a disparity in the distribution of experienced, effective, in-field teachers in low-income versus other school districts. Data is a powerful tool for advocates and policy makers to make a case for the effectiveness or ineffectiveness of a particular policy and to document emerging problems. Determinations about which data to collect are significant, as what gets collected (and conversely what does not) represents a value judgment. There is a lot of wisdom in the old saying "What gets counted gets attention." Likewise, what is not counted is not likely to get attention, and critical concepts that are difficult to measure, such as "high quality," may have data points erroneously assigned to them as proxy measures.

Enforcement Mechanisms

Most federal laws include a set of enforcement mechanisms. Common ones include withholding of funds if violations are determined, fines if violations are determined, future ineligibility for funds if requirements are not fulfilled or violations are determined, and individual complaint and investigation processes that may result in penalties for violations. Federal agencies tend to be hesitant to withhold funds, perhaps because of political backlash that might ensue or concern that withholding funds will not facilitate addressing infractions.

Research

The federal government invests in a significant amount of research in areas ranging from defense, to technology, to science, to health, to agriculture, to education. Research is a well-established role of the federal government. Specific research projects may be undertaken, such as determinations of the most successful strategies to teach reading, or ongoing research may proceed for decades, for example, finding a cure for cancer. Research can be an important tool for advocates, particularly if there are multiple contested aspects of a policy problem or solution. Finding additional information and gaining a greater understanding can be an important component of policy development.

Individual Benefits

Multiple federal programs provide benefits to individuals based on eligibility determination, including Social Security, Medicaid, Medicare, and student financial aid for higher education. In most instances, the individual must apply for the benefit and await a determination by the federal agency as to eligibility. This process may be arduous, as is the case for many applying for Social Security Disability benefits. Eligibility criteria may include such individual data as age, work history, health status, and financial status. Changes in any of these individual circumstances could trigger elimination of the benefit. In some situations, strings are attached. For example, the TEACH grants, a form of student financial aid, require the recipient to teach for a certain period of time in order to avoid having to pay back the grant. In terms of Social Security recipients who are seniors, increased income may trigger increased taxes. Advocates could seek to modify eligibility criteria, eligibility determination processes, or situations that trigger ineligibility.

Tax Code

In addition to determining tax rates for individuals and entities, the tax code can be used to incentivize or support particular behaviors or to redistribute income. In the education arena, teachers are eligible for a tax deduction for any personal funds they spend on school materials up to $250 per year (*Topic no. 458*, 2022). The child tax credit may be available to families of limited means with children in order to enhance their overall economic well-being.

Requirements Related to Implementation by Federal Agency

Some statutes will mandate or prohibit certain implementation strategies by the agency administering a program. For example, a statute may require an agency to utilize the negotiated rule-making process for a particular component of a program. An agency may be given the authority to grant waivers to particular provisions of a law under a certain set of circumstances. An agency may be prohibited from issuing regulations on a certain provision. Agencies may be directed to undertake outreach strategies to potential beneficiaries regarding availability of support. These statutory directives may be in place in addition to general authority of executive agencies to issue guidance, policy letters, and technical assistance materials such as tool kits and FAQs.

WHAT IS GOOD POLICY?

TEXTBOX 4.1.   WHAT IS GOOD PUBLIC POLICY?

I asked many of the experts that I interviewed for this book for their ideas on what constitutes good public policy. Their thoughts are wide ranging and reflect the contested nature of attempting a definition.

"Good policy is informed by research. It builds on what is known to work.

"Good policy is actionable. It can be implemented, and it leads to change that can be sustained over time. It builds capacity at the local level so change will proceed when funding runs out and when politics shifts.

"Good policy impacts those in greatest need. It has particular impact on those who are furthest from opportunity."

—*Anonymous*

"Good policy is something that identifies a recognizable problem and solves it with the least amount of government intervention.

"Good policy solutions help people help themselves. Creating dependency on government to act is not a great idea because government will not always act. Empowering people to solve their own problems is the way to go."

—*David Cleary*

> "Good policy does the most good with the least amount of harm. It is equitable in terms of its impact, and it addresses real problems."
>
> —Jon Fansmith
>
> "Good policy starts with a clearly defined value statement. For example, people with disabilities have a right to be free from discrimination. There must be clarity about the problem, strong evidence as to what the solution should be, a path forward to implementation, and a well-thought-out trajectory for implementation over time— one year, three years, five years, etc. Good policy withstands political shifts."
>
> —Kim Knackstedt
>
> "Good policy making is a negotiation where all involved in the policy writing want to make sure it is successful in implementation."
>
> —Kuna Tavalin
>
> "Policy must be implementable. If it can't be done, what good is it?
> "Good policy requires buy-in from stakeholders who have to live with it. If they don't buy in, they will work around it. Federal policy is a blunt instrument. It can't meet the individual needs of everyone, so there must be buy-in by those who will be involved in putting it into practice."
>
> —Michael Yudin

There is no single metric or standard for determining good policy. Biases become evident when answering this question. Interviewees for this book offered their concepts of good policy as displayed in textbox 4.1. While no policy is perfect, I contend that some are better than others. There are numerous tests that advocates can use along the way to scrutinize policy alternatives in order to promote and develop the best possible policy. These include the following:

- Is the policy likely to contribute to the solution to the problem identified?
- Who are the intended beneficiaries of the policy?
- Have they been part of the policy making process?
- Will there be winners and losers?
- Is the theory of the cause of the problem accurate?
- Are the best policy tools utilized to address this problem?
- Is the policy too complex or underdeveloped?
- Is the capacity to implement the policy in place, or will the policy build that capacity?
- Is the administrative apparatus in place to implement the policy?
- Will the policy generate implementation resistance? If so, how might that be addressed?
- Does the policy create conflict with other policies? If so, how might that be addressed?
- Is the policy solution in balance to the problem being addressed? For example, does the solution cost more than the problem?

- Is there enough flexibility in the policy to adapt to changing circumstances or developments?
- Are accountability mechanisms appropriate?
- Is the time line for implementation reasonable?
- Are the boundaries of the jurisdictions of other relevant entities acknowledged, such as the different roles of the federal, state, and local governments?
- What might the unintended consequences be and could they be ameliorated?

Since policy is always the result of compromise within a political structure, some level of disagreement about its efficacy is inevitable. In addition, a policy that may work for one generation will not work for another. Our most challenging public problems often appear intractable and resistant to policy solutions—such as climate change and poverty. These are not amendable to the quick-fix solutions that policy often seeks to offer within the confines of a political cycle. Incremental change may be the order of the day. Some argue that the education arena has been beset by changing policy so much that the fact that changes occur so frequently—be they good or bad—has a negative effect as there is never enough time for full implementation before another change comes along. This situation creates resistance and weariness among those charged with carrying out policies, so that new policies may be ignored or undermined. In addition, when those who will be affected by the policy are not at the table and do not support the policy, or are unaware of it, the likelihood for success is diminished.

Policy creation is both a long game and a short game. Advocates are wise to keep their eye on the long horizon (e.g., increased equity) as well as the short horizon (e.g., securing additional funds for a particular program). After forty years of working to address the shortage of special education teachers, I can see both the progress made and the long distance there is to travel.

> "Changing policy can be like turning a supertanker. It takes a long time. We are a country of 330 million people and fifty states. I think it is good to have a deliberative process." (David Cleary, personal correspondence, September 15, 2022)

The Americans with Disabilities Act and the Use of Standardized Assessments in Federal Education Policy: Point/Counterpoint

In order to dig deeper into an examination of policy, we will consider two initiatives that represent a significant contrast in how they were developed, why they were developed, their policy requirements, their longevity, and their impact. Scrutiny of the Americans with Disabilities Act of 1990 (ADA) reveals a thoughtful process driven by people with disabilities and their allies, with strategic compromises along the way. The saga of the use of standardized assessments in federal policy from the enactment of No Child Left Behind (NCLB) in 2002, through the 2009 Race to the Top initiative, and finally to the 2011–2017 development and eventual repeal of teacher preparation regulations provides a contrasting narrative. Since its 1990 enactment, the ADA has become part of the fabric of American society, while the use of standardized assessments in federal education policy morphed from a policy solution into a policy problem.

THE ADA: A REMARKABLE POLICY

I had the good fortune to play a small role in the creation of the Americans with Disabilities Act, which was a highlight of my career. I have studied the implementation ever since.[3] The policy has stood firm for over thirty years, with one clarifying amendment; a comprehensive multiagency track record of regulations, guidance, technical assistance, and enforcement; a long history of court cases; continuous applications of the law to new circumstances; numerous failed challenges from policy makers intended to weaken the law; support from Republican and Democratic administrations; and a growing acceptance of people with disabilities as part of the fabric of American society. The intersection of local grassroots activists, savvy policy advocates in Washington, members of Congress, and leaders in the executive branch was critical to the successful creation of the ADA. In many ways, the successful policy that came to be the ADA was the direct result of a strategic and robust advocacy strategy.

In short, the Americans with Disabilities Act of 1990 is a civil rights law prohibiting discrimination against people with disabilities in all areas of public life—including employment, education, transportation, state and local government programs, activities and services, and private and public spaces that are open to the public. In the area of telecommunications, phone and internet companies are required to provide relay services for people with hearing and speech disabilities.

Key features of the ADA that have sustained it over time include the following:

1. *The problem and the solution are well-defined and clearly linked.* The genesis of the ADA was driven by the grassroots advocacy of people with disabilities across the country who repeatedly articulated their experiences with discrimination and lack of access to equal opportunity (*Equality of opportunity*, n.d.). A national leader of the disability community, Justin Dart, led a task force that held town hall meetings in every state in the nation and gathered testimony and written diaries of discrimination from people with disabilities (Disability Rights Education & Defense Fund, 2015). These diaries not only generated support for a solution to the problem; they also brought clarity to the nature and breadth of the problem. In a significant and related development, a small federal independent agency, composed of appointees of then president Ronald Reagan, utilized the legal, business, and disability expertise of council members and staff to draft what would become the framework of the ADA. In 1986,

---

3. See, for example, West (1991, 1996) and West and Yell (2022).

the National Council on Disability issued *Toward Independence*, prioritizing the advancement of federal equal opportunity laws (*Toward independence*, 1986).

2. *The right policy tool is chosen to address the problem.* Since discrimination and lack of equal opportunity were articulated as the problem, the most appropriate solution was a civil rights law.

3. *The policy solution builds on precedent and capacity in terms of legal authority, enforcement mechanisms, and administrative processes.* The ADA had the great policy advantage of building on a long and deep precedent of American civil rights law. The ADA was an extension of the civil rights protections already available to people on the basis of race, color, sex, national origin, age, and religion. In addition, Section 504 of the Rehabilitation Act of 1973—which prohibits discrimination against people with disabilities among recipients of federal funds—had a long track record of implementation. Federal agencies, including the Department of Justice, the Department of Education, and the Equal Opportunity Commission, all had mechanisms in place for the implementation and enforcement of other civil rights laws. Those building blocks served as assurances that the new law could be implemented well.

4. *Technical assistance is built in to enhance implementation.* The ADA includes robust technical assistance components intended to further support implementation of the far-reaching law. This supports people with disabilities in understanding the provisions of the law, their rights under the law, and how they can exercise those rights. It also supports covered entities, including private businesses, specific industries (such as airlines), state and local governments, and employers in understanding how to comply with the law.

5. *Engagement of intended beneficiaries generated contributions to the policy solution and support for that solution, thus mitigating potential resistance.* In sharp contrast to many education laws (for example, No Child Left Behind), those who would be directly affected by the new policy were part of its genesis and ongoing development. The result was tremendous grassroots support for the legislation, as well as ongoing contribution to the development of the provisions of the law as it was under consideration in Congress.

6. *Engagement of potential opponents—or those required to comply with the policy—led to some conflict resolution.* Multiple sectors that would be covered by the ADA generated opposition and raised questions related to cost, feasibility, burden, and intrusion of the federal government on business practices. The transit industry, the health insurance industry, the small business community, the motion picture industry, and the restaurant industry were key among them. At times provisions were negotiated to address concerns, such as principles for determining whether a particular accommodation would constitute an undue burden and thus not be required. Extended phase-in time lines for compliance were developed for some portions of the bill. At other times, limiting amendments were offered to the legislation—and generally defeated. Advocates' engagement of opponents of the bill extensively during the development of the policy led to negotiated policy changes when possible and mitigated a significant level of resistance and policy backlash from covered entities.

7. *Flexibility enables ongoing interpretation of the law to accommodate new circumstances.* The ADA defines individuals with disabilities who are covered by the law. The definition includes three components: having a physical or mental impairment that substantially limits one's ability in certain areas, having a record of such an impairment, or being perceived as having such an impairment. The ADA was amended once, in 2008, in response to Supreme Court cases that provided a limited interpretation of who was covered by the law. The amendments clarified the definition without changing the three key components.

In 2021, during the height of the COVID pandemic, President Biden announced that those with long-haul COVID disease could be considered individuals with disabilities under the ADA (*Guidance on "long COVID,"* 2021). If an individual is determined to have long COVID that would substantially limit their ability in certain areas, they would be covered by the ADA. This application demonstrates the advantage of a definition in policy that can be applied in a range of circumstances rather than a specific delineation of those covered by the law—such as a list of disabilities that people might have.

NCLB AND ITS DERIVATIVES: THE USE OF STANDARDIZED ASSESSMENTS IN FEDERAL EDUCATION POLICY—A CAUTIONARY TALE

Most public policy solutions are complex and fraught with challenges to ensure that the intended result is achieved. These obstacles include lack of resources or capacity to implement, administrative infeasibility, resistance, or lack of commitment from implementers and more. One result of well-intended policy can be that the solution ends up either exacerbating the problem that was intended to be addressed or creating a new problem. The journey of No Child Left Behind and its derivatives offers instructive lessons. This journey features the use of standardized student assessment results in three ways: to measure K–12 school effectiveness, to measure teacher effectiveness, and to measure the effectiveness of teacher education programs.

The move toward expanded data collection used for accountability, with standardized testing at its core, is exemplified by the No Child Left Behind Act of 2001, the Race to the Top initiative of 2012, and teacher preparation regulations developed, and then repealed, between 2011 and 2017.[4] In particular, the high-stakes uses of standardized test results were increasingly contested by researchers and advocates alike (see, e.g., Ravitch, 2013). As noted by Jeffrey Henig in his February 9, 2021, opinion piece:

> Since the federal no Child Left Behind Act was enacted in 2002, the words "data collection" have inspired fear and mistrust in education circles. For

---

4. For more information, see https://www2.ed.gov/documents/teaching/teacher-prep-final-regs.pdf.

many educators, the term signifies bureaucrats' weaponized use of standardized-test scores to monitor and punish districts, schools, and teachers for failing to meet seemingly arbitrary standards of test-score gains. (Henig, 2021)

The 2002 bipartisan adoption of the No Child Left Behind Act was heralded as a great victory—for students, for families, for the education system, for equity, for the future of our nation, and for our economy. It was a culmination of decades of bipartisan consensus that public education was broken. One op-ed at the time noted, "[There is] widening agreement that Washington's present approach to K-12 education policy—an approach that has scarcely changed since LBJ's time—is broken and needs fixing" (Finn et al., 2000). Evidence of student performance declining over time and faltering student test scores in relation to other nations were exhibit A in making the case that the system was broken. The intense focus on test scores led to the creation of an accountability system that would in large measure utilize those test score results to determine progress—a policy solution that, over time, proved itself to be more of a problem than a solution.

The politics surrounding the enactment of NCLB are remarkable. Time-honored and opposing positions by Republicans and Democrats were challenged as public opinion increasingly influenced policy makers on the left and the right to believe that education reform was urgently needed. Galvanized by the 1983 report *A Nation at Risk*, education reform increasingly came to be a central political focus. The report concluded that "our once unchallenged pre-eminence in commerce, industry, science, and technological innovation is being overtaken by competitors throughout the world. . . . If an unfriendly foreign power had attempted to impose on America the mediocre education performance that exists today, we might well have viewed it as an act of war" (Gardner, 1983, p. 9).

In 1988 then presidential candidate George H. W. Bush ran as the "education president." President Bill Clinton, in office from 1993 to 2001, also pushed for education reform, noting a new Democratic commitment to opportunity rather than entitlement, distancing his party from policies of the welfare state. Resistance from the right and the left was evident; however, by 2001, when George W. Bush became president, the seeds of change were planted and leaders in both parties were ready to enact education reform. Republicans felt compelled to support their newly elected president, who came with the credential of a governor who had successfully implemented education reforms that were dubbed "the Texas miracle" (Loyola, 2016). The core components of his initiatives were echoed in NCLB: charter schools, accountability, and school choice. Some Democrats wanted more funding for education and were willing to compromise to get it. Key constituents on both the right and the left were skeptical but were overcome or ignored. Organizations such as the National Education Association and the National Association for the Advancement of Colored People—both important Democratic constituencies who had resisted standards, testing, and accountability measures, including choice—were pushed aside. Republican constituents representing religious, anti-government, and states' rights perspectives—such as the Christian Coalition and the Heritage Foundation—had historically opposed efforts to expand the federal role in education (exemplified by a push to eliminate the federal role in education in the 1980s and 1990s) and were also marginalized (McGuinn, 2006).

So who were the supporters of education reform and NCLB? Ravitch (2013) provides an in-depth analysis, arguing that privatization and corporate involvement were at the center of the movement. Hedge funds, entrepreneurs, multiple foundations, and think tanks adopted the view that public dollars could be seen as investments to be leveraged by the private sector through school choice initiatives such as charter schools. Reformers presented themselves as the solution to the problem that public schools had become. New policy-oriented organizations on the right and the left began to promote reform solutions. With strong allies in the Bush and Obama administrations, the stage was set.

NCLB was enacted with overwhelming bipartisan support. The Senate voted 91–8 to pass the bill, while the House voted 381–41 to adopt it (No Child Left Behind Act of 2001, 2002b). Such bipartisan support for a significant piece of legislation is exceptional. The iconic photo of leaders in both parties at President Bush's signing ceremony for the bill tells the story (*President signs landmark education bill*, 2002). Featuring President Bush flanked by Democratic and Republican leaders of the House Education and the Workforce Committee (Rep. George Miller [D-CA] and Rep. John Boehner [R-OH]) and the Senate Committee on Health, Education, Labor and Pensions (Sen. Ted Kennedy [D-MA] and Sen. Judd Gregg [R-NH]), this was a standout moment in federal education policy history.

NCLB was a reauthorization of the 1965 law originally developed as part of President Lyndon Johnson's War on Poverty, the Elementary and Secondary Education Act (ESEA). It was conceived as an equity-oriented initiative intended to improve education by more equally funding public schools for low-income students and thus offer them greater economic opportunity. The goal of the original law was stated as "to strengthen and improve educational quality and education opportunities in the Nation's education and secondary schools" (Elementary and Secondary Education Act, 1965). Improving educational quality and opportunity invites policy solutions related to equitable distribution of resources targeted to enhance opportunity for children from low-income backgrounds. This policy orientation lasted for thirty years, being gradually overtaken by the reform movement, culminating in the enactment of the No Child Left Behind Act of 2001 (*K-12 Education*, 2008). In contrast to the access-and-equity orientation of ESEA, the stated purpose of NCLB was "to close the achievement gap with accountability, flexibility, and choice so that no child is left behind" (No Child Left Behind Act of 2001, 2002a). It is interesting to note that the goal of the laws shifted from "strengthen and improve educational quality and education opportunities" to "close the achievement gap." "Closing the achievement gap" invites policy solutions that will measure the gap and take action depending on the results.

Data primarily regarding student performance on national and international standardized assessments along with complaints from business and industry that workers were not well prepared were cited. The public and policy makers were concerned, and seeds were sown for curriculum reform (including the development of common core standards [Skinner & Feder, 2014]) and greater accountability. Over time, teacher evaluation began to receive more scrutiny. In general teachers were evaluated based on their credentials and their years of experience. Evaluations were often perfunctory and the result of one observation, which might not even be annual. Critics argued that few teachers were ever released for poor performance and exceptional teachers were not rewarded for their work.

While both the original 1965 law and the 2001 reauthorization in the form of NCLB were intended to improve education, their strategies were quite different. Numerous mandates in NCLB reflected a significant expansion of the federal role in education, with the orientation toward accountability for outcomes rather than access to opportunity. An overview of requirements of NCLB is given below:

- Standards-based assessments would be administered annually to all students grades three through eight in reading and math and at three grade levels in science.
- The state had to create and apply adequate yearly progress (AYP) standards representing benchmarks for student academic achievement. These were to be applied to each school and school district with the goal of all students reaching or exceeding academic proficiency by 2014.
- In a report card fashion, annual public reporting and dissemination to parents of proficiency test results by school, district, and state and by subgroup (students with disabilities, English learners, racial minorities, and children from low-income families) was required. Information on student progress toward AYP, secondary school graduation rates, the number and identity of schools failing to meet AYP standards, and aggregate information on the qualifications of teachers had to be included.
- Accountability provisions for every public school with mandated corrective measures were required when schools did not meet annual yearly progress targets toward 100 percent student proficiency by 2014, including the following:
  - After two years of failing to meet AYP, students had to be offered the opportunity to transfer to a successful public school in the district. Schools in this category were labeled as needing improvement.
  - After three years of failing to meet AYP, students had to continue to be offered the choice of another public school (with transportation support from the district) and supplemental or tutorial services. These schools were considered to be in a state of corrective action.
  - After four years of failing to meet AYP, additional corrective actions were required, with options of replacing relevant school staff, implementing a new curriculum, decreasing management authority at the school, appointing an outside expert to advise the school, extending the school day or year, or changing the internal organization structure of the school.
  - After five years of failing to meet AYP, schools had to restructure by developing alternative governance, such as reopening as a charter school, replacing all or most school staff, or having the state take over the school.

- The law required each state to ensure that teachers were "highly qualified," meaning that they had at least a bachelor's degree, were fully certified, and demonstrated content mastery. Content mastery in the core subjects taught by the teacher was to be measured by a "high, objective, uniform state standard of evaluation"—known as HOUSSE—developed by the state (*K-12 Education*, 2008).

As time went by, the implementation of NCLB developed a strong core of supporters as well as a vocal set of detractors. Some supporters believed its reporting requirements for the performance of subgroups, such as students with disabilities, put a spotlight on them, resulting in greater attention and investment in their success. Some argued that standardized assessments were simply a onetime snapshot of a student's performance on one day and not an accurate measure of performance over time and should not play a role in high-stakes decision making, such as determining if a school is successful. The American Educational Research Association issued a position statement on high-stakes testing, which reads in part:

> If high-stakes testing programs are implemented in circumstances where educational resources are inadequate or where tests lack sufficient reliability and validity for their intended purposes, there is potential for serious harm. Policy makers and the public may be misled by spurious test score increases unrelated to any fundamental educational improvement; students may be placed at increased risk of educational failure and dropping out; teachers may be blamed or punished for inequitable resources over which they have no control; and curriculum and instruction may be severely distorted if high test scores per se, rather than learning, become the overriding goal of classroom instruction. (*Position statement on high-stakes testing*, 2000).

Another concern was that multiple schools were being identified as lagging behind by repeatedly not meeting AYP goals (*Adequate yearly progress*, 2004). In 2007–2008, 35 percent of all public schools were failing to meet AYP for one or more years on the basis of test scores. The percentage of schools in states ranged from 7 to 80 percent. Another study found that schools in California and Illinois that did not meet AYP were composed of 75 to 85 percent minority students, while schools meeting AYP had less than 40 percent minority students (Owens & Sunderman, 2006). Requirements to offer to transfer students to other schools could be challenging in rural areas, where there might not be other schools in the vicinity. In addition, no school was required to accept a student who was seeking to transfer to a higher-performing school. Many argued that the law was never adequately funded to enable full implementation.

Some believed that the goal of every child becoming proficient in math and reading by 2014 was unrealistic and a "one size fits all" approach, ignoring issues like equitable opportunity and resources. In 2019, the state superintendent of education in Alabama, Joe Morton, summed up the sentiments of many critics. He said, in reference to the mandate to reach proficiency by 2014, "There's a fallacy in the law and everybody knows it. . . . That can't happen. You have too many variables and you have too many scenarios, and everybody knows that would never happen" (Stephens, 2010).

In 2012, President Obama announced that ten states would be issued waivers to some of the NCLB requirements (*Educational accountability*, 2012). A total of forty-six states applied, many of them changing state laws in order to meet the requirements of the waiver. The cornerstone requirement for all students to reach proficiency in math and reading by 2014 was waived in exchange for states setting their own achievement goals and their own interventions for failing schools. They were further required to adopt standards for college and career readiness, focus improvement efforts on 15 percent of the poorest performing schools, and develop guidelines for teacher evaluations based in part on student performance. For the first time in federal education policy, funds were tied to teacher evaluation.

The requirement to develop teacher evaluations based in part on student performance led to changes in numerous state laws related to teacher evaluation. The notion of a "quality teacher" or a "highly qualified teacher" changed to the notion of an "effective" teacher, indicating that evidence of student learning was documented. Holding teachers accountable for student learning became a top priority for the Obama administration.

RACE TO THE TOP 2009

When the Obama administration came into office in 2009, the use of test scores as the predominant measure of the success or failure of a school was well established, with vocal critics and supporters. Many thought that Obama might pivot away from such a reliance on test scores, yet the opposite occurred. With the creation of Race to the Top—a $4.3 billion program that was part of the American Recovery and Reinvestment Act of 2009 (*American Recovery and Reinvestment Act*, 2009)—the newly minted secretary of education, Arne Duncan, led the effort to expand the use of test scores. Accountability provisions were extended from measuring student performance, and thus school performance, to measuring teacher performance. The results of standardized test scores became a preeminent component of teacher evaluation systems. If school districts wanted the additional funds available under the Race to the Top program, they would be required to develop teacher evaluation systems that incorporated student growth—which generally translated to student test score results—as a key factor.

In the regulations for Race to the Top, the definition of an effective teacher was offered: "one whose students achieve acceptable rates (e.g. at least one grade level in an academic year) of student growth (as defined by this notice)."[5] Thus, in order to be considered effective, a teacher's students must demonstrate a year's worth of academic progress or more during the school year. The teacher evaluation systems developed under the grant must be based on student growth as a significant

---

5. For more information, see Lomax and Kuenzi (2012).

portion. In efforts to win the grant, multiple states changed their teacher evaluation systems and state laws to include student standardized test performance as a significant component and developed rating systems for teachers. The competition required states to conduct evaluations annually and use teacher evaluations in making key decisions, such as compensation, promotion, retention, and removal of ineffective teachers. Since standardized assessments were only required in certain grades and in certain subjects, there was confusion over how to evaluate teachers whose students were not tested, such as art teachers, history teachers, and more. Over the course of three rounds of funding, almost all states applied. Eighteen states and the District of Columbia were eventually awarded funds, providing each with millions of dollars in exchange for significant changes to their education systems.

One model of measuring teacher effectiveness that became quite popular was value-added modeling, or VAM (Lomax & Kuenzi, 2012). VAM is a statistical method that, among other things, is intended to measure the teacher effect on learning. A number of states were utilizing this tool during the Race to the Top period. Both its supporters and critics were many (Koedel et al., 2015). Critics assert that value-added modeling does not accurately rank teachers in terms of effectiveness and is biased against low-income students and those in lower-resourced schools (Strauss, 2011).

The theory adopted by Secretary Duncan and his team was that poor teachers were the key reason for low student performance. Research was inappropriately cited to support the claim that teachers were the most significant factor in determining student success. What the research does say is that the teacher is the most significant *in-school* factor in determining student success, but out-of-school factors are more influential.[6]

As many states adopted policies to expand the use of standardized student testing for teacher evaluations, researchers balked, as the cardinal rule of psychometrics was being violated: a test should only be used for the purpose for which it is designed. These tests were designed to measure student performance, not teacher quality.

Linda Darling-Hammond, the education lead for President Obama's transition team and then considered to be the pick for his secretary of education, noted in an op-ed, "These test scores largely reflect whom a teacher teaches, not how well they teach. In particular, teachers show lower gains when they have large numbers of new English-learners and students with disabilities than when they teach other students." She goes on to cite accomplished teachers who were fired when their students' test scores declined—including one who worked with immigrant students who do not yet speak English. Her principal said, "I would put my own children in her class" (Darling-Hammond, 2012).

As I watched this debate unfold, I attempted to explain it to my husband, who was a dentist. He was astounded, noting that this approach is the equivalent of holding him accountable for the oral health of his patients when so many

---

6. For a full explanation, see Ravitch (2013).

factors contribute to that outcome—not the least of which is daily brushing! He further argued that if this was the criterion for determining his effectiveness—perhaps influencing his license to practice—he would begin to serve only those who had good oral health to begin with, thus steering away from those who needed his services the most. Over time, the same arguments grew regarding students. Wasn't this a disincentive to teach the kids who were the most behind and the most challenged?

Teachers and their allies began to challenge this practice, particularly as it was expanded to apply to teachers who did not teach students in subjects or grades where standardized tests were utilized—including art and music. Formulas were developed, such as grade or school averages, and applied to teachers who did not teach tested students. Math and reading were prioritized over other subjects, as they were the tested subjects. Teachers were incentivized to structure their teaching so at times it became more like test preparation than instruction.

NCLB represents the first federal education policy requiring schools to be accountable for student achievement as determined by standardized assessments (Mathesz, 2014). The waivers provided for NCLB and the Race to the Top competition further infused the use of student standardized assessment results as a significant aspect of teacher evaluation. The next application of this strategy was to the programs that prepare teachers.

TEACHER PREPARATION REGULATIONS 2011–2017

As Race to the Top continued to unfold, the Obama administration began to shift its attention to the programs that prepare teachers. If teachers are not performing well, shouldn't the programs that prepare them be held accountable? Thus began a seven-year saga of regulatory development and eventual repeal by Congress.

As early as 2009, Sec. Duncan began planting the seeds of the narrative that teacher education was broken. In two speeches in 2009, he proclaimed that "by almost any standard, many, if not most, of the nation's 1450 schools, colleges, and departments of education are doing a mediocre job of preparing teachers for the realities of the 21st century classroom" (Duncan, 2009). He repeatedly noted that he heard from teachers how dissatisfied they were with their teacher preparation programs and cited surveys. He cited the fact that very few states had identified teacher preparation programs as "low-performing"—which is required by the Higher Education Act—noting that this must mean they are not properly monitoring the programs, for surely there are many more low-performing programs (Kuenzi, 2018).

From October 2011 to April 2012, the Department of Education engaged in a negotiated rule-making process to extend the use of K–12 student standardized test scores as an accountability mechanism for school and teacher performance to teacher education programs in higher education. Because members of the negotiated rule-making team could not come to consensus on a proposal, the process failed, and the department took charge to write regulations on its own.

The proposed regulations were published in 2014. They called for states to rate teacher education programs in the state (Teacher preparation issues, 2014). Only those that were highly rated would be eligible for a student financial aid program, called TEACH grants. There was no funding to accompany the proposal, which was estimated to cost or exceed $100 million—about the same amount of funding that went to TEACH grants. The rating system was to comprise four components, with student learning outcomes carrying the most weight (represented by test scores of the K–12 students taught by the graduates of the particular preparation program). No program could be highly rated unless it demonstrated that its graduates were generating acceptable student outcomes—which in virtually every state was measured by the results of K–12 standardized tests. States would be required to rate individual programs, not the entire department. There were estimated to be more than twenty-six thousand individual teacher education programs across the country (Kuenizi, 2018) with some colleges of education reporting over sixteen different individual programs. Programs that were determined to be low performing would lose access to TEACH grants and state financial aid—and possibly access to all federal student financial aid.

During the comment period on the proposed regulations 4,580 comments were received from all fifty states and DC, with approximately 95 percent expressing opposition or grave concern (American Association of Colleges for Teacher Education, 2015). The concerns expressed were multiple, including the following:

- Criteria, such as value-added K–12 student test scores and teacher retention, have not been determined to be valid for the evaluation of teacher preparation programs.
- Multiple factors beyond the control of the preparation program determine teacher impact on students, including the nature of the school in which they teach, the level of support they receive in their schools, their personal motivation, and the motivation of their students.
- States would become the arbiter of eligibility for federal student financial aid, which represents a significant shift for all of higher education and federal higher education policy.
- The capacity to implement this proposal is lacking and cost would be prohibitive.
- The proposal is unworkable, in that there is no capability—likely would never be due to state statutes—to follow program graduates who teach in states other than the one where they were prepared.
- The regulation would have a disproportionately negative impact on minority-serving institutions and programs that prepare teachers for high-need schools and fields.

At an April 25, 2014, event at Dunbar High School in Washington, DC, Secretary Duncan concluded the discussion of the proposed regulations with these words: "If we don't get this done, shame on us." In responding to the proposal, Randi Weingarten, president of the American Federation of Teachers, said the administration should not carry out "a quick-fix, test-and-punish, market-based ranking of programs" (Rich, 2014, p. A12). Linda Darling-Hammond said, "If we evaluated doctors based on that kind of measure, nobody would train AIDS physicians. They'd all train pediatricians who worked in the suburbs where kids are pretty healthy to begin with" (Rich, 2014, p. A12).

In 2015, Duncan stepped down as secretary of education. Also that year, the Every Student Succeeds Act replaced the No Child Left Behind Act and Race to the Top requirements, shifting significant policy decisions from the federal to the state level. Teacher evaluations tied to test results were no longer required by federal policy. In October 2016 the final teacher preparation regulations were released with minimal changes (Teacher preparation issues, 2016). In November, President Trump was elected, and Congress changed hands so that it was controlled by Republicans. In 2017, under the leadership of Republicans, Congress invoked the Congressional Review Act to eliminate the teacher preparation regulations. After a seven-year development effort, the regulations were repealed before they were implemented.

During the development of the teacher preparation regulations, as the Senior Vice President of the American Association of Colleges for Teacher Education, I had the opportunity to talk to a high-ranking official at the Department of Education about the proposal. Our organization was concerned about many aspects of the proposal and the seeming impossibility of implementing it. My question was simple: "Since no state currently has such an accountability scheme in place as you propose, why not pilot it on two or three states and see if it works?" The answer was stark, and I paraphrase: "We cannot wait. This is an urgent matter. We must take comprehensive, bold steps immediately." I left reflecting on his sense of urgency that appeared to be a key rationale for the proposal. I also thought about the schools and colleges of education, which repeatedly told us that, even if they wanted to implement the proposal, the capacity simply was not there.

In reflecting on that conversation, I think about Naomi Klein's theory that promoting a narrative of a severe crisis can be a sound strategy for developing political urgency to adopt a predetermined policy solution. Getting the policy solution adopted took precedence over ensuring that it could be successfully implemented and was a sound approach. Certainly, this is not the only example of such an occurrence. In the end, this approach generated a backlash, leading to a new set of policy changes that eliminated or deemphasized the use of standardized test scores in accountability frameworks and left a residual of skepticism about standardized testing.

Lessons Learned

1. *Broad bipartisan support* does not always mean that policy is sound and sustainable. While both the ADA and NCLB enjoyed broad bipartisan support, only one of the policy regimes survived long-term with continued support, implementation, and adaptation.

2. *Utilization of the wrong policy tools* can generate strong resistance and doom a policy regime. While the ADA was built on a sound foundation laid by previous civil rights laws, the standardized assessment policy regime was not. Student standardized assessments were used for purposes for which they were not designed, and often for high-stakes decision making, generating skepticism and a lack of credibility in decision-making outcomes in areas such as teacher evaluations.

3. *The capacity—or lack thereof—to implement a policy regime* cannot be ignored. The ADA was carefully constructed to utilize existing civil rights implementation capacities and extend them. Strategies such as technical assistance and phasing in requirements over time were essential. The development of teacher preparation regulations is most striking in its lack of consideration of the capacity for implementation. While there was resistance to the content of the policy, the inability to implement it and the significant funds that states would have to commit to do so were given short shrift.

4. *Ensuring the right players at the policy making table matters.* The ADA was generated from the grass roots in conjunction with strong policy leaders in Washington. Together they developed political champions on both sides of the aisle. The entities that would be covered by the ADA—such as restaurants and businesses—had a voice. Compromises were developed. Of course there was opposition, but this was not what it could have been. NCLB was developed by policy makers with selected supporters; however, key constituencies—such as teachers unions and traditional conservative organizations—were marginalized or ignored. Traditional education organizations and entities were positioned as part of the problem and kept at bay. In the development of the teacher preparation regulations, institutions of higher education that prepare teachers were likewise cast as the problem and their concerns ignored. Demonizing the very entities that must carry out the policy did not pan out as a successful strategy.

5. *Elections impact policy.* The fact that President Trump took office in 2017 and that Congress was controlled by Republicans opened the door for the revocation of the teacher preparation regulations. Had the Republicans not been in charge, it is doubtful the regulations would have been repealed. Rather, they would likely have had a long, slow, fraught implementation, much like NCLB, with resistance growing and eventual dissolution. The sound policy provisions in the ADA, in addition to strong support from the disability community and its allies—as well as numerous Democratic and Republican presidents and congressional champions—served to sustain the law through multiple presidencies and turnovers in Congress.

TAKEAWAYS: POLICY

1. How policy problems are defined shapes policy solutions.
2. The choice of policy tools utilized to address a policy problem may enhance or deter the likelihood of policy success.
3. The determination of what constitutes good public policy is fraught with bias. However, scrutiny of multiple variables (such as who is at the policy making table, the likelihood of successful implementation, and amelioration of unintended consequences) promotes the probability of effective policy.
4. The contrasting narratives offered by the Americans with Disabilities Act of 1990 and the No Child Left Behind Act of 2001 and its derivatives reveal that bipartisan support is not a proxy for policy success or longevity, that utilizing the wrong policy tools can doom policy, that the lack of capacity to implement policy will curtail its effectiveness, that marginalizing the voices of key actors during policy deliberations has consequences, and that elections impact policy.

CHAPTER 5

Advocacy

· ·

Putting It All Together

Don't agonize, organize!

—House Speaker Nancy Pelosi (D-CA),
interview on MSNBC *Andrea Mitchell Reports*, 2022

For busy professionals, advocacy feels like an "add-on" to an already demanding schedule. Most people want to have their voices heard by policy makers, but they do not have an accessible or straightforward road map for engaging in the policy dialogue. Getting involved seems messy and obtuse with questionable results. "What difference can one person make?" is a common refrain. But we are not at the table at our own peril. Today, more than ever, policy decisions affect our lives, our professions, our families, our communities, our nation, and our world. It is tempting to throw up our hands and walk away, but in so doing we are turning over our power to others—others who may not share our expertise or our values but who *will* have their voices heard.

Advocacy activity can be reframed as an integral part of the work you are already involved in—not an "add-on" or an extra task to be piled onto an already overloaded to-do list. As you think about yourself as an advocate, consider the following:

- You are the employer of elected officials—you hold the power to hire them and to fire them. Ultimately, they report to you—the voter, the constituent. Research from the Congressional Management Foundation, which reported results from a survey of over 260 congressional staffers, found that constituent visits were the most influential factor on legislators who were undecided about an issue (*Communicating with Congress*, 2011).
- As an educator or other professional, you have experience and knowledge that is unique and informative for policy making—in other words, you are an *expert*.
- Policy makers want to hear from you. (This does not mean they will agree with you, and that is okay. You can speak to your view of their positions at

· ·

the ballot box.) You can keep them informed about what is happening in their district or state; you can provide examples of needs and successes; you can inform decision making with expertise.

To position yourself as an effective advocate, consider both your individual voice and your voice as part of a collective, most probably an organization or an association. Your individual role is amplified when you join with like-minded colleagues or constituents to make your case. Your individual role as a constituent (voter) is paramount, as most elected officials will seek reelection, and those who are new to politics will court your vote in order to prevail. Joining forces with like-minded others communicates to Congress that there is a broad level of support or opposition for a particular position, which is appealing as a member weighs their position on a policy matter.

> "The policy making process is slow. It's so important to have a long-view perspective. It might take thirty years of advocacy to see the results you want. This is why it is important for individuals to tap into organizations with broad agendas and established access to policy makers. This also helps us reach across dividing lines to broaden our agendas, for example, from education to civil rights." (Ashley White, personal correspondence, September 23, 2022)

While this book's focus is on advocacy at the federal level, the framework presented is equally relevant at the state level. In some policy areas, including education, the federal government increasingly defers policy decisions to the state. Some policy makers, particularly Republicans, believe in a limited role for the federal government and that states are in a better position to determine policy matters, as they are closer to the people and the challenges they face. In many areas of policy, particularly in education, there is a significant role for both the state and federal governments. Advocating at both levels is essential.

> "We have to think more about state advocacy. For a long time we have separated our advocacy work into state and federal efforts. They need to be coordinated, especially now as many key decisions are being made at the state level." (Ashley White, personal correspondence, September 23, 2022)

I have often been asked, "How do I pick a policy issue for my advocacy?" The best response I heard to this question came from an insightful colleague, Erika Hagensen (Balancing work and life, 2019). She said to consider what makes your blood boil or your heart sing. In other words, check in with your passion. What do you feel most strongly about? What are you most committed to? Your passion is what will sustain you through defeats and frustrations of the long game. Your passion is what will motivate you to write the thirty-fourth email about an issue you care about. Your passion is what will drive you to show up at the next town hall meeting after a long day at work.

Policy advocacy is generally associated with promoting a policy solution. While this is the ultimate goal, educating policy makers about policy problems is also essential, as is preventing potentially damaging or ineffective policy proposals from moving forward. A colleague who worked at the White House once shared with me that the vast majority of his work was preventing various players in the administration from moving on policy ideas that would be detrimental to his area of policy. Government relations experts in Washington know that at least half of their work involves strategy to keep a proposal from becoming a reality. For example, when a president issues a budget proposal and calls for the elimination of a program that you advocate for, the prevention strategy kicks into gear. Or when a member of Congress introduces a bill that is in opposition to your position, your advocacy work will revolve around preventing it from moving forward.

TEXTBOX 5.1. AN EXTRAORDINARY ADVOCATE: EUNICE KENNEDY SHRIVER

Eunice Kennedy Shriver, sister of President John F. Kennedy, is known for her monumental philanthropic work, in particular her founding of Special Olympics, a program designed to provide athletic opportunities for people with intellectual disabilities (*Eunice Kennedy Shriver's story*, n.d.). I had the great good fortune to work for Mrs. Shriver for a number of years supporting her advocacy work. She was a tenacious advocate. From her I learned some key lessons about advocacy. First, your passion will drive you. Her passion was generated from her sister Rosemary, who had an intellectual disability and because of that encountered limitations on the opportunities that were available to her. Mrs. Shriver deeply felt the injustice of this and set out to open doors that had been closed to her sister. Second, be relentless. Mrs. Shriver used her vast network to engage people across multiple sectors to educate them, charm them, and make her case. She had deep relationships from across the political spectrum. Third, never give up. If one route did not pan out, she was ready for the next. She would find a way. To this day, I hear her voice in my mind, "Let's go, get busy!"

ADVOCATING WITH CONGRESSIONAL OFFICES

When developing an advocacy strategy, it is important to know the membership of the committees and subcommittees with jurisdiction over the policy area that is the target of the advocacy. Members of Congress generally seek to serve on particular committees because they have an interest or background in the area and it may be of particular interest to their constituents. The work of the committee targeted will involve oversight and monitoring of the policy area selected. For example, if the goal is to change a component of education policy—for example, address the affordability of college—the key committees to target would be the House Committee on Education and Labor[1] and the Senate Committee on Health, Education, Labor and Pensions (HELP).[2] Furthermore, there may be a subcommittee of that committee to further target. In this case, that would be the Higher Education and Workforce Subcommittee in the House. At this time, the Senate HELP Committee does not have a subcommittee with jurisdiction over higher education, so the full committee would be the target. Even when Congress moves massive bills with multiple policy provisions, such as a reconciliation bill, if there is a matter in the bill that is under the jurisdiction of a particular committee, the leaders of those committees will likely be consulted.

As a constituent, it is critically important to be familiar with your representative as well as the two senators from your state. These policy makers are in Washington to represent their constituents. It does not matter if you voted for them or against them or if you did not vote at all. You are still a constituent if you live in their district or state. Sometimes advocates think it is not worth communicating with their representative or senator if their views are not in line with their advocacy goals. This is not the case. As a constituent, being in touch with your delegation always matters. Sometimes a personal connection will trump a different point of view—for example, if the member's son is friends with your son, or if the member's alma mater is the place where you work. Sometimes a mutually shared concern will be more significant than opposing political views. For example, if you are advocating on behalf of people with disabilities, you may find that a member of your delegation may have a family member with a disability. Rep. Cathy McMorris Rodgers (R-WA) is the mother of a child with Down syndrome. Her experience led her to found and cochair the Congressional Down Syndrome Caucus and to introduce and promote disability legislation.

> "Constituents will always find an open door, where nonconstituents will not. Lawmakers are small businesses and constituents are their customers." (Kuna Tavalin, personal correspondence, August 17, 2022)

---

1. For more information, see https://edlabor.house.gov/.
2. For more information, see https://www.help.senate.gov/.

As a rule of thumb, members want to know what their constituents have to say. The more they know about what is happening in the area they represent, the better prepared they are for the policy work they encounter. As a knowledgeable constituent, you can help your representative, your senators, and their staff understand what is going on in their district or state so that this information informs their decision making.

You can find out who your representative and senators are on the Web.[3] Members' websites allow you to contact the member's office in Washington, sign up for newsletters, review the member's priorities, and more. You can also call the member's office by dialing the Capitol Switchboard at (202) 224-3121. You will be directly connected to the member's personal office. You can inquire about how to schedule an appointment, learn how to share your views with the members, and find out what staff person covers the issue you are concerned about. This is the staff person you will want to build a relationship with. Many offices prioritize meetings and communication with constituents over other interested parties. There will be information about how to directly contact their office, follow them on Twitter, sign up for newsletters, attend breakfasts, and participate in town halls. Some offices will only communicate with constituents via their websites, thereby privileging their information and opinions.

Many congressional offices have communications vehicles that are only available to constituents—such as routine breakfasts on Capitol Hill or town hall meetings in the district or state. For example, for seventy-seven years the Nebraska delegation has hosted a regular breakfast with any constituents who are in DC in order to dialogue with them and provide briefings (Fischer, 2021).

TEXTBOX 5.2. GETTING STARTED WITH YOUR CONGRESSIONAL DELEGATION

- Determine the senators and representative for whom you are a constituent. Put your address in the "Find Your Members" search box (https://www.congress.gov/members/find-your-member) and your delegation will pop up.
- What committees do they serve on?
- Do you have any personal connections with them, such as the same hometown or same alma mater?
- Sign up for their newsletter.
- Follow them on Twitter, Facebook, Instagram.

---

3. For more information, see https://www.govtrack.us/congress/members.

First and Foremost: Build a Relationship

> "The time to make relationships is before you need them. You build relationships so that when something challenging comes up, you can rely on those relationships." (Kuna Tavalin, personal correspondence, August 17, 2022)

Advocacy is a long-term proposition. As such, a foundational relationship is key to achieving your advocacy goals. You want to have the foundation of a relationship developed through meetings and regular communication before a crisis hits and you have an urgent request. Establishing yourself as a reliable and knowledgeable resource to a congressional office is always goal number one. Policy makers and their staffs hear from literally hundreds of interested parties every day on a wide range of issues with a wide range of opinions. Policy makers and policy staff turn over regularly as a result of elections and job changes. How do you become someone the office remembers? How do you become a "go-to" constituent with eyes and ears on the ground to keep them informed about what is happening back home? How do you develop trust as someone who can help them with your expertise when needed? Below are essential ingredients.

> "DC is all about relationship building. You want to be trustworthy. You want to be the person they call when questions come up." (Lindsay Fryer, personal correspondence, September 22, 2022)

Prepare for Meetings

Before engaging with members of Congress, you want to do your homework (West, 2018). The four Ps can be instructive. Find out what you can about the *people*. Check the websites of your congressional delegation and determine their priorities, the history of their votes, and bills that they have introduced or supported. Consider whether you might have personal connections with them (e.g., your son went to high school with their daughter). Determine if they have a personal connection to your issue (e.g., if you are addressing issues related to education, perhaps they were once an educator). Understand their general set of beliefs (e.g., perhaps they believe in a small role for the federal government). Get a sense of what other organizations or individuals generally support or engage with the official. Also, have a sense of the organizations or people who oppose your position.

In terms of *politics*, know the political party membership of your congressional delegation. Know whether or not they are "in cycle" (i.e., in reelection mode) as well as how vulnerable they might be. Determine if they are senior members or junior members and whether they hold leadership positions.

For *process*, understand where there might be opportunities to have your issue addressed. Is there a bill that has been introduced that you would like your representative to cosponsor? Is Congress in the midst of crafting a funding bill that could provide funds for your targeted program? Knowing what moving trains are on the tracks will help you to craft your specific requests or "asks."

In terms of *policy*, be prepared on the issue you will advocate for. Know how the issue is manifesting in the state or district of the elected official. For example, if you are concerned about lack of access to health care, be prepared to provide data about that lack of access and its impact in their district or state. Know the status of how the policy is being addressed—for example, if there is a bill pending that is relevant and who the supporters and critics are as well as their views. Finally, know the opposition. Understand what the arguments are against your position and be prepared to respond to them.

TEXTBOX 5.3. REQUESTING MEETINGS WITH YOUR CONGRESSIONAL DELEGATION

If you are scheduling a meeting in conjunction with a national organization, follow their guidance for scheduling, including matters such as what letterhead and email to use (e.g., personal or professional). If you are scheduling a meeting as an individual constituent, the following guidance is offered:

- Check the websites of the members of your congressional delegation to determine how to request a meeting. Generally, an email to the scheduler is recommended. Another option is to call the office. You can dial (202) 224-3121 and reach the Capitol Switchboard, which will connect you to any congressional office. If you do not hear back within a few days, follow up.
- You may want to schedule a meeting on behalf of a few like-minded constituents with the same policy concern. Numbers amplify your message.
- Seek to meet with the member of Congress directly or the staff person who covers the issue you are concerned about (such as education).
- In your request for a meeting, use your personal email or letterhead, and identify yourself as a constituent as well as an expert in your field. Briefly note what policy area you would like to discuss, noting matters of local concern and how the federal government might make a difference.
- Indicate dates and times for your meeting request and whether you prefer a virtual or in-person meeting—which could be either in Washington or when the member or their staff are back in the district or state.

Provide Background Information, Data, and Stories

> "Your average Senate office has about one hundred meetings a week. How can you be sure they will remember you? You have to break through. Compelling stories and good data presented in a way it can be understood are important. People will remember a good story." (Michael Yudin, personal correspondence, August 12, 2022)

Educating congressional offices is often a key part of your meeting. The congressional office you meet with may or may not be familiar with your policy concern and with the possible policy measures that could address it. Providing information about both the problem and the solution is an effective way to structure your time. For example, if your issue is the shortage of educators, you could begin by describing the dimensions of the problem with data—nationally, for your state, and locally. How many vacancies is the local school district anticipating this year? How many positions were filled by under- or unqualified people last year? What does the pipeline look like for the future? Then you could pivot to a program that offers a solution. In our example, that might be the Teacher Quality Partnership Grant program authorized by the Higher Education Act. Offering a fact sheet on the program is helpful in case the congressional office is not familiar with it.[4] More funding for this program could make a difference in addressing the shortage. Finally, you will want to be prepared with a story. Stories can be most persuasive in delivering your message. A story from personal experience is particularly powerful. In our example, a person who was the beneficiary of the Teacher Quality Partnership Grant program could talk about how that program enabled them to become a successful teacher in a shortage area in the congressional district, and how without the grant they would have been unable to fulfill their dream of becoming a teacher in an underresourced school.

Refine Your Message So It Will Be Heard by Your Audience

Your homework has enabled you to understand important background about the office you are targeting. First, remember that the person you are meeting with is unlikely to be an expert, like you. In general, it is not advisable to use jargon or acronyms from your field. If you assume that these are familiar, you may leave the meeting with the staff or member not understanding what you said. You might want to begin your meeting by asking about their familiarity with your policy issue. The response will guide you in determining how you will communicate with them.

---

4. For an example, see https://aacte.org/federal-policy-and-legislation/teacher-quality-partnership-grants/.

Second, be succinct. As Cunningham and Wycoff (2013) reported in the lessons learned from their analysis of researchers interacting with policy makers: "Less is more." Policy makers and their staffs are quite busy and their portfolios are large, so leaving them with a cogent message is critical. It is not uncommon for meetings to last just fifteen minutes, so a succinct message or "elevator speech" is critical. For experts, it is often tempting to provide detailed information about an analysis and outline the pros and cons, as this is often called for in academic settings. However, such a presentation could result in your audience losing interest. As one observer noted: "If you try to sell an idea by saying, 'Well, this might work but on the other hand, there are problems with it, but the data show this, but there are problems with the data, so we have to qualify it, but nevertheless I think we should perhaps try this out,' you won't get anywhere. You have to go in there and say, 'This is the greatest thing to come along in years'" (Kingdon, 2010, p. 127). Of course, overselling your position is not a good way to build a trusting relationship, but it is important to be persuasive.

> "Be concise. Think about your elevator pitch. This is the most important thing you will bring to policy makers. They don't have time for a thirty-minute conversation about the issue. The pitch should be short." (David Cleary, personal correspondence, September 15, 2022)

The homework you have done can further help you shape your message. If you are meeting with a conservative Republican, you may want to present your issue and your "asks" differently than if you are meeting with a liberal Democrat. For example, with a Republican, you may need to make the case that the issue you would like to see addressed is in the federal purview. Particularly in areas like education, some more conservative members may see education as the purview of state and local government and believe in a minimal role or no role for the federal government. Knowing this, you may want to directly address the unique role of the federal government in relation to state and local government. For example, the long-established federal commitment to equal access to education for students with disabilities, exemplified by the Individuals with Disabilities Education Act, plays a significant and unique role in our nation's history of public education. All legislators, but particularly Republicans, may want to have a sense of the "ROI," or return on investment, for the federal expenditure and how the funds will be monitored for accountability. Providing such information is persuasive in establishing your understanding of the need to answer to voters and taxpayers.

> "Effective advocates adapt their language for a particular member of Congress, their political party, and their region of the country in order to resonate with the office. You can't deliver the message the same way to everyone." (Kuna Tavalin, personal correspondence, August 17, 2022)

In reinforcing your message, consider what third-party endorsers may have a ready audience with the policy maker you are pursuing. Might there be local high-profile policy elites, politicians, or community leaders who are well established with the congressional office who have ready access and would share your message? At times the same message will be heard by one messenger and ignored when it is delivered by a different messenger. The messenger can be as important as the message.

Be Prepared with No More Than Three "Asks"

"Asks" is DC slang for requests. Members of Congress and their staffs expect those they meet with to have requests. While that might seem a little abrupt, particularly at a first meeting, know that without those asks the staffer or member may think you have not done your homework and that you are wasting their time. The work of Congress is decision making and action. Congressional offices need to know precisely what you want them to do. Since a meeting will generally last between fifteen and thirty minutes, the asks should be on the tip of your tongue. In fact, I once encountered a staffer who was running short on time begin the meeting with a constituent by asking, "What do you want?" Fortunately, she was ready to answer that question on the spot.

> "When I met with people who just wanted to share their research and had no ask, I wondered why we were meeting." (Lindsay Fryer, personal correspondence, September 22, 2022)

It is best if asks can be straightforward and potentially answered by yes or no. While you might not get an answer during the meeting, you have opened the door for follow-up. Requests such as "Will you cosponsor H.R. 2653, the Diversify Act?" are straightforward and easy for a congressional office to relate to. Asking to cosponsor a particular bill shows that you have done your homework. It is also something that is easily within the purview of a congressional office. Asks should be achievable by the congressional office. If one of your asks is "Can you develop a bill to eradicate poverty?" you might not get very far. Another way to approach this would be to target a specific existing program and request a revision in it or an increase in funding for it. For example, "The Child and Dependent Care Tax Credit really helps to lift families out of poverty. Would you support a provision in the upcoming reconciliation bill to make that credit permanent?"

Congressional offices have many ways of showing such support. For example, they could submit a letter to the Committee on Appropriations that includes your request as a priority, they could sign a "Dear Colleague" letter being circulated by other members of Congress supporting this request, or they could speak personally to the committee chair or ranking member and indicate this as a priority for them. Finally, an ask could be broad and invite follow-up—for example, "Would you be interested in working on a new bill to address the critical infrastructure needs in science labs in higher education? I'd love to make some recommendations about what is needed."

"Be able to tell policy makers what they should *do* with your information and ideas. Make the ask. Request specific actions—the more specific the better." (Anonymous, personal correspondence, September 1, 2022)

No more than three asks is recommended, and one ask is sufficient. In my experience three or fewer is a reasonable number to manage—for both the advocate and the policy maker. Making ten requests might indicate that you do not have your priorities in order. That is also a lot to ask of a congressional office that conducts multiple meetings a day and handles multiple requests. Try to make it reasonably easy for your request to be a "win" for both you and the office whenever possible.

Knowing the status of the legislative processes that are in play is key in determining requests. For example, a good time to request an increase in funding for a program is after the president has submitted their budget to Congress and the relevant committees are beginning to think about writing their appropriations bills. Chapter 3 provides detailed information about congressional processes. Being aware of them will enable you to find the right timing for your requests.

You will want to let those you meet with know that you would like to follow up and stay in touch on your requests—in addition to providing any additional information they may need.

QUICK TIPS FOR A SUCCESSFUL MEETING WITH A CONGRESSIONAL OFFICE

- Note the meeting is likely to last fifteen to thirty minutes. Plan accordingly.
- Make sure you are on time. (If you are going in person, this may require leaving time to go through security.)
- Thank the staff or member for finding time to meet with you.
- Introduce yourself as both a constituent and an expert in your policy area.
- Succinctly state what you would like to talk about in the meeting (e.g., the critical shortage of early childhood care providers and the impact that has on employment in your state and what could be done to address this challenge).
- Provide information, data, and a personal story. Have "leave behinds" ready such as one-page fact sheets on the policy problem and on relevant federal programs.
- Make your asks.
- Ask if there is any more information they would like on the topic.
- Ask what the relevant policy priorities are for their office and determine if there is an overlap with your policy priority.
- Thank them for the meeting and request their email to follow up. Let them know you are available to be a resource to them with eyes and ears on the ground in the district or state. Leave your contact information.
- Follow up with a thank-you email, any information they requested or that you believe would be useful, and to find out the status of your asks.

Offer Invitations to Speak or Visit

Members of Congress and congressional staff are generally quite receptive to invitations to visit your program or campus or to engage via Zoom. Such visits give them an opportunity to learn more about what is happening in their district or state and to introduce themselves to constituents. If the representative or senator is up for reelection, they may be particularly receptive to such invitations, as they will be actively campaigning and looking to win votes.

I have had many wonderful experiences inviting congressional staff to speak to my doctoral classes. They are generally eager to share information about their jobs, their portfolios, how they make decisions and gather information, and how students can be engaged in the policy making process. This is true of both Democratic and Republican staff—even when they do not agree with your policy positions. They also like to hear from students—about their experiences in the field and their research. When Hill staffers are former educators, they are happy to share their journeys from the classroom to Capitol Hill.

Members of Congress are back in their district or state frequently. Coordinating a visit with their scheduler or the office in the state or district is a good way to get on their schedule. Before making such an invitation, be sure to coordinate with relevant colleagues or supervisors in your setting. For example, if you are a teacher, you would want the approval of the principal, who may want to make the member's presence a schoolwide event.

> "Face-to-face meetings matter a lot, particularly meeting with real people from the state who care. People underestimate the importance of advocacy back home versus in DC." (David Cleary, personal correspondence, September 15, 2022)

Don't Get Mad or Argue or Talk Politics

Some congressional offices simply will not agree with you. They may argue that your policy issue is not one for the federal government to address. They may argue that while they would like to address your concern, the federal deficit is too dire and they cannot support any more spending. They may hold ideological positions that are in stark opposition to yours, such as when a public education advocate engages with an office that supports vouchers. When getting pushback from an office, the best response is to listen. Understand their perspective. Acknowledge that you hear them. Continue to make your case, but in the end, you may agree to disagree. Regardless of such a fundamental difference in perspective, most congressional offices will still want to have information about what is happening in their district. It is always better to be in the arena making your case than sitting on the sidelines. Perhaps they will hear a new argument from you or be persuaded by a constituent story. Perhaps you will discover a personal connection with the office. At a minimum, your goal remains to build a relationship and become a resource.

> "The biggest mistakes advocates make are not having a clear ask and being angry. You will never get someone to agree with you if you belittle them or they feel like they are being disrespected. It's like a first date and you want to make a good impression." (David Cleary, personal correspondence, September 15, 2022)

Finally, congressional offices have a strict dividing line between their offices and campaign/political matters. The House Committee on Ethics[5] and the Senate Select Committee on Ethics[6] outline these parameters. In general, government funds are not to be used for reelection purposes. While there is a limited role that certain staff members may play in coordinating with reelection campaigns, those roles are not usually assigned to the legislative staff with whom you are likely to be meeting. Discussing politics and election matters, such as fund-raisers, should not be part of your conversation. Your purpose is to address policy, not politics. Knowing the

---

5. For more information, see https://ethics.house.gov/.

6. For more information, see https://www.ethics.senate.gov/public/index.cfm/home.

political context of your advocacy is essential, as outlined in chapter 2; however, politics should not be part of an advocacy conversation about policy. If you want to get involved in a campaign, look online and you can easily find out how.

Always Follow Up

It's good to think of your interaction with congressional offices as dating someone you like. It takes a while to get to know them, and you want to leave your encounter anticipating the next one with optimism. Follow-up is key. If you have left your meeting with a promise to follow up or with a request for additional information, be sure to follow up within a few days. Remember that the congressional timetable is fast. When information is requested, it may be needed immediately. Asking what the deadline is for providing requested information is always a good idea. When following up on a request, note that it may take some time for the office to address your request. For example, if you requested that the office add your request to a list of appropriations priorities for submission to the leaders of the Committee on Appropriations, there may be a time line involved that has not yet materialized.

A follow-up thank-you email is essential. You want to be sure to leave the meeting with the email address of the person you met with. Thanking them for their time and acknowledging their work, reviewing your concern and asks, and offering to be an ongoing resource for information are the key ingredients of a thank-you follow-up.

Keep Showing Up

Interaction with congressional offices is an ongoing endeavor. Frequency matters in building a relationship. You could give yourself a biweekly reminder to think about something you could share with the congressional office to stay in touch. Offices love to hear good news about their district or state. If someone in your teacher education program won an award, share that with the office. If there is a local newspaper article or an op-ed that reinforces your message, send that to the office.

Social media is an important way to stay in touch. Virtually every member of Congress has a Twitter handle, a Facebook page, and an Instagram account. They all have websites whereby you can contact them, sign up for their newsletters, and learn about town hall meetings. Phone calls are a particularly good way to weigh in on a current matter. The people who answer the phone in a congressional office generally keep running tallies of constituents who call and their views—best expressed as "support" or "oppose" on an upcoming vote. When the numbers reach a certain threshold, they are reported by the staff to the member of Congress, who takes note of how their constituents are viewing a matter. Regular emails staying in touch with the staff are effective. Participating in town hall meetings back in the district or state demonstrates your tenacity and your ongoing desire to be a resource to the congressional office. You can develop a multifaceted approach to ensure your interaction is frequent and ongoing.

Add Your Voice to a National Organization

Virtually all national membership organizations with a policy and advocacy portfolio host an annual, biannual, or even quarterly session where they bring their members to Washington or offer an online convening so that constituent voices can be heard directly by members of Congress. The advantages of participating in one of these organizational efforts are many. When participating in an event hosted by a national association, you will be advised by government relations experts whose day job is to know what is happening in Congress and the administration regarding your priority policy areas. These experts will brief you on background; suggest priorities and strategies for meetings with Hill staff; recommend asks that reflect the organization's key concerns; provide briefings from Hill staff, members of Congress, representatives of the executive branch, and representatives of other national organizations; and support you in developing and practicing for your own advocacy meetings. They will provide background materials, or "one-pagers," about policy topics or federal programs that are suitable to present to congressional offices during your meetings, such as those offered by the American Association of Colleges for Teachers Education (aacte.org). They will facilitate your collaboration with others from your state who are attending the session so that you send a joint message to your congressional delegation from multiple constituents.

Many national membership organizations also utilize "action alerts," whereby you can simply go on to their website and send a short advocacy message to your congressional delegation with a timely and specific request—for example, to cosponsor a bill or to vote in support of a particular measure. When members of Congress hear from a sizable number of constituents about one specific policy request, that request is likely to gain traction. See, for example, the Council for Exceptional Children's Action Alert Center at https://exceptionalchildren.org/search?query=action+alerts.

"Membership in a national association amplifies your voice and your power. When the organization can show it speaks for a lot of people, the message will spread to a broader audience. Politicians are aware of the number of people an organization represents—the more people, the more influence." (Jonathan Fansmith, personal correspondence, August 16, 2022)

In short, membership in a national organization will amplify your voice so that Congress knows your perspective is shared by many others. There is power in numbers. Advocacy is both an individual sport and a team sport.

ADVOCATING WITH THE EXECUTIVE BRANCH

As advocates, it is important to know which offices of the White House and which federal agencies are involved in your issue areas. There are likely to be many, including staff of the White House at OMB and DPC. With their overarching authority for multiple federal agencies and ensuring the unfolding of the president's agenda across the entire federal government, they can be quite influential in moving or blocking a policy initiative. In addition, small independent federal agencies, which often have unique missions and direct contacts in the White House, may be pivotal for advocacy. If engaging with an executive agency, determine if the person is a civil servant (government employee with no political affiliation) or a political appointee who serves so long as the president is in office.

ARTIFACTS FOR ADVOCACY

Multiple resources from both the legislative and executive branches are readily available to inform your advocacy work. These resources can be used to inform you about the four Ps and provide critical background. They may be prospective—alerting you to upcoming events—or retrospective—providing recordings of past hearings or press releases from committee chairs. The Congressional Research Service offers a guide to resources for conducting legislative research (*Legislative history research*, 2016). Resources are ever changing as events unfold. Checking websites and searching online regularly will enable you to stay up to date. Below are some key resources that will deepen your understanding of policy making and enhance your effectiveness as an advocate.

Committee and Subcommittee Activities: Hearings, Markups, and More

At the nucleus of the policy work of Congress lies committees. The committee of jurisdiction over the issues you are working on is a key resource for you. For example, if you are concerned about education matters, the website of the Committee on Education and Labor in the House of Representatives[7] should be a favorite for you. Consider what can be found here. There are recordings of hearings, written testimony of witnesses, lists of committee and subcommittee members, press releases, a schedule of upcoming events, a description of the jurisdiction of the committee, letters written by the chair of the committee, a list of legislation pending in the committee for consideration, committee reports that accompany legislation the committee has adopted, fact sheets, and a form to fill out to receive the newsletter. Virtually all hearings and markups are also streamed live from

---

7. For more information, see https://edlabor.house.gov/.

committee websites. Watching them provides an excellent opportunity to get up to speed on the matter but also to learn the perspectives of the members of the committee through the statements they make and the questions they ask.

Note that often, particularly in the House, the committee website is hosted by the chair of the committee and reflects the chair's priorities and views, not those of the entire committee. The ranking minority member of the committee often has very different views that may be found on a separate website. For example, as of 2022, Ranking Member of the Committee on Education and Labor Virginia Foxx (R-NC) hosts a website for the Republican members of the Committee.[8] It features her press releases and a separate newsletter for sign-up.

Other Statements from Members of Congress

Whenever either the House or the Senate is in session, it can be watched live via C-SPAN, or it can be reviewed from videos as well as an official daily written record. All official proceedings are transcribed in the *Congressional Record*. Archives are available for review and research going back to 1913 on https://www.congress .gov/congressional-record.

In addition to dialogue on the floor of the House or Senate, members of Congress often communicate through letters—sometimes to chairs of committees about their priorities, concerns, or objections and sometimes to representatives of the administration. Some communications are internal, and others are intended for public consumption. A common vehicle is the "Dear Colleague" letter, which several members of Congress will sign and submit to the chair of a committee or to leadership, clarifying a request or a concern (see textbox 3.4, "Dear Colleague" Letters in the House and Senate). Such letters can indicate widespread support for the perspective in the letter when numerous signatories are included.

Status of Bills Introduced

In your advocacy work, you may want to point to a specific bill that has been introduced as you urge your member of Congress to become a cosponsor. All bills that have been introduced, in either the House or the Senate, can be found on the Congress.gov website. Bills can be searched by the year they were introduced, the name of the bill, the member who introduced the bill, and more. In addition, you can find out if there are cosponsors and who they are, whether a bill has been marked up in committee, a summary of the bill, and the text of the bill. You can search for all bills that have been introduced in a particular content area, such as education. You can also link to a committee to determine what bills have been referred to that committee.

---

8. For more information, see https://republicans-edlabor.house.gov/.

Reports from the Congressional Research Service

I think of the Congressional Research Service (CRS) as the brain trust that supports Congress. When I worked on Capitol Hill, we routinely met with and relied on CRS staff members to provide background information and analysis, especially if we were considering a new and far-reaching policy proposal. CRS is a division of the Library of Congress, which is part of the legislative branch of the federal government. It was designed to support Congress with impartial information and analysis.

Given the routine turnover among congressional staff and members of Congress, an institutional memory with deep policy knowledge and history plays a significant role in grounding policy decisions. CRS is staffed by content experts in every area of policy that the federal government addresses, many of whom spend their careers there. The staff respond to requests from congressional offices for summaries or background information or analysis about the potential impact of a policy provision or the status of legislation, such as appropriations bills. In addition, CRS routinely issues reports on salient topics of the day. Whatever your policy priority, you will want to search online for CRS reports on the subject. Reports are available to the public.

Documents from the Government Accountability Office

The Government Accountability Office (GAO) provides heads of executive agencies and Congress with fact-based nonpartisan information intended to improve government and save taxpayer dollars. It carries out audits, evaluations, and investigations and provides legal analysis at the behest of members of Congress. GAO frequently provides testimony to Congress and may issue legal decisions. Sometimes legislation will include mandated studies and reports from GAO. For example, in the CARES Act, GAO was required to issue bimonthly reports

> "Three things I constantly check are CRS and GAO reports and committee websites. There is no writing I have done without utilizing CRS and GAO reports. These weren't things that I knew existed before I began to understand policy as a doctoral student. Since I now understand that policy is central to all my research, I tap into these resources regularly.
>
> "I sometimes use hearings that are recorded on committee websites in my classes. For example, when I was in the House, the committee conducted a hearing on trauma-informed care. I use this hearing in my class for preservice teachers. In general, instructors in higher education do not realize these resources on committee websites are available or that they even exist." (Ashley White, personal correspondence, September 23, 2022)

on the impact of COVID-19.[9] Congress and executive agencies are generally quite attentive to GAO reports, as they often address high-profile matters. All of GAO's publications are online and available to the public. Like CRS, GAO is an important source of information and background for advocates.

Developments from the White House and Federal Agencies

Whenever the White House is pushing a major initiative, such as a new budget proposal, there will be multiple sets of information about it available on their website, including press releases, fact sheets, summaries, and videos of the president. Likewise, when a federal agency issues new guidance, a new fact sheet, a letter to interested parties, a proposed regulation, or set of priorities, it will be available on their website. Programs run by a department will be listed with summaries, competition dates and requirements, lists of grants recipients, and more. The *Federal Register* is the key communication vehicle for the executive branch, serving as the official vehicle for the federal government regarding rules, proposed rules, and notices, for example, of negotiated rule-making sessions. It also includes executive orders from the White House and other presidential documents. It is published every weekday. You can sign up for notifications related to your area of interest.

As noted in chapter 3, another set of offices of the executive branch that routinely issues high-profile reports are the inspector generals (IGs). With IG offices distributed across numerous federal agencies, they are designed to be independent and nonpartisan with the goal of preventing and detecting waste, fraud, and abuse throughout the federal government. IGs may conduct investigations and evaluations and issue reports to Congress with findings and recommendations. Such reports generally garner significant attention and can be helpful in understanding both the political and policy aspects of your advocacy work.

CONNECTING RESEARCH, PRACTICE, AND POLICY

"In higher education, advocacy must become a part of our academic work. Advocacy through policy work would be valued more if it were a consideration in tenure. Now the triumvirate is publishing, teaching, and service—and people don't conceptualize policy advocacy as service." (Ashley White, personal correspondence, September 23, 2022)

Experts and scholars in most fields do not have a direct path to enabling their work to inform policy. Historically, academic endeavors have not been integrally related to policy making, as discussed in chapter 1; however, that is changing. Courses

---

9. For more information, see https://www.gao.gov/coronavirus.

in education policy and politics are increasingly being offered in graduate education programs. Doctoral students are encouraged to pursue policy fellowships or internships in the offices of members of Congress, with national associations, and in federal executive agencies. National associations and the federal government are investing in connecting research, practice, and policy through funded policy fellowships. These include the American Educational Research Association's Congressional Fellowship, the U.S. Department of Energy's Albert Einstein Distinguished Educator Fellowship Program, the American Association for the Advancement of Science's Science and Technology Policy Fellowships, and the Joseph P. Kennedy Jr. Foundation's Public Policy Fellowship. Some institutions of higher education have begun policy fellowships in support of linking research and scholarship to policy. Stanford University has developed the Scholars in Service program, which places and supports faculty in a range of settings where they can inform and affect policy, including offices of members of Congress, the White House, and federal agencies.

"Internships on the Hill are powerful experiences for researchers and advocates. I can't recommend them enough, especially for people of color, disabled persons, and other marginalized groups. Congressional offices are always looking for interns. Even if you intern for three weeks, or with an interest group or a federal agency, you will learn so much. If you want to influence change, you have to learn how things work, and the best way to do that is to experience it from inside the process." (Ashley White, personal correspondence, September 23, 2022)

In addition, doctoral programs can encourage scholars to connect their research to policy throughout their programs. This could be done through activities and assignments that encourage scholars to make that connection. Regularly tweeting out research findings or pursuits and links to research articles with policy implications can make a difference. An admired colleague, Professor Colleen Thoma of Virginia Commonwealth University, suggested that perhaps the dissertation should include a chapter 6: "Implications for Policy."

"Doctoral students need to know they can and should be a part of policy making. They need to understand that it is essential to our work as researchers and advocates of our programs, of teachers and students, and for public education in general. All the research and writing in the world won't change policy. People on the Hill aren't looking for you. You have to find them." (Ashley White, personal correspondence, September 23, 2022)

Research indicates that the doctoral course I developed and taught on behalf of the Higher Education Consortium for Special Education, the Short Course in Education Policy and Politics, generates continued policy advocacy work by participants as they carry out their various professional roles (Nagro, Shepherd, West, & Nagy, 2018; Nagro, Shepherd, Knackstedt, et al., 2020).

PARTICIPATING IN A COMMITTEE HEARING OR A TOWN HALL MEETING

If you have established yourself with a congressional office as an expert, or if the national association to which you belong promotes you as an expert on a particular topic, you may be considered to provide testimony at a committee hearing. This is a great honor and can be quite persuasive as hearings are generally well attended by members of Congress and virtually always livestreamed to the public and archived on committee websites.[10] Your testimony becomes an official part of the committee record and is used to inform the committee's decision making. Having a platform to provide findings and recommendations in this forum can be very influential. The staff of the committee provide guidance in preparing for the hearing. In this forum, being succinct remains critical. Witnesses generally have just five minutes to present their perspective. Committee chairs take that seriously and will indicate when your time is up. You may submit written testimony that is much longer and will provide an opportunity for more background. That is also submitted as part of the official record. If you are fortunate enough to have been invited to testify before a hearing, you will want to have a good understanding of the relevant four Ps and consult with a government relations expert at the national association where you belong who can guide you in developing your remarks.

> "The silver bullet in testimony is lived experience. This can break down walls of political and policy differences." (Kuna Tavalin, personal correspondence, August 17, 2022)

Another way to have input into a hearing is to submit possible questions to a member of Congress who sits on the committee so that they may ask those questions of the witnesses during the hearing. Committee staff will often reach out to constituents and experts and request suggestions for such questions. This input assists the policy maker in asking pertinent questions relevant to their district or state and that reflect expert understanding.

Most members of Congress routinely hold town hall meetings with their constituents, especially during election years. Times and dates are posted on the

---

10. For more information, see https://www.help.senate.gov/hearings.

member's website, where you can sign up to speak or find directions as to how to sign up. These are excellent opportunities to engage with your elected officials, as your representative or senator is away from the hectic pace of Washington in a more relaxed environment with more time to listen attentively. The same strategies apply as when preparing for a meeting with a congressional office. Attending with a group of constituents, and frequently participating in town hall meetings, will amplify your message.

IMPACT OF THE COVID-19 PANDEMIC ON ADVOCACY ACTIVITIES

Like all other activities in our society, advocacy has been affected by the COVID-19 epidemic. Prior to the pandemic, in-person meetings in Washington were a staple of the advocacy experience. Going to Capitol Hill to the office of your senator and representative or to a federal agency is a memorable experience. The unplanned situations are often highlights for advocates—running into a senator in the hallway and saying hello, riding the mini-train that connects the Senate and House office buildings to the Capitol, and eating in one of the many dining rooms in congressional office buildings leave lasting impressions. These provide a sense of being part of the "action" and demystify the operations of Congress or an executive agency.

As of 2022 advocacy activities have taken on a hybrid nature, with many meetings taking place online or by telephone, but increasingly in person as buildings open up further. Congressional offices report increased interaction with constituents through video and phone connections and increased use of websites. Furthermore, many offices report a likelihood that virtual connections with constituents and advocates will continue to be a robust part of their engagement. Advocates have experienced success with virtual advocacy and the expanded opportunity to bring in constituents without the need to travel to Washington. As the situation continues to evolve, you may want to check with the office you are visiting to see if they have COVID-specific protocols.

> "The combination of COVID and January 6 means that federal agencies and Congress are not as accessible as they used to be. There is a general feeling of nervousness. It doesn't feel like a warm and inviting environment like it used to. It's not as easy to access and navigate." (Lindsay Fryer, personal correspondence, September 22, 2022)

IMPACT OF THE JANUARY 6, 2021, EVENTS AT THE CAPITOL ON SECURITY MEASURES

The breach of the Capitol on June 6, 2021, resulted in a significant rethinking of security at the Capitol and congressional office buildings—all of which are attached by underground tunnels. As of 2022, the Capitol Visitors Center, which provides public access to the Capitol, was reopened to the public and increased access is anticipated. Members of Congress, along with the Capitol Police and the Architect of the Capitol, continue to devise new safety protocols. You may want to check with the office you are planning to meet with to see if there are additional security requirements beyond the usual entry through security screening devices.

IN CLOSING

As you close this book, I hope you do so with excitement and determination. The four Ps will inform your advocacy journey no matter what your particular role or issue area may be—as a constituent, an expert, an interested party, or all three. Know that your engagement makes a difference and that if you are not at the table, someone else will take your seat, and they may add you to the menu. Don't let that happen. Take your seat at the table and don't ever leave. This is my call to action.

TAKEAWAYS: ADVOCACY

1. Let your passion determine the policy issues for your advocacy.
2. The first rule of advocacy is to build a relationship with the office of the policy maker you hope to work with.
3. Do your homework before meeting with the policy maker's office.
4. Be sure to have data, information, a personal story, and no more than three "asks" when you meet with your congressional delegation.
5. Stay in touch with your congressional delegation regularly, even when they do not agree with your position.
6. Craft your message so that it will be heard by your audience.
7. Advocacy is as much about educating and preventing poor policy from progressing as it is about promoting effective policy solutions.
8. Advocate as an individual and as part of a national organization.
9. Explore the rich set of policy artifacts to inform your advocacy, including committee reports, CRS reports, GAO reports, IG reports, and documents found in the *Federal Register*.
10. Connect your expertise to your policy interests.
11. Consider speaking at a town hall meeting sponsored by a member of your congressional delegation.
12. Be aware of the potential impact of the COVID-19 epidemic and of the events of January 6, 2021, at the Capitol in terms of protocol implications for advocacy meetings with congressional offices.

Wrapping Up

....

Being at the Table, Not on the Menu

1. There is always more to learn.
2. Do your homework . . . over and over again.
3. Set up accounts on Twitter and Instagram; follow your congressional delegation. Tweet at them about your policy-relevant research, information about your policy area, and relevant data from their state or district.
4. Sign up for newsletters and announcements—from your congressional delegation, from relevant committees, from the *Federal Register*, and from relevant news outlets.
5. Attend town hall meetings with members of your congressional delegation.
6. Politics matters—there is no escaping it.
7. Procedures and processes: make them your friends so that they will not become your enemies.
8. Individual relationships are the foundation of advocacy.
9. Share personal stories about your policy area; these are what will be remembered the most.
10. Meetings with congressional staff are as important as meetings with members of Congress.
11. The squeaky wheel gets the grease: volume and frequency count.
12. Know when to declare victory and when to hold out (i.e., know "when to hold 'em and when to fold 'em").
13. Policy making is a short game and a long game; you gotta play both.
14. Cultivate champions among policy makers; when your issue is a priority for them, they will go to bat for it in the room where it happens.
15. Pay attention to election cycles and their impact on individual policy makers.
16. One person can make a huge difference.
17. Frame your policy work as part of your professional role, not as an "add-on."
18. As a constituent, you are the employer of elected officials. You hire 'em and you fire 'em—at the ballot box, that is. Show up like the employer.
19. You are an expert in your area, whatever that may be. You have information and knowledge that the policy maker does not have. Show up like an expert.
20. Educating others about your policy issues is part of advocacy.

....

21. Check your policy proposal: Is there capacity to implement it? Are all relevant voices at the table? Who is advantaged and who is disadvantaged? Will there be unintended consequences? Are you using the right policy tools?
22. Preventing a potentially damaging policy proposal from moving forward is as important as promoting an effective policy solution.
23. Know your allies and your opponents. Adjust accordingly.
24. Language matters—in policy and in messaging: *shall* versus *may*, *investment* versus *expenditure*.
25. Policy making will not tolerate a vacuum: if you are not at the table, someone is in your seat.
26. Strive to support the policy maker and the staff in doing their jobs well.
27. Be a trusted resource—eyes and ears on the ground.
28. Remember the power of third-party endorsers, people who can amplify your message and may be more effective at delivering it than you are.
29. Remember that the world of policy making is a different culture from yours. Learn the norms and follow them as you engage.
30. Always show up as part of the solution.
31. It's a team sport. Build your team.

References

....

A guide to the rulemaking process. (2011, January). Office of the Federal Register. https://www.federalregister.gov/uploads/2011/01/the_rulemaking_process.pdf

About. (n.d.). U.S. Government Accountability Office. https://www.gao.gov/about

About the committee system. (n.d.). United States Senate. https://www.senate.gov/about/origins-foundations/committee-system.htm

Abrams, A. (2021, March 11). One year into the pandemic, the white house aims to prioritize people with disabilities. *Time.* https://time.com/5946183/white-house-disability-policy-director/

ADA history—In their own words: Part one. (n.d.). Administration for Community Living. https://acl.gov/ada/origins-of-the-ada

Adequate yearly progress (AYP): Implementation of the No Child Left Behind Act (2004, July 28). EveryCRSReport.com. https://www.everycrsreport.com/reports/RL32495.html

Agency use of guidance documents. (2021). Congressional Research Service. https://www.everycrsreport.com/files/2021-04-19_LSB10591_9477746a9161f3ee6f2d127a70eb84cdcec6e4df.pdf

American Association of Colleges for Teacher Education. (2015). Internal memo.

American Recovery and Reinvestment Act of 2009 (P.L. 111-5): Summary and Legislative History. (2009, April 20). EveryCRSReport.com. https://www.everycrsreport.com/reports/R40537.html#:~:text=ARRA%20provides%20almost%20%24800%20billion,departments%20and%2011%20independent%20agencies

American Rescue Plan Act, H. R. 1319, 117th Cong. (2021). https://www.congress.gov/bill/117th-congress/house-bill/1319

Americans with Disabilities Act, Anderson, J. E. (1999). *Public policymaking* (4th ed.). Houghton Mifflin.

Appointment and confirmation of executive branch leadership: An overview (R44083). (2021, March 17). Congressional Research Service. https://fas.org/sgp/crs/misc/R44083.pdf

Appropriations 101. (2022, June 22). Committee for a Responsible Federal Budget. https://www.crfb.org/papers/appropriations-101

Bacchi, C. (n.d.). *Introducing WPR.* WordPress. https://carolbacchi.com/about/

Bacchi, C. (2012). Introducing the "what's the problem represented to be?" approach. In A. Bletsas & C. Beasley (Eds.), *Engaging with Carol Bacchi: Strategic interventions and exchanges* (pp. 21–24). University of Adelaide Press. https://www.adelaide.edu.au/press/system/files/media/documents/2019-04/uap-engaging-ebook.pdf

Balancing work and life with your unique abilities. (2019, March). *DIVERSEability Magazine.* https://diverseabilitymagazine.com/2019/03/balancing-work-life-abilities/

Barlow, R. (2021, January 19). Biden's top four priorities, explained by leading BU experts. *BU Today.* https://www.bu.edu/articles/2021/bidens-top-four-priorities-explained-by-leading-bu-experts/

Bendix, W. (2016). Bypassing congressional committees: Parties, panel rosters, and deliberative processes. *Legislative Studies Quarterly, 41*(3), 690–691.

Berman, P., & McLaughlin, M. W. (1976). Implementation of educational innovation. *Educational Forum, 40,* 345–370.

....

Biden, J. R., Jr. (2021, January 20). *Executive order on advancing racial equity and support for underserved communities through the federal government.* White House. https://www .whitehouse.gov/briefing-room/presidential-actions/2021/01/20/executive-order -advancing-racial-equity-and-support-for-underserved-communities-through-the -federal-government/

Birkland, T. A. (2016). *An introduction to the policy process: Theories, concepts, and models of public policy making.* Routledge.

Brenson, L. (2020). *Racial diversity among top staff in Senate personal offices.* Joint Center. https://jointcenter.org/racial-diversity-among-top-staff-in-senate-personal-offices/

Broadwater, L., Cochrane, E., & Pariapiano, A. (2022, April 1). As earmarks return to Congress, lawmakers rush to steer money home. *New York Times.* https://www.nytimes .com/2022/04/01/us/politics/congress-earmarks.html?referringSource=articleShare

Brown, E. (2017a, March 8). Senate overturns Obama-era regulations on teacher preparation. *Washington Post.* https://www.washingtonpost.com/local/education/senate -overturns-obama-era-regulations-on-teacher-preparation/2017/03/08/b8cf127a-041c -11e7-b9fa-ed727b644a0b_story.html

Brown, E. (2017b, March 9). Senate scraps Obama regulations on school accountability. *Washington Post.* https://www.washingtonpost.com/local/education/senate -scraps-obama-regulations-on-school-accountability/2017/03/09/e9279932-04e5-11e7 -b1e9-a05d3c21f7cf_story.html?utm_term=.4c3133fe4b0b&itid=lk_inline_manual_14

Brudnick, I. A. (2020). *Support offices in the House of Representatives: Roles and authorities* (RL33220). Congressional Research Service. https://sgp.fas.org/crs/misc/RL33220.pdf

Carey, M. P. (2021). *Negotiated rulemaking: In brief* (R46756). Congressional Research Service. https://crsreports.congress.gov/product/pdf/R/R46756/2

CDC: 1 in 4 US adults live with a disability. (2018, August 16). Centers for Disease Control and Prevention. https://www.cdc.gov/media/releases/2018/p0816-disability.html

Cioffi, C., & Saksa, J. (2022, February 9). Hill staffers are organizing. What could their unions look like? *Roll Call.* https://rollcall.com/2022/02/09/hill-staffers-unionizing -what-could-that-look-like/

Committee for Education Funding. (2017). *Why 5¢ makes sense: Increase our investment in education to 5 cents of every federal dollar.* https://cef.org/advocacy/5-cents-makes-sense-old/

Committees. (n.d.). United States Senate. https://www.senate.gov/committees/index.htm

Committees of the U.S. Congress. (n.d.). Congress.gov. Retrieved January 7, 2022, from https:// www.congress.gov/committees

Communicating with Congress: Perceptions of citizen advocacy on capitol hill. (2011). Congressional Management Foundation. https://www.congressfoundation.org/storage/docu ments/CMF_Pubs/cwc-perceptions-of-citizen-advocacy.pdf

Congress on social media 2020: Pandemic year brings increase in social dialogue, decrease in legislation. (n.d.). Quorum. https://www.quorum.us/wp-content/uploads/2020/12 /Quorum_Report_CongressOnSocialMediaFINAL.pdf

Congressional careers: Service tenure and patters of member service, 1789–2021 (R41545). (2021, January 5). Congressional Research Service. https://sgp.fas.org/crs/misc/R41545.pdf

Congressional Research Service. (2017). *Committee types and roles.* https://crsreports .congress.gov/product/pdf/RS/98-241

Constitutional amendments and major civil rights acts of Congress referenced in Black Americans in Congress. (n.d.). History, Art & Archives: US House of Representatives. https:// history.house.gov/Exhibitions-and-Publications/BAIC/Historical-Data/Constitution al-Amendments-and-Legislation/

Core Opportunity Resources for Equity and Excellence Act, S. 37, 114th Cong. (2015). https://www.congress.gov/bill/114th-congress/senate-bill/37?q=%7B%22search%22 %3A%5B%22S.+37%22%5D%7D&s=8&r=3

Cost, J. (2018, February 26). The NRA is not your typical interest group. *National Review.* https://www.nationalreview.com/2018/02/nra-members-gun-owners-make-power ful-voting-bloc-motivated-by-ideology/

Council of State Governments. (2021, May 4). *The impact of 2020 census data on Congressional seats*. WordPress. https://web.csg.org/tcs/2021/05/04/the-impact-of-2020-census-data-on-congressional-seats/

Cunningham, D. H., & Wycoff, J. (2013). Policy makers and researchers schooling each other: Lessons in educational policy from New York. *Association for Education Finance and Policy, 8*(3), 275–286. https://direct.mit.edu/edfp/article/8/3/275/10171/Policy-Makers-and-Researchers-Schooling-Each-Other

Darling-Hammond, L. (2012, March 20). Value-added evaluation hurts teaching. *Education Week*. https://www.edweek.org/teaching-learning/opinion-value-added-evaluation-hurts-teaching/2012/03

Delaney, J. (2021, January 7). The horror of the Confederate flag in the U.S. Capitol. *Boston Globe*. https://www.bostonglobe.com/2021/01/07/opinion/horror-confederate-flag-us-capitol/

Desjardins, L. (2022, August 16). How Congress overcame deep differences to pass major legislation. *PBS News Hour*. https://www.pbs.org/newshour/show/how-congress-overcame-deep-differences-to-pass-major-legislation

Disability Rights Education & Defense Fund. (2015, August 24). *The making of the ADA—Justin Dart* [Video]. YouTube. https://www.youtube.com/watch?v=ywTVusm_WAo

Discretionary spending in fiscal year 2020: An infographic. (2021, April 30). Congressional Budget Office. https://www.cbo.gov/publication/57172

Duncan, A. (2009, October 22). *Teacher preparation: Reforming the uncertain profession*. Ed.gov. https://www2.ed.gov/news/pressreleases/2009/10/10222009a.html

Eckman, S. J. (2021). *Apportionment and redistricting following the 2020 census* (IN11360). Congressional Research Service. https://crsreports.congress.gov/product/pdf/IN/IN11360

Educational accountability and secretarial waiver authority under section 9401 of the Elementary and Secondary Education Act (R42328). (2012, June 1). Congressional Research Service. https://www.everycrsreport.com/files/20120601_R42328_3d55caf06417d087c4c3edbf0950dc9b46ed0122.pdf

Elementary and Secondary Education Act of 1965: H. R. 2362, 89th Cong., 1st sess., public law 89-10 (1965).

Equality of opportunity: The making of the Americans with Disabilities Act. (n.d.). National Council on Disability. https://ncd.gov/publications/2010/equality_of_opportunity_the_making_of_the_americans_with_disabilities_act

Eunice Kennedy Shriver's story. (n.d.). Special Olympics. https://www.specialolympics.org/eunice-kennedy-shriver/bio

Every Student Succeeds Act. Pub.L. 114-95. 129 Stat. 1802. (2015). https://www.congress.gov/bill/114th-congress/senate-bill/1177

Fact sheet: The President's budget for fiscal year 2022. (2022). White House. https://www.whitehouse.gov/wp-content/uploads/2021/05/FINAL-FY22-Budget-Overview-Fact-Sheet.pdf

Farley, A. N., Leonardi, B., & Donnor, J. K. (2021). Perpetuating inequalities: The role of political distraction in education policy. *Education Policy, 35*(2), 163–179.

Federal grants to state and local governments: An historical perspective on contemporary issues (R40638). (2019, May 22). Congressional Research Service. https://fas.org/sgp/crs/misc/R40638.pdf

Federal net interest costs: A primer. (2020, December). Congressional Budget Office. https://www.cbo.gov/publication/56910

Filibusters and cloture in the Senate (RL30360). (2017). Congressional Research Service. https://crsreports.congress.gov/product/pdf/RL/RL30360

Finn, C., Manno, B., & Ravitch, D. (2000, December 14). *Education 2002: Getting the job done—a memorandum to the President-Elect and the 107th Congress*. Thomas B. Fordham Institute. https://fordhaminstitute.org/national/research/education-2001-getting-job-done-memorandum-president-elect-and-107th-congress

Fischer, D. (2021). *Nebraska breakfast*. https://www.fischer.senate.gov/public/index.cfm/nebraska-breakfast

Ford, G. R. (1975, December 2). *Statement on signing the Education for All Handicapped Children Act of 1975.* National Archives. https://www.fordlibrarymuseum.gov/library/speeches/750707.htm

Fowler, F. C. (2013). *Policy studies for educational leaders* (4th ed.). Pearson Education.

Gaffney, J. M. (2021). *Executive orders: An introduction* (R46738). Congressional Research Service. https://crsreports.congress.gov/product/pdf/R/R46738

Gardner, D. P. (1983, April). *A nation at risk: The imperative for educational reform: A report to the nation and the Secretary of Education, United States Department of Education.* National Commission on Excellence in Education. https://files.eric.ed.gov/fulltext/ED226006.pdf

Garvey, T. (2017). *A brief overview of rulemaking and judicial review* (R41546). Congressional Research Service. https://sgp.fas.org/crs/misc/R41546.pdf

Gazis, O., & Becket, S. (2020, August 18). *Senate Intelligence Committee releases final report on 2016 Russian interference.* CBS News. https://www.cbsnews.com/news/senate-report-russian-interference-2016-us-election/

Glassman, M. (2018, July 24). *House turnover rates explained.* Legislative Procedure. https://www.legislativeprocedure.com/blog/2018/7/24/thinking-about-house-turnover

GovTrack. (2021). *Statistics and historical comparisons.* https://www.govtrack.us/congress/bills/statistics

Grumet, J. (2019, October 31). *Congress can be partisan and productive to benefit citizens.* The Hill. https://thehill.com/opinion/campaign/468354-congress-can-be-partisan-and-productive-to-benefit-citizens

Guidance on "long COVID" as a disability under the ADA, Section 504, and Section 1557. (2021). U.S. Department of Health and Human Services. https://www.hhs.gov/civil-rights/for-providers/civil-rights-covid19/guidance-long-covid-disability/index.html

Handicapped Children's Protection Act, Pub. L. No. 99-372 100 Stat. 796 (1986). https://www.govinfo.gov/content/pkg/STATUTE-100/pdf/STATUTE-100-Pg796.pdf#page=1

Hartranft, B. (n.d.). *How a bill becomes a law flowchart.* Congressional Webpage. https://congressionalwebpage.weebly.com/how-a-bill-becomes-a-law.html

HECSE Short Course. (2023). Higher Education Consortium for Special Education. https://hecse.net/events/hecse-short-course/

Henig, J. (2021, February 9). "Data" has become a dirty word to public education advocates. It doesn't have to be. *Education Week.* https://www.edweek.org/policy-politics/opinion-data-has-become-a-dirty-word-to-public-education-advocates-it-doesnt-have-to-be/2021/02

Herszenhorn, D. M. (2016, June 28). House Benghazi report finds no new evidence of wrongdoing by Hillary Clinton. *New York Times.* https://www.nytimes.com/2016/06/29/us/politics/hillary-clinton-benghazi.html

History of bipartisanship. (2021, March). Bipartisan Policy Center. https://bipartisanpolicy.org/history-of-bipartisanship/

Holyoke, T. T. (2021). *Interest groups and lobbying pursuing political interests in America* (2nd ed.). Routledge.

House committees. (n.d.). History, Art & Archives: United States House of Representatives. https://history.house.gov/Education/Fact-Sheets/Committees-Fact-Sheet2/

House Committee on Appropriations. (2022, June 30). *Appropriations committee approves fiscal year 2023 labor, health and human services, education, and related agencies funding bill* [Press release]. https://appropriations.house.gov/news/press-releases/appropriations-committee-approves-fiscal-year-2023-labor-health-and-human#:~:text=WASHINGTON%20%E2%80%94%20The%20House%20Appropriations%20Committee,%E2%80%93%2013%20percent%20%E2%80%93%20above%202022

How old is Congress? (2017). Quorum. https://www.quorum.us/data-driven-insights/the-current-congress-is-among-the-oldest-in-history/

Hudiburg, J. A. (2019, May 21). *House rules changes affecting committee procedure in the 116th Congress (2019–2020)* (R45731). Congressional Research Service. https://crsreports.congress.gov/product/pdf/R/R45731

Incumbents defeated in 2018 congressional elections. (n.d.). Ballotpedia. https://ballotpedia
.org/Incumbents_defeated_in_2018_congressional_elections

Infoplease Staff. (2020, March 17). *Timeline of U.S. government shutdowns.* Infoplease. https://
www.infoplease.com/history/us/timeline-of-us-government-shutdowns

Introduction to the legislative process in the U.S. Congress (R42843). (2020). Congressional
Research Service. https://sgp.fas.org/crs/misc/R42843.pdf

Jabbow, G. (2011, January 6). *Schoolhouse rock—how a bill becomes a law* [Video]. YouTube.
https://www.youtube.com/watch?v=FBpdxEMelR0

Jones, C. O. (1984). *An introduction to the study of public policy* (3rd ed.). Brooks/Cole.

Jundt, T. (2010). *Ill fares the land.* Penguin.

K-12 Education: Highlights of the No Child Left Behind Act of 2001 (P.L. 107-110) (RL31284).
(2008, January 7). Congressional Research Service. https://crsreports.congress.gov
/product/pdf/RL/RL31284

Keeping All Students Safe Act, H. R. 3474, 117th Cong. (2021a). https://www.congress.gov
/bill/117th-congress/house-bill/3474?q=%7B%22search%22%3A%5B%22keeping+all
+students+safe+act%22%2C%22keeping%22%2C%22all%22%2C%22students%22%2C
%22safe%22%2C%22act%22%5D%7D&s=1&r=1

Keeping All Students Safe Act, S. 1858, 117th Cong. (2021b). https://www.congress.gov
/bill/117th-congress/senate-bill/1858?q=%7B%22search%22%3A%5B%22keeping
+all+students+safe+act%22%2C%22keeping%22%2C%22all%22%2C%22students%22
%2C%22safe%22%2C%22act%22%5D%7D&s=1&r=2

Kingdon, J. W. (1989). *Congressmen's voting decisions.* University of Michigan Press.

Kingdon, J. W. (2010). *Agendas, alternatives and public policies* (2nd ed.). Longman.

Klein, N. (2007). *Shock doctrine the rise of disaster capitalism.* Henry Holt and Company.

Knott, K. (2022, September 14). New Title IX rules get 235,000 comments. *Inside Higher Ed.*
https://www.insidehighered.com/news/2022/09/14/thousands-weigh-new-title-ix
-rules

Koedel, C., Mihaly, K., & Rockoff, J. E. (2015). Value-added modeling: A review. *Econom-
ics of Education Review, 47,* 180–195. https://www.gsb.columbia.edu/mygsb/faculty
/research/pubfiles/11584/value-added.pdf

Kraft, M. E., & Furlong, S. R. (2021). *Public policy, politics, analysis, and alternatives* (7th ed.).
Sage.

Kuenzi, J. J. (2018, November 16). *Teacher preparation policies and issues in the Higher Education
Act* (R45407). Congressional Research Service. https://fas.org/sgp/crs/misc/R45407.pdf

Ladson-Billings, G. (2008). A letter to our next president. *Journal of Teacher Education, 59*(3),
235–239.

Ladson-Billings, G. (2013). Lack of achievement or loss of opportunity? In P. L. Carter &
K. G. Welner (Eds.), *Closing the opportunity gap: What America must do to give every child an
even chance* (pp. 11–22). Oxford University Press.

Legislative history research: A guide to resources for congressional staff. (2016, July 6). Congressional Research Service. https://www.everycrsreport.com/files/20160706_R41865
_4f340c8f2dfb2a04feaea853f72a60ec2d1a9bde.pdf

Liptak, A., & Kao, J. (2022, June 30). The major Supreme Court decisions in 2022. *New York
Times.* https://www.nytimes.com/interactive/2022/06/21/us/major-supreme-court
-cases-2022.html

List of members of the United States Congress by longevity of service. (n.d.). In *Wikipedia.*
https://en.wikipedia.org/wiki/List_of_members_of_the_United_States_Congress_by
_longevity_of_service

Lobbying. (n.d.). Internal Revenue Service. https://www.irs.gov/charities-non-profits
/lobbying

Lomax, E. D., & Kuenzi, J. J. (2012, December 11). *Value-added modeling for teacher effectiveness*
(R41051). Congressional Research Service. https://sgp.fas.org/crs/misc/R41051.pdf

Loyola, M. (2016). Almost a miracle. *City Journal.* https://www.city-journal.org/html
/almost-miracle-14734.html

Lynch, M. S. (2020, December 3). *Lifting the earmark moratorium: Frequently asked questions* (R45429). Congressional Research Service. https://crsreports.congress.gov/product/pdf/R/R45429

Lynn, L. E. (1978). *Knowledge and policy: The uncertain connection.* National Academy of Sciences.

Manning, S. (2019, June 10). *"What's the problem represented to be?" A policy analysis tool designed by Carol Bacchi and some recent applications in the area of early childhood education policy.* Blog of the New Zealand Association for Research in Education. https://nzare blog.wordpress.com/2019/06/10/wpr-ece/

Manríquez, P. (2022, July 15). "Dear White Staffers" speaks: Inside the effort to unionize capitol hill. *New Republic.* https://newrepublic.com/article/167058/dear-white-staffers-instagram-interview-unionize-capitol-hill

Martin, E. W. (2013). *Breakthrough: Federal special education legislation 1965–1981.* Bardolf & Company.

Mathesz, J. M. (2014, June 6). *An historical perspective to examine how federal policy influenced the definition and evaluation of teacher effectiveness since 1950* [Unpublished doctoral dissertation]. Seton Hall University. https://scholarship.shu.edu/dissertations/2026

May, J. V., & Wildavsky, A. (Eds.). (1978). *The policy cycle.* Sage.

McGuinn, P. J. (2006). *No Child Left Behind and the transformation of federal education policy 1965–2005.* University Press of Kansas.

McLaughlin, V. L., West, J. E., & Anderson, J. A. (2016). Engaging effectively in the policy-making process. *Teacher Education and Special Education, 39*(2), 134–139.

Mead, L. M. (2018). Teaching public policy: Linking policy and politics. *Journal of Public Affairs Education, 19*(3), 389–403. https://www.tandfonline.com/doi/abs/10.1080/1523 6803.2013.12001742

Miles, M. B., & Huberman, M. (1984). *Qualitative data analysis: A sourcebook of new methods.* Sage.

Nagro, S. A., Shepherd, K. G., Knackstedt, K., West, J. E., & Nagy, S. J. (2020). Bridging the gap between research and policy: Fostering advocacy and policy engagement in special education doctoral students. *Journal of Disability Policy Studies, 30*(4), 233–243. https://doi.org/10.1177/1044207319849930

Nagro, S. A., Shepherd, K. G., West, J. E., & Nagy, S. J. (2018). Activating policy and advocacy skills: A strategy for tomorrow's special education leaders. *Journal of Special Education, 53*(2), 67–75. https://doi.org/10.1177/0022466918800705

Nakamura, R. T., & Smallwood, F. (1980). *The politics of policy implementation.* St. Martin's Press.

Natow, R. S. (2017). *Higher education rulemaking.* Johns Hopkins University Press.

Nelson, L. (2017, February 7). How Betsy DeVos became Trump's most controversial nominee. *Vox.* https://www.vox.com/policy-and-politics/2017/2/1/14475290/betsy-devos-confirmation-trump-resist

Nichols, J. (2017, July 28). Disability-rights activists are the real heroes of the health care fight. *National Review.* https://www.thenation.com/article/archive/disability-rights-activists-are-the-real-heroes-of-the-health-care-fight/

No Child Left Behind Act of 2001, P.L. 107-110, 20 U.S.C. § 6319 (2002b). https://www.con gress.gov/bill/107th-congress/house-bill/1/text

No Child Left Behind Act of 2001, Pub. L. No. 107-110 115 Stat. 1425 (2002a). https://www .govinfo.gov/content/pkg/PLAW-107publ110/pdf/PLAW-107publ110.pdf

Number of registered active lobbyists in the United States from 2000 to 2021. (2022, September 30). Statista. https://www.statista.com/statistics/257340/number-of-lobbyists-in-the-us/

Office of Sen. Mike Enzi. (2020, December 2). *Senator Mike Enzi delivers farewell speech on Senate floor.* KULR-8. https://www.kulr8.com/news/wyoming/senator-mike-enzi-delivers-farewell-speech-on-senate-floor/article_d78f74ce-34ed-11eb-bac4-8723f05faab9.html

Oleszek, W. J. (2020). *The "regular order": A perspective* (R46597). Congressional Research Service. https://www.everycrsreport.com/files/2020-11-06_R46597_099cacea85260793d 4b361950c17a3e2b57165e4.pdf

Oleszek, W. J., Oleszek, M. J., Rybicki, E., & Heniff, B. (2020). *Congressional procedures and the policy process* (11th ed.). CQ Press.

Owens, A., & Sunderman, G. L. (2006). *School accountability under NCLB: Aid or obstacle for measuring racial equity.* Civil Rights Project at Harvard University.

Palazzolo, D. (2021 February 11). *Bipartisanship in Congress isn't about being nice—It's about cold, hard numbers.* The Conversation. https://theconversation.com/bipartisanship -in-congress-isnt-about-being-nice-its-about-cold-hard-numbers-153850

Petersen, R. E. (2021, April 23). *Congressional staff: Duties, qualifications, and skills identified by members of Congress for selected positions* (R46262). Congressional Research Service. https://sgp.fas.org/crs/misc/R46262.pdf

Position statement on high-stakes testing. (2000, July). American Educational Research Association. https://www.aera.net/About-AERA/AERA-Rules-Policies/Association-Policies /Position-Statement-on-High-Stakes-Testing

President signs landmark education bill. (2002). White House: President George W. Bush. https://georgewbush-whitehouse.archives.gov/news/releases/2002/01/images /20020108-1_20020108-1-515h.html

Presidential appointee positions requiring Senate confirmation and committees handling nominations (RL30959). (2017). Congressional Research Service. https://www.everycrsreport .com/files/2021-12-28_RL30959_6d0d6e63f911075d984705eff1cbef0cedec4fce.pdf

Pressman, J. L., & Wildavsky, A. (Eds.). (1984). *Implementation.* University of California Press.

Price, D. E. (2021). *The congressional experience: An institution transformed* (4th ed.). Taylor and Francis.

Rainey, R., & Ramsey, A. R. (2022, August 1). Punching in: High court signals coming curbs on agency deference. *Bloomberg Law.* https://news.bloomberglaw.com/daily-labor -report/punching-in-high-court-signals-coming-curbs-on-agency-deference-28

Ravitch, D. (2013). *Reign of error.* Alfred A. Knopf.

Rich, M. (2014, April 26). Obama Administration plans new rules to grade teacher training programs. *New York Times.*

Ripley, R. B., & Franklin, G. A. (1986). *Policy implementation and bureaucracy* (2nd ed.). Dorsey Press.

Rosalsky, G. (2020, November 17). *Are there too many political appointees?* National Public Radio. https://www.npr.org/sections/money/2020/11/17/935430860/are-there-too -many-political-appointees

Rybicki, E. (2021). *Senate consideration of presidential nominations: Committee and floor procedure* (RL31980). Congressional Research Service. https://sgp.fas.org/crs/misc/RL31980.pdf

Saturno, J. V. (2020a). *Authorizations and the appropriations process.* Congressional Research Service. https://sgp.fas.org/crs/misc/R46497.pdf

Saturno, J. V. (2020b). *Introduction to the federal budget process* (R46240). Congressional Research Service. https://crsreports.congress.gov/product/pdf/R/R46240

Schaeffer, K. (2021, January 28). *Racial, ethnic diversity increases yet again with the 117th Congress.* Pew Research Center. https://www.pewresearch.org/fact-tank/2021/01/28 /racial-ethnic-diversity-increases-yet-again-with-the-117th-congress/

Schnell, M. (2022, July 7). *Staffers in eight House offices become first to begin unionization process.* The Hill. https://thehill.com/homenews/house/3564191-staffers-at-eight-house-offices -become-first-to-unionize/

Schuster, B. S. (2013). Highly qualified teachers: Moving forward from *Renee v. Duncan. Harvard Journal on Legislation, 49*(2012), 151–173. https://harvardjol.com/wp-content /uploads/sites/17/2013/09/Schuster1.pdf

Skinner, R. R., & Feder, J. (2014, September 2). *Common core state standards and assessments: Background and issues* (R43711). Congressional Research Service. https://sgp.fas.org/crs /misc/R43711.pdf

Smith v. Robinson, 468 U.S. 992 (1984). https://supreme.justia.com/cases/federal/us /468/992/

Some think tanks blur line between research and lobbying. (2016, August 10). Philanthropy News Digest. https://philanthropynewsdigest.org/news/some-think-tanks-blur-line -between-research-and-lobbying

Spiering, C. (2012, September 6). Actress Kerry Washington warns voters: "Politics is think-ing about you." *Washington Examiner.* https://www.washingtonexaminer.com/actress -kerry-washington-warns-voters-politics-is-thinking-about-you

Sponsorship and cosponsorship of House bills (RS22477). (2019). Congressional Research Ser-vice. https://sgp.fas.org/crs/misc/RS22477.pdf

Sponsorship and cosponsorship of Senate bills (98-279). (2021). Congressional Research Service. https://sgp.fas.org/crs/misc/98-279.pdf

Statistics and historical comparison. (n.d.). GovTrack. https://www.govtrack.us/congress /bills/statistics

Stephens, C. (2010, August 12). *Times watchdog report: No Child Left Behind on the way out, but not anytime soon.* Advance Local Media. https://www.al.com/breaking/2010/08 /times_watchdog_report_no_child.html

Straus, J. R. (2017). *"Dear colleague" letters in the House of Representatives: Past practices and issues for Congress* (R44768). Congressional Research Service. https://www.everycrs report.com/files/20170222_R44768_74705ebfee214b3a6788c25889029d61d83bd45a.pdf

Strauss, V. (2011, November 25). Should value-added models account for poverty? *Wash-ington Post.* https://www.washingtonpost.com/blogs/answer-sheet/post/should-value -added-models-account-for-poverty/2011/11/23/gIQAhwaotN_blog.html

Tackling teacher shortages, House Subcommittee on Labor/HHS/Education Appropria-tions, 117th Cong. (2022) (testimony of Jane E. West). https://docs.house.gov/meetings /AP/AP07/20220525/114831/HHRG-117-AP07-Wstate-WestJ-20220525.pdf

Tackling teacher shortages. (2022, May 25). House Committee on Appropriations. https:// appropriations.house.gov/events/hearings/tackling-teacher-shortages

Teacher preparation issues. (2014, December 3). *Federal Register, 79*(232), 71820–71892. https://www.govinfo.gov/content/pkg/FR-2014-12-03/pdf/2014-28218.pdf

Teacher preparation issues. (2016, October 31). *Federal Register, 81*(210), 75494–75622. https://www.govinfo.gov/content/pkg/FR-2016-10-31/pdf/2016-24856.pdf

Teachers and Parents at the Table Act. H. R. 3246, 115th Cong. (2017). https://www .congress.gov/115/bills/hr3246/BILLS-115hr3246ih.pdf

The Congressional Review Act (CRA): Frequently asked questions (R43992). (2021). Congressio-nal Research Service. https://sgp.fas.org/crs/misc/R43992.pdf

The federal budget in fiscal year 2020: An infographic. (2021, April 30). Congressional Budget Office. https://www.cbo.gov/publication/57170

The Lobbying Disclosure Act at 20: Analysis and issues for Congress (R44292). (2015, Decem-ber 1). Congressional Research Service. https://crsreports.congress.gov/product/pdf/R /R44292/4

The Office of the Parliamentarian in the House and Senate (RS20544). (2018). Congressional Research Service. https://crsreports.congress.gov/product/pdf/RS/RS20544

Title IX and sexual harassment: Education Department proposes new regulations (LSB10268). (2019). Congressional Research Service. https://crsreports.congress.gov/product/pdf /LSB/LSB10268

Topic no. 458 educator expense deduction. (2022, November 1). IRS. https://www.irs.gov /taxtopics/tc458#:~:text=If%20you%27re%20an%20eligible,unreimbursed%20trade%20 or%20business%20expenses.&text=This%20deduction%20is%20for%20expenses%20 paid%20or%20incurred%20during%20the%20tax%20year.

Toward independence: An assessment of federal laws and programs affecting persons with disabil-ities—with legislative recommendations. (1986). National Council on Disability. https:// www.ncd.gov/publications/1986/February1986

Types of legislation. (n.d.). United States Senate. https://www.senate.gov/legislative/com mon/briefing/leg_laws_acts.htm

U.S. department of education fiscal year 2021 budget summary. (n.d.). https://www2.ed.gov /about/overview/budget/budget21/summary/21summary.pdf

U.S. Department of the Treasury. (n.d.). *Debt limit*. https://home.treasury.gov/policy-issues/financial-markets-financial-institutions-and-fiscal-service/debt-limit

Washington Journal. (2022, August 18). *David Pepper on threats to Democracy in state legislatures* [Video]. C-Span. https://www.c-span.org/video/?522347-3/washington-journal-david-pepper-discusses-threats-democracy-taking-place-state-legislatures&live#

Watkins, Z. L. (2008). *Lobbyists and interest groups: Sources of information* (RS20725). Congressional Research Service. https://www.senate.gov/reference/resources/pdf/RS20725.pdf

West, J. E. (Ed.). (1991). *The Americans with Disabilities Act from policy to practice*. Milbank Memorial Fund.

West, J. E. (Ed.). (1996). *Implementing the Americans with Disabilities Act*. Blackwell and Milbank Memorial Fund.

West, J. E. (2018). Calling all teachers flexing your advocacy muscles to address teacher shortages. *Midwest Symposium on Leadership in Behavior Disorders: Rethinking Behavior*, 2(1), 43–48. https://www.pageturnpro.com/Midwest-Symposium-for-Leadership-in-Behavior-Disorders/86925-RETHINKING-Behavior-Fall-2018/flex.html#page/45

West, J., & Yell, M. (2022). The 30th anniversary of the Americans with Disabilities Act: An interview with Dr. Jane West. *Journal of Disability Policy Studies*, 0(0). https://doi.org/10.1177/10442073221118863

Wilhelm, B. (2019, January 3). *Statutory inspectors general in the federal government: A primer* (R45450). Congressional Research Service. https://sgp.fas.org/crs/misc/R45450.pdf

Wilhelm, B. (2022). *Statutory inspectors general in the federal government: A primer* (R45450). Congressional Research Service. https://sgp.fas.org/crs/misc/R45450.pdf

Wright, P. A., & West, J. E. (2019). *When to hold 'em and when to fold 'em*. https://dredf.org/news/publications/disability-rights-law-and-policy/when-to-hold-em-and-when-to-fold-em/

Wright, P., as told to West, J. (2000). *Know when to hold 'em and when to fold 'em*. Disability Rights Education and Defense Fund. https://dredf.org/news/publications/disability-rights-law-and-policy/when-to-hold-em-and-when-to-fold-em/

Young, J., & National Council on Disability. (1997). *Equality of opportunity: The making of the Americans with Disabilities Act*. National Council on Disability.

Zoch, A. (2020, October 29). *The "average" state legislator is changing slowly*. National Conference of State Legislatures. https://www.ncsl.org/research/about-state-legislatures/who-s-the-average-state-legislator-depends-on-your-state-magazine2020.aspx

Zota, R. R. (2019, December 12). *TEACH grants: A primer* (R46117). Congressional Research Service. https://www.everycrsreport.com/files/20191212_R46117_e36c0dd734077a69c624165c6b4bf0034c526855.pdf

Zweigenhaft, R. L. (2021, March). *Diversity in presidential cabinets: From the least diverse in 30 years to the most diverse ever*. Who Rules America? https://whorulesamerica.ucsc.edu/power/diversity_in_presidential_cabinets.html

Index

civil rights: ADA and, 111; as policy tool, 104–5

Civil Rights Act, 50, 80, 87, 104

Civil Rights Data Collection, 105

Cleary, David P., 161; on bipartisanship, 42, 89; on constituents, 21; on election cycles, 36; on elevator speech, 133; on good policy, 107b; on majority party, 32; on meetings, 137; on partisanship, 40; on Senate, 3; on timeframe, 109

Clinton, Bill, 113

Clinton, Hillary, 82

closed rule, 86

cloture, 87–88

coalitions, 14–15

Code of Federal Regulations (CFR), 93

Cole, Tom, 41–42, 75b

collective actions: and advocacy, 126; national organizations and, 139; and policy adoption, 51

College Cost Reduction and Access Act, 73

command: and policy adoption, 54; and policy implementation, 54

committee(s), 4–6; and bills, 65; conference, 69; functions of, 62; resources on, 140–41; on rules, 86–87; standing, 66t; types of, 4–5

committee chairs, term limits and, 33

Committee for Education Funding, 14–15

Committee on Health, Education, Labor and Pensions: jurisdiction of, 81b; website of, 140

Committee on Rules, 68

Common Cause, 11

common good, debate on, 99

communication: on budget, 75; on Capitol Hill, 26b, 141; in different cultures, 24t, 25–26; persistence in, 139–40; with representative, 21, 129, 132–34

compromise, 53

concurrent resolutions, 64b; budget, 72

condition, versus problem, 48

conference committee, 69

confirmations, 38–39, 83–85

conflict resolution, ADA and, 111

Congress: advocating with, 128–39; demographics of, 28; in iron triangle, 2–4; and judiciary, 17, 17b; lawmaking operations of, 69–81; majorities and minorities in, 32–33; procedures in, 60–88; and social media, 18–19

Congressional Budget Act, 72

Congressional Progressive Staff Association, 6

Congressional Research Service, 33, 62; reports from, 142

Congressional Review Act, 85, 93

Congressional Workers Union, 6

constituents, 20–22; and advocacy, 128; definition of, 20; influence of, 20b; interests of, and policy adoption, 52

Constitution, courts and, 16

continuing resolution, 76

Core Opportunity Resources for Equity and Excellence Act, 102

corporations: associations of, 11; NCLB and, 114

cosponsorship, 66b

Council for Exceptional Children, Action Alert Center, 139

courts. See judiciary

COVID pandemic, 73, 112, 146

crises: and agenda setting, 50; and problem versus solution, 100

Cruz, Ted, 19

culture, of policy making, 23–27, 24t

currency, in different cultures, 24, 24t

cyclical framework, 47–58, 48f

Darling-Hammond, Linda, 118, 121

Dart, Justin, 110

data collection: NCLB and, 112; as policy tool, 105–6

Data for Progress, 20

data reports: and agenda setting, 49–50; and evaluation, 57; and meetings, 132

"Dear Colleague" letters, 65b, 141

@Dear_White_Staffers, 6

debt limit, definition of, 77n7

decision criteria, and policy adoption, 51

decision memos, 26b

decision rules, and policy adoption, 52–53

deeming resolution, 73

Defense Reauthorization Act, 80

deference, and policy adoption, 52

Delaney, Josh, 29b

DeLauro, Rosa, 41–42, 75b

delegation, congressional, 128; getting started with, 129b; information on, 129; invitations for, 136; relationship building with, 130; requesting meetings with, 131b; statements from, 141

Democratic Party: and bipartisanship, 40–42; and Twitter, 19

design of policy, and implementation, 56

DeVos, Betsy, 39, 70–72

Dingell, John, 34, 45

disability rights, culture of, 23–27, 24t

4 Ps, xix–xxiv, xx*f*
PACT Act, xvii
Parent Training and Information Centers, 20*b*
parliamentarian, 85–86
Parrino, Sandra, 10
partisanship, 7–8, 40–42, 61
passion, and issue selection, 127
Pell Grants, 77–78
Pelosi, Nancy, 7n5, 125
people, 1–30; in four-P framework, xx, xx*f*; importance of relationships with, 6–8; and meeting preparation, 130
Pepper, David, 3
permanent authorization, 80–81
persistence, and advocacy, 139–40
persuasion, and policy adoption, 53
phone calls, 139
planning, process knowledge and, 46, 47*b*
policy, 99–123; in four-P framework, xx, xx*f*; and meeting preparation, 131; and politics, 31–32; research and, 143–45. *See also* good policy
policy entrepreneurs, 59
policy frames, 101
policy issues, selection of, 127
policy making: culture of, 23–27, 24*t*; interest groups and, 13
policy streams, 47, 58–60
policy tools, 94, 103–7; selection of, 122
policy window, 59
political action committees, 14
political party affiliation: and message refinement, 133; and policy adoption, 51–52
politics, 31–43; in four-P framework, xx, xx*f*; and meeting preparation, 131; NCLB and, 113; and policy, 31–32; as policy stream, 58–59
polls, 19–20
precedent, 17; ADA and, 111
preconference, 69
president, 34–35; and budget, 70; information from, 143; and nominations, 38–39, 83–85; powers of, 8–9; signing bill, 69. *See also* executive branch
press, 18–19
privatization, NCLB and, 114
problem definition, in process cycle, 48–49, 48*f*
problems: ADA and, 110; versus condition, 48; as policy stream, 58–59; versus solution, 100–3
process, 45–97; in four-P framework, xx, xx*f*; literature on, 47–60; and meeting

preparation, 131; understanding, and advocacy, 45–46, 47*b*
professional associations, 11
proposals, as policy stream, 58–59
public interest groups, 11–12
public opinion, 19–20; and policy adoption, 52

Race to the Top 2009, 117–19
Ravitch, D., 114
Reagan, Ronald, 110
reapportionment, 3
reauthorization, 56–57, 80
reconciliation, 73
redistricting, 3
Reed, Jack, 102
Reginfo.gov, 91
regular order, 60, 62–69; steps in, 62, 63*f*; variations from, 61
Regulations.gov, 91
regulatory plan, 91
Rehabilitation Act of 1973, Section 504, 111
Reid, Harry, 88
relationships: and advocacy, 130; with constituents, 21–22; importance of, 6–8
representation, 101; importance of, 27–30
Republican Party: and bipartisanship, 40–42, 89; and message refinement, 133; and Twitter, 19
requests, 134–35
research: and advocacy, 143–45; and agenda setting, 49–50; on implementation, 54–55; as policy tool, 106; on process, 47–60
researchers, as policy elites, 23
resistance, and evaluation, 58
resource constraints, and evaluation, 58
riders, 77
Rodgers, Cathy McMorris, 128
Roosevelt, Franklin D., 1
Roy, Chip, 19
rule making, 90–94; negotiated, 94
rules, 68, 85–86

Safer Communities Act, xvii
Sanders, Bernie, 51
Schoolhouse Rock, 60
Schumer, Chuck, 6
security, at Capitol, 147
Senate, 3; and confirmations, 38–40, 83–85; and cosponsorship, 66*b*; and "Dear Colleague" letters, 65*b*; election cycles and, 35–36; filibuster and cloture in, 87–88; rules of, 85–86; standing committees, 66*t*

seniority, 4, 33–34
Shriver, Eunice Kennedy, 127b
Sierra Club, 11
signing statements, 69, 70b
simple resolutions, 64b
Smith v. Robinson, 17b
social justice, and problem representations, 101–3
social media, 18–19; and advocacy, 139; Trump and, 8
Social Security, 106
solutions: ADA and, 110–11; versus problems, 100–3
spending: in 2020 budget, 78f; types of, 77–78
staffers, congressional, 4–6; characteristics of, 1; demographics of, 28–29; personal experience of, 5b
standardized tests: and achievement gap concept, 101; and policy, 109–21
standing committees, 4–5, 66t
state level advocacy, 126
stopping bad policy, 127; interest groups and, 13
stories, for meetings, 132
strategizing, process knowledge and, 46, 47b
subcommittees, 5; appropriations, 74t, 75b; referral to, 67; resources on, 140–41
supermajority, 40
supplemental appropriations bills, 77
support agencies, congressional, 6
Supreme Court, 17b; decisions, and agenda setting, 50; politicization of, 88
systemic procedural occurrences, and agenda setting, 50

table, presence at, 102–3, 149–50; importance of, 122
Tavalin, Kuna, 162; on coalitions, 14; on constituents, 128; on education, 23; on good policy, 108b; on message refinement, 134; on minority party, 33; on process, 45; on relationships, 7, 130; on testimony, 145
tax code, as policy tool, 107
teacher evaluation: NCLB and, 115–16; Race to the Top and, 117–18
teacher preparation, 119–21
Teachers and Parents at the Table Act, 56
TEACH grants, 73, 106, 120

technical assistance components, ADA and, 111
tenure, in different cultures, 24–25, 24t
testimony, 145; on appropriations, 75b
think tanks, 12
Thoma, Colleen, 144
302(a), 72, 74
302(b), 74
Thurmond, Strom, 87
time/timing: and advocacy, 125–26; in different cultures, 24t, 25; and policy making, 7, 109; and process, 45–46, 47b; and requests, 135
Title IX, 95b, 104
town hall meetings: and advocacy, 139–40; participating in, 145–46
trade associations, 11
transition teams, 37–40
Triage Cancer, 19
Trump, Donald, 8, 72, 95b, 121
Twitter, 18–19

unanimous consent, 68
unauthorized appropriations, 76
unified government, 40–41
unions, congressional staffers and, 6, 29

value-added modeling (VAM), 118
values: and accountability, 105; and policy, 99
veto, 69
veto override, 69
views and estimates, 72
Voting Rights Act, 104–5

Washington, Kerry, 31
Weicker, Lowell, 5b, 20b
Weingarten, Randi, 120–21
White, Ashley L., 163; on advocacy, 143; on diversity, 27, 101; on interest groups, 13; on internships, 144; on resources, 142; on state level advocacy, 126; on time, 126
will, and implementation, 55
WPR framework, 102
Wright, Pat, 22

Young, Don, 34
Yudin, Michael K., 163; on bipartisanship, 41; on good policy, 108b; on grassroots, 22; on nominations, 39; on policy tools, 94; on stories, 132

About the Interviewees

....

Interviewees were chosen because of their deep knowledge, experience, and insightful perspectives related to the policy making world in Washington. All have held positions with the U.S. House or Representatives, the U.S. Senate, the executive branch (White House or a federal agency), or Washington-based interest groups. Some have held positions with two or three or all of these sectors. One interviewee requested anonymity, as noted below.

David P. Cleary served as staff director on the Senate Health, Education, Labor and Pensions (HELP) Committee for ranking Republican Sen. Richard Burr (R-NC). He has served in a range of policy positions in Washington for twenty-five years—in the House, the Senate, and in the U.S. Department of Education. He began his service at the U.S. Department of Education, where he worked for five years, moving on to the House Education and Workforce Committee, working for Chairman John Boehner (R-OH) from 2003 to 2005. From 2006 to 2011, he served as subcommittee staff director for Sen. Lamar Alexander (R-TN) on the Senate HELP Committee's Children and Families Subcommittee. From 2011 to 2013, he served as Sen. Alexander's legislative director. In 2013 he became the staff director for the Senate HELP Committee and then Sen. Alexander's chief of staff from 2013 to 2021. Beginning in 2021, he assumed the role of staff director for Sen. Richard Burr (R-NC), ranking Republican on the HELP Committee. David holds an M.P.A. from George Washington University.

Jonathan Fansmith is senior vice president for government relations at the American Council on Education (ACE), where he has held multiple roles since 2004. Jon has been central to carrying out ACE's mission—to convene, organize, mobilize, and lead advocacy efforts that shape effective public policy related to higher education. Jon has led the association's work on the federal budget and appropriations process. He is an expert on student aid policy and led the organization's work in areas such as reauthorization of the Higher Education Act and COVID-19 relief funding.

Fansmith is a former president and member of the executive committee of the Committee for Education Funding, a coalition of over one hundred national organizations seeking to secure adequate federal support for the nation's educational system. He has served as coordinator of the Student Aid Alliance, a coalition

....

of over eighty higher education organizations focused on student financial aid, and is a member of the Think College National Coordinating Center Accreditation Working Group, which was created by the 2008 Higher Education Opportunity Act. Jon holds an M.A. from Johns Hopkins University.

Lindsay Fryer served as senior vice president at Penn Hill Group, where she provided government relations and policy strategy services to a range of organizations. Prior to joining Penn Hill in 2016, she worked as an education committee staff member in both the Senate and the House. In the Senate, where she worked from 2014 to 2016, she was senior education policy advisor to Chairman of the Senate HELP Committee Sen. Lamar Alexander (R-TN). In this role she carried out the legislative agenda for the committee in areas ranging from elementary and secondary education to student privacy. She was the principal negotiator and drafter for Sen. Alexander on the Every Student Succeeds Act. Working for the Committee on Education and the Workforce in the House from 2011 to 2014, Lindsay managed a portfolio of issues for Chairman John Kline (R-MN) related to K–12 education, higher education, older Americans, juvenile justice, runaway and homeless youth, and child abuse prevention. Prior to working in Congress, Lindsay worked at the American Institutes for Research, where she contributed to a range of research projects and reports. Lindsay holds a B.A. from Boston College and an M.Ed. from Harvard University.

Kimberly Knackstedt is senior fellow and codirector of the Century Foundation's Disability Economic Justice Collaborative, where she began in 2022. Kim has six years of experience working in Congress, on committees for both the Senate and the House. She began working on the Senate HELP Committee in 2016 as a Joseph P. Kennedy Jr. Public Policy Fellow. From 2017 to 2019, she worked as disability policy advisor for House Committee on Education and Labor Chairman Bobby Scott (D-VA). From 2019 to 2021, she returned to the Senate, where she served as senior disability policy advisor for Chair Patty Murray (D-WA) on the HELP Committee. In January 2021, Kim was appointed by President Biden as the first director of disability policy for the Domestic Policy Council in the White House. Kim holds a Ph.D. from the University of Kansas. Kim was a participant in the first short course Jane West taught in 2015.[1]

Kuna Tavalin has been a partner at Stride Policy Solutions, a government relations firm in Washington, DC, since 2018. From 2004 to 2008, she worked as a legislative staff member in the offices of Senator Jim Jeffords (I-VT) and Sen. Sherrod Brown (D-OH), covering a range of issues, including poverty, foster care, transportation, immigration, and housing. From 2009 to 2018, Kuna primarily worked in a number of settings providing government relations and policy advice to multiple

---

1. For more information on HECSE Short Courses, see https://hecse.net/events/hecse-short -course/.

education and disability-related nonprofit organizations. Kuna holds an M.A.T. from Smith College.

Ashley L. White is an assistant professor at the University of Wisconsin–Madison. Before joining the university in 2020, Ashley held a range of positions related to public policy development. She served as the Joseph P. Kennedy Public Policy Fellow in 2019 to 2020 on the Committee on Education and Labor for Chairman Bobby Scott (D-VA). In the summer of 2018, she worked for her own congress-woman, Kathy Castor (D-FL). In the summer of 2017, she interned at the U.S. Department of Education.

Ashley also serves as the Inaugural Educational Fellow for the National Association for the Advancement of Colored People (NAACP), advancing civil rights through education. Ashley's orientation to her work is ensuring that policy solutions are grounded in research, with a focus on multiply marginalized students and students with disabilities and equitable outcomes for all. Ashley holds a Ph.D. from the University of South Florida. She was a participant in the short course Dr. West taught in 2017 and has served as a coinstructor for that course for several years.

Michael K. Yudin is a principal at the Raben Group, where he works as a policy and government affairs consultant to nonprofit organizations and public agencies. Before joining the group in 2016, Michael worked for twenty-five years in various positions in Congress and the executive branch. From 2010 to 2016, he served the Obama administration in the Department of Education as both assistant secretary for the Office of Special Education and Rehabilitative Services and acting assistant secretary for the Office of Elementary and Secondary Education. From 2001 to 2010, he was a Senate staffer, serving as legislative director for Sen. Jeanne Shaheen (D-NH), senior counsel to Sen. Jeff Bingaman (D-NM), and HELP Committee counsel to Sen. Jim Jeffords (I-VT). From 1991 to 2001, Michael served as an attorney at the Social Security Administration and the U.S. Department of Labor. Michael holds a law degree from the Western New England College School of Law.

Anonymous is a former Senate staff member, member of the Biden transition team, and a Biden political appointee at the U.S. Department of Education.

About the Author

Jane West is an independent education policy consultant based in Washington, DC. She began her policy work as an intern in the U.S. Senate for Sen. Lowell P. Weicker (R-CT) in 1983, where she went on to serve as staff director for the Subcommittee on Disability Policy of the Committee on Health, Education, Labor and Pensions (HELP). She has been active in policy making for over forty years, working for a range of federal government agencies as well as national organizations, including the Presidential Task Force on the HIV Epidemic, the National Council on Disability, the Social Security Administration, the U.S. Department of Education, the American Association of Colleges for Teacher Education, the Joseph P. Kennedy Jr. Foundation, the National Network of State Teachers of the Year, the Higher Education Consortium for Special Education, and the Teacher Education Division of the Council for Exceptional Children.

She has written and spoken extensively on policy and advocacy in education and disability and served on the faculties of the University of San Francisco, Johns Hopkins University, the University of Maryland, and Virginia Commonwealth University, designing and teaching public policy courses. She holds a B.A. from the University of California at Santa Barbara, an M.A. from Columbia University, and a Ph.D. from the University of Maryland.

For more information, see https://www.janewestconsulting.com/.